THE POETRY OF
BASIL BUNTING

Basil Bunting at Briggflatts (photo: Derek Smith)

VICTORIA FORDE

The Poetry of Basil Bunting

BLOODAXE BOOKS

ISBN: 1 85224 047 4 hardback edition
1 85224 048 2 paperback edition

First published 1991 by
Bloodaxe Books Ltd,
P.O. Box 1SN,
Newcastle upon Tyne NE99 1SN.

Bloodaxe Books Ltd acknowledges
the financial assistance of Northern Arts.

Cover reproduction by V & H Reprographics, Newcastle upon Tyne.

Typesetting by EMS Phototypesetting, Spittal, Berwick upon Tweed.

Printed in Great Britain by
Bell & Bain Limited, Glasgow, Scotland.

Contents

Sister Victoria Forde with Basil Bunting at Greystead, 1982.

Preface

From the time in 1970 when I first started corresponding with Basil Bunting until his death in 1985, the poet, his life, and his poetry became better and better known to me. Although in 1970 Bunting's poetry was the subject of my dissertation, people who knew him told me not to even bother asking him anything about his poetry, that he would refuse to discuss it. Fortunately, I ignored their advice and risked the chance of his not answering a letter. But Bunting did answer, at first briefly, and then more and more in detail during the two years it took me to complete the study.

After my work was finished, he read it meticulously – and then sent six sheets of suggested corrections. Many were simply remarks of a modest man, others were enlightening comments. For example, instead of T. S. Eliot being 'long-time friend and critic', Basil suggested 'old acquaintance' as 'more correct'. From that time on, he was interested in my getting the manuscript published. One comment that kept me encouraged was in his letter [2 June 1981] from his new home in Greystead:

> I'm afraid I'm indifferent to things like [some recent publications and a film to be made about him]. But I am not indifferent to your thesis. It turned up when I began to unpack my books, and I looked through it again. I hope [the publisher] gets on with it...I'd be willing, if you approve, to go through the proofs when there are any before [the publisher] sends them on to you to remove a few blemishes (but not of course to modify any of your interpretations or opinions). If this seems desirable to you, please write...

Unfortunately, the original publisher had severe financial problems, so this book has not the unique hallmark that only Basil's proof-reading would have given it.

In January and February 1982 when he came down to London where I lived for the semester, he introduced me to editors and publisher friends. Once he invited me to accompany him to dinner with representatives of Oxford University Press and Anvil Press. It was Peter Jay of Anvil who later sent the manuscript to Bloodaxe Books. Aside from the desire of getting the entire manuscript published, Basil seemed quietly pleased every time I published an article about his work or spoke at a conference, usually giving permission to use anything he had written in letters, most often casually, with 'never a boast or a see-here'.

Since I wrote the original work chiefly from 1970 to 1972, when I was barely acquainted with Basil and before the recent appearance of so many critical publications on his poetry, his work was more easily appraised according to the qualities I saw in it. Now, in 1990, though it is more difficult to criticise the work of a long-time friend, especially one who has died so recently, it is easier to be more certain of my evaluations after years of re-reading his poetry and considering others' criticism. Volumes have been written about the poet and his work as various bibliographies attest. It is not my intention to incorporate all of this. To fulfil Basil's wish, it seems enough to publish the original work with only a few additions which provide further light on certain works not already considered as fully as others.

As far as his biography is concerned, because in 1970 Basil Bunting was not as well known as today, I wrote a brief introductory biography to place his work in its proper perspective. If this would have been filled in completely, it could easily have become the focal point with its fascinating adventures. Now, twenty years later, I have added some details and a summary of the years up to his death.

This revision has been enriching by putting me in touch with Basil's two daughters, Roudaba and Bourtai, in the United States, and his sister Joyce in Northumberland. They have been especially generous with information only they could supply. Maria and Tom Bunting in England have been most kind to me ever since I met them in 1982, treating me as a good friend who admires their father and his work. Tom's help in securing the gracious permission of the Estate to use the collections of letters requires an additional note of appreciation, as does John Halliday's help as the Estate's Executor.

To Bunting's friends, Louis Zukofsky, Tom Pickard, Peter Quartermain, Michael and Penny Henshaw, Richard Caddel, George MacBeth, and Derek Smith (who provided photographs), I owe an acknowledgement also.

I wish to express my deep gratitude to Professor John Matthias, my dissertation advisor at the University of Notre Dame, who introduced me to Basil Bunting and whose guidance and enthusiasm has supported me for years. I am obliged to Dr Donald Sniegowski and Dr John Garvick for their discriminating criticism and interest in the original study. At that time Dr Eugene Leahy of

PREFACE   9

the University of Notre Dame and Dr Arthur Lawrence and Dr
Lewis Artau of St Mary's College most graciously helped me with
music, and Dr Henry Carter's knowledge of classical Spanish and
Italian was invaluable. Jaafar Moghadam and Khosrow Moshtarikhah at Notre Dame and Reza Shanehsazzadeh at Mount St
Joseph untiringly answered questions, researched and translated
Persian poetry for me. I wish to thank the Harry Ransom
Humanities Research Center at the University of Texas at Austin
and the University of Chicago Library for all their help and for
their permission to use manuscript collections. Cheryl Albrecht
and her staff at the Mount St Joseph Library have given me
assistance I could not do without. Richard Caddel read the
typescript and made many helpful suggestions.

Extracts from Basil Bunting's *Collected Poems* (1978) are reprinted by permission of Oxford University Press and the Ode
'Now we've no hope of going back' from *Collected Poems* (1985) by
permission of Moyer Bell Ltd. Both the BBC and Tyne Tees
Television Ltd gave permission for use of material from pro-
grammes featuring Basil Bunting.

    'Basil Bunting's Persian Poems' was published in *Juggler*
(University of Notre Dame, Spring 1973); 'The Odes' and
'Translations and Adaptations' in *Basil Bunting: Man and Poet*,
edited by Carroll F. Terrell (National Poetry Foundation, Inc.,
Orono, ME, 1980); and 'Latin Translations' as 'Basil Bunting's
Debt to Ezra Pound and the Classics' in *Classical and Modern
Literature Quarterly*, 1 (Fall 1980), 25-37.

    Without assistance from the University of Notre Dame, the
Schmitt Foundation, the University of London, and my community, the Sisters of Charity of Cincinnati, graduate studies and
the revision of this manuscript would not have been possible. I am
also grateful to the College of Mt St Joseph for financial help and
the time for the final revision.

    Sister Eugene Fox, SC, my lifelong mentor, spent hours proof-
reading the copy, suggesting changes always for the best. My
family, especially my father and my sisters Justine and Jacquelyn,
and my friends, especially Ruth Bockenstette, SC, gave me their
faithful and confident support from the beginning. To each of them
I owe a special debt of gratitude.

    Without Basil Bunting's courteous responses to my many letters
and his warm friendship over fifteen years, this manuscript would
be quite different. My only regret is that he is not alive to see the
publication of this effort to make his poetry better known. My
sincerest hope is that this book may help others delight in his 'lines
of sound drawn in the air'.

Basil Bunting at Briggflatts, 1984 (photo: Derek Smith)

Introduction

During most of the eighty-five years of Basil Bunting's life, he worked to write poetry as close to music as possible. From the beginning he believed that poetry should skilfully take over some of the techniques that he knew only in music. For him interest in sound was essential to writing good poetry, and he concluded that 'if you're interested in sound, you're almost certainly going to be interested in music too'.[1]

Working alone in England in his youth, he was enthusiastic about the kind of cadences that Whitman produced in poetry at the time contemporaries, such as Liszt, were doing the same in music. Later he was encouraged by his discovery that T. S. Eliot also was attempting something along musical lines by writing 'Preludes'. As a young man he enjoyed Byrd, Bach, and Beethoven, but he admits he got off on the wrong foot trying to imitate Beethoven's sonatas with their extremely violent contrasts of speed and tone. It was not until he learned from Scarlatti and Corelli that he was satisfied with the models for the music in his poems.

A traveller to three other continents, Bunting learned his craft among recognised contemporary poets at the same time that he was studying the skills of great poets of the past, especially those who were never far from music in their work. In the Preface to his *Collected Poems* he acknowledges many by name:

> If ever I learned the trick of it, it was mostly from poets long dead whose names are obvious: Wordsworth and Dante, Horace, Wyat and Malherbe, Manucheri and Ferdosi, Villon, Whitman, Edmund Spenser; but two living men also taught me much: Ezra Pound and in his sterner, stonier way, Louis Zukofsky.

Practising with poetry in many languages – Latin, French, Italian, Persian, and an Italian translation of Japanese, he wrote translations and adaptations which helped him create the musical form he was searching for. Throughout a lifetime seldom unaffected by war, hard work, and poverty, he worked to carve out odes and sonatas in musical patterns whose complete shape was in each line.

A kind of modern Renaissance man, Bunting wrote poetry as close to music as possible as an integral part of an eventful life.

Even the briefest biographical outline suggests a life so full, it is difficult to see how at certain periods he had any time for writing. Yet it is from his experiences that he produced his best and most mature works.

'You can't write about anything unless you've experienced it, you're either confused in your subject matter or else you get it wrong.'[2] Without ever going outside his experiences, Basil Bunting could have written volumes of poetry with full authority. To earn a living, he was poet, music critic, barman, magazine sub-editor, sea captain, RAF squadron leader, intelligence officer, diplomat, newspaper correspondent and journalist for several papers, and university lecturer. In a more personal vein he was an only son, brother, lover, husband, father, grandfather, great grandfather, and friend. Just the beginning of a list of his friends reads like the index of a great modern literature book: Ezra Pound, Louis Zukofsky, W. B. Yeats, Ford Madox Ford, Mina Loy, William Carlos Williams, Lorine Niedecker, Marianne Moore, Ted Hughes, Hugh Mac-Diarmid, Robert Duncan, Tom Pickard and Jonathan Williams as well as 'acquaintance' T. S. Eliot, and the list goes on. Though his friendships spanned several continents, this linguist and world traveller remained a Northumberland man all his life until he died there. For those who know his life well, all this fits into place; for those who do not, it needs some sorting out.

Knowledge about Bunting's life, his love of music, and the other major influences on his poetry lead directly to a greater understanding of his work. However, standing in the way of this possibility for some are the stumbling blocks of Bunting's own pronouncements.

Bunting described his poetry as 'lines and patterns of sound drawn in the air which stir deep emotions which have not even a name in prose'.[3] To appreciate his poetry then, one does not need to theorise about poetry, which Bunting disparaged, but simply recognise the art of his craftsmanship, his skill with 'the relation to one another of lines and patterns of sound'. In other words, one must appreciate his music and its meaning. But for a few disciples his pronouncement against literary criticism puts up a barrier between them and those others who want to discuss the craftsmanship instead of just listening to the music. However, not only did Bunting himself write criticism, his own written and spoken criticism about literature and music as well as his writings about criticism itself further clarify his ideas about poetry and music.

For certain critics his 'Statement' about poetry has provided them with building blocks for a wall that prevents attention from being focused on the poetry itself. His often quoted dicta: 'Poetry, like music, is to be heard...Poetry is seeking to make not meaning but beauty' needs no explaining, as Bunting has said, to those who get their poetry by ear. For those who take issue with his 'Statement', he explains further in interviews and writings during his lifetime.

One final obstacle must be dealt with before the way is cleared for a discussion of the poems. Though Bunting modestly credits poets of the past and present for helping him learn 'the trick' of writing poetry, he quietly insists over and over that in the end his poetry is his own. The two most influential 'living' teachers, in Bunting's own words, were Ezra Pound and Louis Zukofsky, with a minor role played by T. S. Eliot. It seems important to review these influences to put them in perspective from the beginning.

Therefore, besides a knowledge of his biography and an overview of Bunting's poetics and criticism, a consideration of the major contemporary influences on his poetry is useful for the fullest understanding of his work. But all these are surely secondary. Here each topic will be briefly discussed only as an introduction to the heart of the matter, Bunting's poetry, its music and its meaning.

Bunting at Greystead Cottage, 1982 (photo: Derek Smith)

CHAPTER 1

Basil Bunting: A Life

Although Basil Bunting declared repeatedly throughout his life that he did 'not believe in biography', as the years went by, he allowed more and more details to be known. From his birth in Scotswood-on-Tyne on 1 March 1900, until his death in Hexham on 17 April 1985, he called Northumberland his home. In one of his best biographies, Jonathan Williams' *Descant on Rawthey's Madrigal*, [D][1] he remembers he was born 'amid rejoicings for the relief of Ladysmith during the Boer War'. Two years later the only other child in the family was born, his sister Joyce.

To a fellow Northumbrian, David Gordon, Basil boasted that his mother Annie Cheesman Bunting, the daughter of Annie Foster and Isaac Taylor Cheesman, a local mine manager, was related to most of the Border families, including the Charltons, one of his favourites, and he delighted in stories of border raids he grew up on.[2] A cursory look at the family tree reveals a Nancy Robson whose family is listed as 'Scottish Border thieves' with one who 'was hung for sheep stealing'.

Always close to her son, Basil's mother generously took into her home for three years the child of a woman Basil was associated with during the Twenties in London. With an adventuresome spirit she travelled to Rapallo in Italy and to London to be with him before, during and after his first marriage. Although during his marriage she had a flat of her own both in Rapallo and in London, after Marian and the children left, she moved her furniture into Basil's London flat to live with him there. Marian, Basil's first wife, who got along well with her, remembered her as a beautiful woman who took good care of herself and her beautiful things, her fine linens and china.

Later, when Mrs Bunting lived with Basil, his second wife, and their family in Wylam, just outside Newcastle, she proved the hardiness of the stock she came from by making shopping trips

Basil Bunting with his sister, cousin and maids, 1905.

from Wylam to Newcastle alone though she was in her nineties. In fact, she lived to be ninety-four and had been out shopping by herself just before she died. She loved reading mysteries, Basil told me, and the only way he knew she was dead was because she did not turn the page of the story she was reading.

Basil's father, Thomas Lowe Bunting, the son of Mary Lowe Bunting and Joseph Bunting, was a remarkable doctor who had received a gold medal at Edinburgh for his M.D. thesis on the histology of lymphatic glands. Finding no living in that, he shifted to radiography and remained a hard-working general practitioner serving the miners at Montague Pit until he died of angina in 1925.

But before he died, he had influenced his two children, Basil and Joyce, in ways that shaped their lives, especially in their love of Northumberland. As an experienced climber himself, he saw to it that Basil at ten began climbing big boulders. Walking and climbing were sometimes serious undertakings, and at twelve a friend was giving climbing lessons to Basil who remembers him as 'occasionally a little impatient, what the hell'. With a shake of his head, Bunting described to me the simple preparations for climbing in those years, relishing the story about the time that his father and a group of climbers struggled to the top of a mountain in Switzerland only to find a shepherd there, calmly eating his lunch and enjoying the view. However, as late as 1982 he still shuddered to remember the time he was alone, climbing in the fog, when he slipped to a chalk ledge between two steep sides about a thousand feet from his starting point at the base.

Though he had difficulty walking without a cane during the last few years of his life, Basil spoke to me proudly of the vigour which until those final years had kept him walking about twenty miles every afternoon. Even in 110° heat he walked daily in Persia, and once in 129° without a hat. In this connection he told me about Ezra Pound in Italy inviting him to take 'a long walk'. He laughed at himself, remembering that after his extensive preparations, Ezra was satisfied with only one or two turns around the promenade, about two and a half miles.

But his stories about walking were peripheral. He told Jonathan Williams that as early as 1905, 'his first conscious memory was of poetry [he] wanted to write – a genuine childhood desire, an instinct'. By reading, very early, bits of 'the less recondite Wordsworth' and others to Basil and Joyce, his father planted in them the seed of his love of more serious poetry. Joyce wrote to me that it amuses her to think that 'up to the age of 8 or 9 if asked what I would be when I grew up, I always said, "a poetess". But this soon faded' – though she was drawn to writing limericks from having enjoyed Edward Lear. Basil for the rest of his life lived the conviction that his business was to be a poet [D]. Joyce remembers 'when Basil was 12 years old, our parents encouraged us and a cousin to write poems about a holiday we had had in the Lake District by offering a small prize and Basil won it'.

Images for poetry were stored early in his life. One such vivid memory of Scotswood-on-Tyne, now a suburb of Newcastle, was of the three carts which used to be drawn up to the bank of the Tyne to carry the salmon caught in nets. Though his education was carried on partially at home with a governess, he could have seen fishing scenes often on his way to school in Newcastle where his formal education began. Later he attended Ackworth, a Quaker boarding school in the West Riding of Yorkshire. Here he learned

Basil Bunting (right), c. 1913.

to love the rhythms of the Scriptures and the narrative skill of some chapters, especially the early chapters in the Second Book of Kings.

At the Quaker school at Leighton Park in Berkshire, which he attended until he was seventeen and a half, he came across an early edition of Whitman's *Leaves of Grass* pushed behind other books in the school library. Enthusiastic about the musical prose cadences, he 'wrote an essay which won more or less a national prize to the great annoyance of his school teachers. And this caught the eye of an old gentleman living in Sheffield who got on his pushbike and rode thirty or forty miles in order to call on the fifteen year old critic of Whitman. That was no less a person than Edward Carpenter, who'd been one of Whitman's closest friends.'[3]

A key to Basil Bunting's poetry, his deep appreciation of music, he attributed to his father and his aunt, a fine pianist who provided good music for him to listen to. Though he himself never played an instrument, he admitted he did have a good amateur voice which later helped him to read his poetry musically. Basil, present at many of the performances at services as well as practices of the Newcastle Bach Choir, acknowledges a debt to the director, Dr Whittaker, from whom he learned a great sense of music and art in general. This man who stressed the value of Northumbrian music collected Northumbrian folk songs and tunes and occasionally used them in his own compositions. At this time Dr Fellowes had just rediscovered the Great Service of Byrd in Durham, and in 1924 Whittaker conducted the first performance.

A teacher Basil remembered with respect was Miss Fry who encouraged him to take Quaker doctrine seriously. Supported by her but not his family, though one uncle was a Quaker, Bunting refused service in World War I. Years later Ezra Pound in a letter to Rabindranath Tagore mentioned this as a telling factor in a character reference: 'I think Bunting is about the only man who did six months in jail as conscientious objector during the armistice, i.e., after the war was over, on principle that if there was a war he wouldn't go (Quaker)...'[4]

Almost on his eighteenth birthday, he had been arrested in Newcastle and began a sentence of eighteen months in jails – 'Wormwood Scrubs for the most part, Winchester gaol for a good lump at the end, but in between various military gaols and guardrooms.' His reticence about that experience gives a clear feeling of prison conditions. Seeing others set free through their hunger fasts, he also tried one for about eleven or twelve days,

Studio portrait, 1917.

Portrait of the artist as a young man.

Bunting with nephew shortly after his release from prison in 1919.

but the Governor of Winchester Prison had an ingenious notion. He was not allowed to forcibly feed you, the Suffragettes had seen to that..., but every morning he had delivered to my cell a perfectly beautiful freshly roasted chicken and I had to sit there looking at this chicken and not eating it...a bit difficult. Ezra was much impressed with that and put it in the Cantos.

One of the last one or two to be released in late 1919, he was given a pass for a fortnight or so. With his father's encouragement not to report back, he began living in London at first in 'a nice extraordinary hotel'. Some four years later he received a letter from the Governor of Winchester Prison stating, 'You are this day discharged out of my custody', though he had not been near his custody for years.[5]

As a student at the London School of Economics, he had helped to alleviate harsh prison conditions by contributing footnotes to a book by Graham Wallas, one of the founders of the Fabian Society. This book was used as 'the main evidence before the Royal Commission that reformed the prisons' though Bunting modestly suggested to me that his work was 'infinitesimally small'.

It was about this same time – in 1919 – that Bunting first encountered Pound's and Eliot's works. Though he felt the resemblance of Eliot's 'Preludes' to Chopin's was 'slight and superficial', he 'was delighted to discover that there were actually people doing what I had merely worked out in my head was the kind of thing that ought to be done. This was a revelation that it really could be done, that it wasn't a hopeless trade.'[6]

True to his childhood conviction, Bunting had always written poetry, but he had only had one poem, 'Keep Troth', published in 1917 in the *Leightonian*. Another prize-winning poem and essay, published probably in 1916 or 1917 in the Leeds evening paper, the *Mercury*, has never been found. However, at this time Bunting felt encouraged even by a rejection from a London editor who told him, 'You must try a little harder and you'll have it.' In later years he cautioned other poets to use a very large waste paper basket as their most important tool.[7] Much to the dismay of researchers, he practised this himself, preserving only one small fragment of the earliest poem he wrote in 1923.

However, in 1922, bored with economics, he left school without graduating and became secretary to Harry Barnes, MP. In his new position, Bunting's first trip out of England to Scandinavia included an unsuccessful attempt to enter Russia.

During this time his sister, following in her father's footsteps, was studying at Edinburgh University, graduating in 1924 with the

Basil Bunting in 1923.

degree of Bachelor of Medicine and Surgery (MB CRB). Working
as an 'ordinary doctor', Joyce described her practice as 'partly
assistant to doctors in general and partly in the School Medical
Service' (4 April 1987).

More restless, Basil cleared off to France with no money at all to
work in Paris as road digger, artist's model, and barman.[8] Here, he
met Pound 'playing a swashbuckling kind of chess' [D]. Writing to
a friend in 1932, Bunting recalled the situation:

> I believed then as now, that his *Propertius* was the finest of modern
> poems. Indeed, it was the one that gave me the notion that poetry wasn't
> altogether impossible in the XX century. So I made friends. I was
> digging roads outside of Paris for a living. I got locked up for a colossal
> drunk. It was Ezra who discovered me...and perjured himself in the
> courts to try to get me off. When I came out of quod, and was working at
> the Jocky, he introduced me to Ford Madox Ford and I became sub. ed.
> and sec. to the *Transatlantic Review*.[9]

Before he quarrelled with Ford and was succeeded by Ernest Hemingway, Bunting was not only 'sub. ed. and sec.': he told Jonathan Williams he also bathed the baby and answered the telephone, corrected proofs, and even changed a few words in a Ford Conrad novel. During this time Ford wrote to A. E. Coppard: 'If you know the route you are coming by and the time of the train we will either meet you or have you met by Bunting – a dark youth with round spectacles, in a large Trilby hat and a blue trench coat who shall hold a copy of the *Transatlantic Review* and smile.'[10]

His loyalty and appreciation for Ford was never so evident as in his preface of *Selected Poems: Ford Madox Ford* (1971) which he edited. Here he strongly defended him against biographers who missed the goodness of Ford as a friend and a writer. But his sharpest retaliation was aimed at Hemingway who wrote 'an unlaughable caricature' in *A Moveable Feast*, 'a lie...deliberately assembled to damage the reputation of a dead man'.[11]

Decades afterwards, Bunting's life in Paris was hinted at a little more in a London bookshop where we had stopped during a walk. While enjoying books of beautiful reproductions of painters and sculptors of the twenties in Paris and earlier, he slowly turned the pages, examining them carefully. Once he chuckled remembering that in Paris they had used a piece by a famous sculptor pictured there for a doorstop. In February after I had sent him for his birthday the Giorgione book he had admired, he replied: 'What a pleasant birthday present! It has gone on to my shelf next to the Balthus, but not until I'd read it through and inspected the pictures. All they have to say about Giorgione is quite different from what they would have said fifty years ago, and that is interesting too' (28 February 1982).

In Paris in 1923 Bunting kept in touch with Pound who was giving Ford advice and even contributing to the *Review*. So it was not surprising that after a visit to England in December and January during which he decided to leave Ford, he travelled to Rapallo, Italy, with Pound's address in hand. Disappointed not to find him, he liked the place enough to stay on alone. However, he describes the joy of their reunion in a letter and in an interview. In the letter he explains: 'So afterwards I climbed a mountain, and on top of the mountain, to my astonishment, Ezra appeared. So I saw more of him. He was busy writing his first opera, and I was busy with poems. I am glad no one would print me then. All those have been destroyed.'[12] In Jonathan Williams' *Descant* he gives more details:

One day I walked up the mountain. I had to walk in those days, there were no cable railways and no roads. I walked up the mule track and there was a little inn at the top. As I passed the inn somebody rushed out of the doorway and began shouting, 'Bunting!' 'Bunting!' And I looked round and there to my astonishment was Ezra Pound, followed almost immediately by Dorothy, running after me up the mountain. Ezra was very pleasant, and it was from that meeting that I can say that I became one of Pound's friends...I never lost touch with him again.

For a while Bunting made a living on sand boats from Rapallo and the Tuscany coast, but this first stay in Rapallo was cut short by his return trip to England before his father died in 1925. During these months in England he was the British correspondent for the *Rivista di Roma*, but he packed this in when he 'discovered that that enterprising review hadn't the remotest intention of ever paying for its contributions'.[13]

The highlights of this stay in England in the eyes of outsiders was Basil's meeting with T. S. Eliot, D. H. Lawrence, and members of the Bloomsbury Group. The telling detail that Basil recalls is his deference to Eliot when he suggested that reading Dante would improve his poetry; the young poet was too modest to tell Eliot that not only had he already read Dante but he 'knew a good deal of the *Inferno* by heart'. Basil's replies to me about various members of the Bloomsbury Group were pithy:

Q. Roger Fry?
A. Fidgety.
Q. Clive Bell?
A. (Dismissed with 'hmph').
Q. Forster?
A. Nice enough chap, but the whole Bloomsbury Group didn't really like anyone not wealthy, with an inheritance, and educated.

By 1927 Bunting was a regular at a pub in Charlotte Street behind Tottenham Court Road, an area then full of cheap restaurants and artists' studios:

> I used to go to Kleinfeldt's to meet Nina Hamnett, and then people came to meet both of us there, and, gradually, from being a quiet place where a small number of people met from time to time, it became more and more crowded [D]

Otto Theiss, the American literary editor of the *Outlook*, knew he could reach Bunting there when he called him to take on the job of music critic. Bunting leaves it to others to decide the extent of his musical background. He told Theiss he didn't know 'a damn thing' about music, but he admits that before the twenties ended, when he had money as critic to buy scores, he could read them and hear pretty much the way the music went. Anyone who has read all his articles in the *Outlook* would take his 'Not a damn thing' with a large pinch of salt.

After he wrote about Elizabethan composers, Philip Heseltine sought him out at Kleinfeldt's along with Cecil Gray, and during those conversations Bunting declares he learned much about sixteenth-century music. In a television interview he told Jonathan Williams that criticism was 'not art in any sense. I was merely a journalist who knew nothing whatever about music pretending to be a music critic. That went well enough. England was full of highbrow papers in those days...I even wrote High Tory leaders [for the *Outlook*] though I was a Socialist.'[14] Bunting wrote to me that he was sorry the *Outlook* articles and the early journalism even existed: 'A young man earning his weekly guineas is not particular what he writes. Indeed, the *Outlook* told me that when I wrote sober I was too highbrow for them, so mostly I wrote drunk, and goodness knows what foolish things I may have written. Besides, I hardly recognise the author: I am not the same person I was fifty, forty, thirty years ago, and I don't think I would like my early self very much if I met him – too conceited by far, and even more ignorant than I am today' (28 February 1972).

In 1928 when 'the *Outlook* died of a libel action that it didn't want to face', it was rough going until he met Margaret de Silver, a wealthy American widow of one of the founders of the Civil Liberties Union who spent almost all her fortune subsidising 'artists, poets, politicians, lawyers, and civil liberties'[D]. After she left London, Theiss informed him that she had agreed to subsidise Bunting with two hundred pounds a year for two years. This liberating gift enabled him to get away from London to the rural area he loved best; for about six months he lived in a shepherd's cottage in the Simonsides in Northumberland, seven miles to the cigarette shop and four miles to the pub. What he learned here about the training of sheep dogs he distilled into poetry.

After those six months, Bunting relates that he then cleared off to Germany first – but for a very short time. He found he didn't like the Germans at all, so he returned to Rapallo. His settling in, however, was unsettled by a chance encounter in Venice where he met his future wife, Marian Gray Culver from Eau Claire, Wisconsin. With a freshly earned M.A. in English from Columbia, Marian was touring Europe as a graduation gift from her father. To broaden her experiences she had visited her brother who was studying medicine in Vienna and then she had travelled on to

Venice.

While Marian, an attractive American with burnished red hair, was on her balcony looking down on a Venetian festival, a handsome young Englishman stopped on the walk beneath and began explaining the celebration to her. Three days after this romantic encounter she moved in with Bunting, who was eight months older. Returning alone to the States, she spent some time teaching and doing social work until Bunting followed, ostensibly to see Margaret de Silver and to find a job. A year after they had met, Basil and Marian were married in Riverhead, Long Island, on 9 July 1930. On their marriage certificate, Basil, 30, listed his residence as Rapallo, and Marian, 29, listed hers as Wading River, New York. This marked the beginning of their brief attempt to live in the States. Home was 62 Montague Street while Marian taught English in the New York City school system and Bunting tried to find work without using all the letters of introduction Pound had given him.

However, these months gave Bunting the opportunity to cultivate his lifelong friendship with Louis Zukofsky whom he had first met in Rapallo. Besides Zukofsky, Bunting and his wife's circle of friends in New York included René Taupin, William Carlos Williams, Adolf Dehn, and Tibor Serly. When Zukofsky left in September for a year of teaching at the University of Wisconsin at Madison, Bunting saw him there also when he and his wife visited her family nearby.

Years later Bunting recalled this era of American Prohibition as a comedy. He told me that once in Rhode Island when Margaret de Silver said she would have to go to New York because she was out of whiskey, Bunting forestalled her by going out and asking the first policeman he saw where he could find a bootlegger. 'You came to the right person,' the officer replied. 'I'm the only bootlegger in town!'

But not comic at all were the eight months Bunting tried to earn money by writing reviews for *The Nation*, the *New York Times*, and music criticism for a Philadelphia paper. The Depression year, 1930, was the worst possible time to eke out a living in the United States. It was not difficult for Pound to convince him that he might as well be unemployed in Rapallo as in New York. According to Bunting, 'It was better to go back and see how long we could live on nothing in Italy – rather than the very short time you can live on nothing in the United States' [D]. Though Margaret de Silver had stopped funds when Basil had married, she did help pay for their

Self portrait in mirror, 1929.

Caricature of Bunting, published in Italy, 1931.

trip to Rapallo in January 1931.

A year later, in 1932, he wrote of those years:

> I was for some years in England, earning a very meagre living and
> growing stupid. Then I kicked, decided that I'd rather not earn a living
> than write any more reviews for weeklies, and have been better for it
> ever since. I tried my own North Country for a while, and it wasn't so
> bad but I got very little done that I wanted to keep, so I took advice and
> went to Berlin and it was the worst thing I ever did. In the end to save
> my sanity I went suddenly to the station and bought a ticket for Italy to
> look up Pound again. And here I've been ever since, with the exception
> of eight months in the States to get married.[15]

Reminiscing thirty years later, he added details about life in Rapallo
after he and his new wife returned:

> So off to Italy again. We settled down at Rapallo half-way up the
> mountain, and on the whole it was a very pleasant time. I got a good deal
> of poetry written, I enjoyed conversation, enjoyed sailing my boat,
> enjoyed the sunshine. And enjoyed having a baby. My first daughter
> [Bourtai]. Pound was there and various other people. Yeats was there. I
> saw a good deal of Yeats. But of few others. I don't enjoy literary society
> and literary conversation. [D].

The Pounds lived down the hill from the Buntings and for a time
Yeats lived in Rapallo for six months of each year. At first Yeats was
not interested in Bunting whom he named as 'one of Pound's more
savage disciples'.[16] But that changed so much that throughout his
life Bunting proudly recalled the surprise that Yeats gave him. At a
dinner for Bunting, Yeats, the host, dramatically recited one of
Basil's poems from memory – so dramatically, in fact, that for a
time the author did not even recognise it. Later Yeats's father, the
painter Jack Butler Yeats, gave the first Bunting child a playhouse,
and W. B. Yeats himself became a friend of Basil's mother, a great
reader of astrology books. For the rest of her life she remembered
with pride that she had read Yeats's horoscope.

In March 1930 *Redimiculum Matellarum* (Necklace of Chamber
Pots) was published privately in Milan. Bunting could never have
foreseen that today rare copies of this collection are kept in the
Bodleian at Oxford, in the Humanities Research Center at the
University of Texas at Austin, and that William Carlos Williams's
copy is kept at Yale.

With the help of Pound, *Villon* was featured in the October issue
of *Poetry*, the first of many poems Harriet Moore and her editors
published. This must have helped convince the poet that recognition, long due, had finally begun. In December discussions about
an English edition of *Poetry* began, but this did not become a reality

until much later. In February 1931 though, Zukofsky's much celebrated Objectivist issue of *Poetry* contained Bunting's 'The Word' ('Nothing').

A new member had joined the Rapallo group when his mother arrived to be with her son in the spring of 1929. Later that year she had her furniture brought down from Newcastle. If she had left Italy when Basil went to the United States, she had returned and moved into her own apartment before Basil and his wife arrived in Rapallo in February 1931 since Marian remembered her already there and well liked by Dorothy Pound.[17] Since Mr and Mrs Homer Pound and Jack Butler Yeats were also in Rapallo at various times, her arrival swelled the ranks of parents who had made their homes near their talented sons.

Poems dated 1931 prove this was a productive time – *Chomei at Toyama*, 'Vestiges', 'Attis' and *Aus dem zweiten Reich*. In Rapallo the Villa Michele Castruccio, Sestiers Borzoli, with its 330 steps on Montallegro, was the Buntings' home. But in November 1931 Marian travelled to the Protestant hospital in Genoa for the birth of their first child, Bourtai, named after the nine-year-old wife of Genghis Khan. The fifty-dollar Lyric Prize *Poetry* awarded Bunting for *Villon* came just in time to pay the hospital bill. Too poor to afford pre-natal care, Marian suffered serious complications. She had to spend nearly a month in the hospital, and then several weeks at Mrs Bunting's apartment recuperating.

Early in 1932 the new family returned to Borzoli, but then shortly afterwards they moved to a small penthouse on the Corso Cristoforo Colombo situated on the Gulf of Tigullio. Here they watched and took pictures of every new development of their first child. During these years they were in illustrious company. An article Bourtai keeps from her mother's collection is headlined 'Prominent Literati Arriving At Rapallo To Pass Winter Season' (5 January 1932). Part of it reads:

> Gerhardt Hauptmann, venerable figure of the literary constellation, is shortly due from Switzerland...
>
> Ezra Pound is here busily working upon his new opera, which should shortly be completed. He is living with his parents at the beautiful home of William B. Yeats, who is in Dublin arranging for the presentation of one of his dramas.
>
> Nancy Wilcox McCormick, Chicago sculptor, recently stayed with Mr and Mrs Homer Pound, parents of the poet, after coming from London where she completed a bust of Gandhi...
>
> The poet, Basil Bunting, whose wife is from Wisconsin, is rejoicing in the arrival of a baby daughter born in the Protestant Hospital at Genoa. The daughter was christened Bortai Bunting in honor of Genghis

Rapallo photographed by Bunting, with his boat in the foreground.

ABOVE: Bunting on the beach with Marian at Rapallo, 1933.
BELOW: Rapallo, 1933, with Marian (left) and Helen Lehmann.

Khan. Since this has happened Mr Bunting has given birth to two lines
of inspired verse each month.
...Edmond Dodsworth, Italian translator of William Blake and W. H.
Husdon, recently moved here...
   Max Beerbohm, with his wife Florence Kahn, former actress from
Tennessee, is busy in his white villa on the Ambrogian Hill.
   The Princess San Faustina, née Jan Campbell of New York, is a
prominent

– and here Marian Bunting cut the article; the most important
people had been noted.

   In February 1932 *Poetry: English Number* was finally published,
the issue for which Bunting with Michael Roberts was partly
responsible. Once again *Poetry* readers were able to enjoy his
writing, both poetry, 'Muzzle and Jowl', and prose, 'English Poetry
Today'. Even more encouraging was the appearance of *An
Objectivists' Anthology* edited by Zukofsky and published by George
Oppen in France.

   In a television interview near the end of his life, Bunting implied
that writing poetry was something he had to do. But as a young man
it was almost impossible to earn his living from writing poetry or
articles for magazines and newspapers as hard as he tried. Among
other things, in 1932 he contributed an article on Pound and one
on Eliot to the *New English Weekly* as well as articles to the *Paris
Tribune* and the *New York Sun*. In another television interview
Bunting explained that Pound could get about two hundred pounds
for an article now and again, but that he, of course, could not get
half a crown for an article, let alone a few hundred pounds.[18]
Bourtai remembers her mother telling her that Ezra Pound was
always concerned and generous, giving Basil clothes which were,
however, too large for him to use.

   As one of the core group of *Il Mare's Supplemento Letterrario*, his
name was on their official stationery after Pound's and two Italians
at the time Pound began a concert series designed to elevate the
popular taste. Bunting insists his connection was quite incidental.
His self-effacement or perhaps his feelings about the "overpower-
ing" Olga Rudge who had a part in it may have kept him from
associating himself with this project closely.

   To make the circle of poets and artists in Rapallo even more
complete, in August 1933 Zukofsky arrived. This welcomed guest,
met at Genoa by Bunting, outstanding in a red jacket, stayed with
the Pounds. Except for breakfast he ate all meals with the Buntings
for which Pound paid. Tea with Ezra and Dorothy which lasted for
hours every afternoon became a ritual for these two younger

poets.[19] Money had poured in after the birth of Bourtai, especially from Margaret de Silver, so that Bunting had bought a crude sailboat which Zukofsky enjoyed sharing some days.

Although Marian was not a part of the inner circle of poets, she was active in her own sphere. Since she had been a tennis champion at the University of Wisconsin, she entered a tournament in Italy, but was beaten badly. She joined in all the social events of the group, particularly one famous celebration of Robert Burns. Haggis was imported from Scotland and washed down with neat whisky until guests were doing outlandish things – indoors throwing cheese at each other and outdoors sailing around the lake wildly, and the like. Marian remembered that no one dared put his or her head out of doors for days for fear of meeting the looks of the shocked Italians.

Once the Buntings returned from an outing to claim Bourtai from the babysitter, Ezra Pound, only to find him feeding the baby whisky and exclaiming, 'She likes it! She likes it!'

However, by September 1933, the same month that *Chomei at Toyama* appeared in *Poetry*, rising costs and the fear of war and imprisonment made Bunting feel compelled to move his family to the Canary Islands. Believing that Bunting's mother would help her prevent this move, Marian tried to use all their money to pay bills, but on the day that Mrs Bunting was to arrive they left for the Canary Islands. The odd jobs that Bunting could find became so scarce he had little money, but with help from Margaret de Silver and Marian's family, they were able to live for a few months on Tenerife, the largest of the Canary Islands.

According to Bunting, the scenery was very good and the climate delightful [D]. But Bourtai remembers unusual weather too, red rain once or twice when the Sahara sand coloured it, a hurricane which lifted the thatched roof of a peasant's cottage straight up in the air, and all the trees down in the garden. Frighteningly, the window before which Marian was holding her youngest daughter while she was looking out at the chaos was broken immediately afterwards. Bourtai recalls moving several times, once from Hotel La Orotava to a favourite place, a small house at Salto del Barranco among banana plantations near Puerto Cruz. Here a woman living next door invited them to help themselves from her garage full of bananas whenever they wanted.

One high point within this financially depressing time was the first major appearance of Bunting's poetry in an important British publication. Ezra Pound's *Active Anthology* dedicated to Bunting

Bunting in Barcelona, 1933.

Barcelona, 1933.

and Zukofsky, 'two strugglers in the desert', published by Faber & Faber in October 1933, contained a large selection of Bunting's work which could never be honestly ignored from then on.

A second high point was the birth of his second daughter Roudaba on 4 February 1934, in Santa Cruz.[20] Naming her after the mother of Rustam in the epic of Persia showed the strong influence that learning Persian had on his personal life. Earlier when Pound had wanted to hear more of the poetry of the *Shahnamah*, Bunting had begun learning the language.

For her part Roudaba remembers the painful roll calls in each new school class as the unusual name was spoken until she finally shortened it to the less noticeable Rou. Although she was too young to remember life in the Canaries, she does remember her father as the dapper young man in photographs of this time and recalls hearing of the lively parties in Italy of 'Haas, Mas, and Baz', Eugene Haas, Masoliver, and Basil. Both daughters remember the Drerups well, and Rou still keeps a picture of 'Carlos and Gertruda' who became their friends, alleviating some of the isolation both families felt. Carlos photographed Bunting and painted his portrait, and Bourtai remembers the annual Christmas card with its drawing by Carlos sent to them for years afterwards.

One day when her parents took Bourtai to buy a puppy from a poor man, they found his large family in one room with one bed. In it was a girl Bourtai had been told was dying. As they took away her puppy to sell to the Buntings, she was crying, and Bourtai felt paralysed in this situation. To this traumatic childhood experience Bourtai, now a city attorney in the States, attributes much of her deep concern about poverty and injustice.

Bunting admitted he 'got very gloomy in the Canaries and wrote a poem called 'The Well of Lycopolis', which is about as gloomy a poem as anyone would want' [D]. So still searching for a living, he travelled to the Algarve in southern Portugal with help from Margaret de Silver. Here he found all he had hoped for, but Marian was not convinced of the wisdom of travelling with two small children and no money to a place that was fifty miles from a town and a doctor. While Basil was away, with the help of the Drerups, Marian moved from their house which Carlos and Gertruda Drerup were waiting for to the pension Las Arenas run by Dr Isadore Luz and Baron and Baroness von Louen. The Baroness was the widow of the Kaiser's youngest son, a mentally deficient boy who committed suicide when she ran away with the Baron. Since by Hitler's order the Germans could not spend their money outside of Germany, there were not many tourists. So the proprietors took in the Buntings at low rates. The last part of their two years in Santa Cruz, the Buntings lived in a beautiful house, Casa Fortuna.

Both children learned Spanish quickly and even translated for their parents at times, but this facility was lost after their later move to London. One Spanish political jingle they can still recite begins with the vowels, 'Ah, eh ee, o, oo', to rhyme with 'La cabeza de Lerroux', that is, 'The head of Lerroux', the Premier of Spain at the helm of a weak provisional government. Bunting offhandedly mentioned that his work there was occasionally interrupted by chess games with a man from St Helena and Francisco Franco, military governor of the Islands [D]. This military government was a shadow of the growing unrest with Fascist groups vying with supporters of the Republic. Bourtai remembers jumping with joyful excitement, unknowingly, when a bomb exploded in the tennis court of her wealthy little English friend, Rosamund Clark.

The Roehn Rebellion and massacre outraged both Germans and English, but the Germans who heard an address by Hitler on the wireless were convinced that the Führer knew best. Sympathisers with the Popular Front, the Buntings followed political events closely. Though Marian was the one who attended meetings, Basil's name was soon on Franco's list. Realising they were sitting on a powder keg and fearing imprisonment once more, he bought tickets for Southampton. Immediately upon their arrival in England, the headlines shouted the beginning of the Spanish Civil War in June 1936 and the ports in the Canaries were closed. Soon after, Bunting wrote one of his rare political essays, 'The Roots of the Spanish Civil War', for *The Spectator*.

Life in England must have been quite difficult for the family, living for a time with Mrs Bunting in London and for a time alone. But the children were kept free from these concerns. Bourtai can vividly picture the Christmas tree her grandmother trimmed for them and the quintuplet dolls she loved to undress completely so that her mother and grandmother would have to dress them up again. Like an echo from Basil's own early education, Bourtai remembers both her parents reading to her from an early age, especially 'The Cat Who Walked by Himself' from the *Just So* stories. The music Basil taught her to appreciate was quite different from Byrd's Service, but more in line with the bawdy songs he enjoyed all his life: 'Rollicking Bill the Sailor', for one, and an American Civil War shanty she still sings, for another.

Bunting in Santa Cruz, 1934.

Santa Cruz, 1934: Minoletti, Masoliver, Bunting, Haas.

While they were living at South Hill Mansion with a view of Round Pond at Hampstead Heath, she obediently kept away from the swans though she was always allowed to run excitedly to meet the hot cross bun man. She also remembers being frightened when she rode the elephant at the London Zoo where her parents had taken her.

Rou's clearest and happiest memory is riding on her father's shoulders with Bourtai walking, holding his hand, to see the Punch and Judy shows. Bourtai's memory is of her own turn on his shoulders so she could look down into the crowd to see where Punch had thrown out the baby. That he was preparing his children to love the kind of entertainment he himself enjoyed is evident from a letter he sent me fifty years later: 'Years ago I would have said take your students to the pantomime at the Elephant, but they pulled down the Elephant long since, and though there may still be theatres in the suburbs or in south London where they keep up the old Victorian pantomime, the lush ones in Central London are just what you might see anywhere – no real fun' (1 December 1981).

A list of five articles published in 1936 reveals that Bunting was submitting pieces to *The Spectator*, the *New English Weekly*, and *The Criterion*. Throughout his life Bunting was reticent about his 'acquaintance', T. S. Eliot, the influential editor of *The Criterion*, who only infrequently published his work. Once in April 1936, he printed a group of four book reviews and one poem, 'From Faridun's Sons' by Firdusi, which Bunting omitted from his *Collected Poems*; once in July, two book reviews, one signed 'BB'; and much later in April 1938, another book review.[21] Not only did Eliot's lack of support hurt the possibility of being recognised more widely; Bunting's hostile review of Malcolm Muggeridge's book on Samuel Butler in the *New English Weekly* (1 October 1936), turned this other influential author against him and seemed to be the final blow to his chances of being noticed by the important critics in London.

Financial difficulties were affecting the family more seriously than ever before. Though Marian believed in the exceptional quality of Basil's poetry all her life, lack of money was a serious concern for her. In early January 1937, pregnant and with the loan of one pound from Mrs Bunting, she moved away with their two daughters. After gaining legal custody of the children, she left Europe for her home in Eau Claire, Wisconsin, where their son Rustam was born on May 15. That the ocean voyages, this time on the Queen Mary, were traumatic for Bourtai is evident from her memories of huge waves which threatened to overwhelm the ship and which she dreamed of long afterwards. Bunting reports it stoically years later: '...my wife presently quit me and took the children with her and went to America' [D].

For the winter Bunting tried 'to face up to the difficulty of life' by sailing on his own six-tonner, the *Thistle*, around Essex, helping out the herring fishermen on the south coast of Devon and seine-net men on the shore [D]. In the spring when Karl Drerup visited him, Bunting was with his mother who had moved in with him in London when his family left. But he must have still owned the *Thistle* since he remembers buying it for one hundred pounds and selling it a year later for two hundred pounds. His financial difficulties and deep sadness about not being able to visit his children were clearly expressed in letters to Zukofsky all during this time and well into the forties as well as in letters he wrote to Marian.

Not for certification which his bad eyesight prevented, but just to know enough to handle a boat intelligently, he enrolled in the Nellist Nautical Academy in Newcastle, 'a cramming school for people who want certificates', yet one which 'used to turn out half the Merchant Navy officers in Britain', according to Bunting. Though Bunting never stopped writing, as an April 1938 book review in *The Criterion* and another in *The Nation* the next July prove, from April 1938 until the start of World War II, Bunting found work again in New York and Los Angeles, sailing a big schooner and other boats [D].

Recalling this time, Lorine Niedecker explained to Cid Corman:

> Basil Bunting – yes, I came close to meeting him when he was in this country in the 30s. Some mention at the time of his going into the fishing business (he had yeoman muscles LZ said and arrived in NY with a sextant) with my father on our lake and river but it was the depression and at that particular time my dad felt it best to 'lay low' so far as starting fresh with new equipment was concerned and a new partner – the market had dropped so low for our carp – and I believe BB merely lived a few weeks with Louie without engaging in any business.[22]

From June on he had been in close contact with kindred spirits, Louis Zukofsky, William Carlos Williams, Kenneth Patchen, René Taupin, Carl Drerup as well as Charles Reznikoff, John Rodker, Austin Dobson, and Jacques Kahane. In 1939 Britain declared war and Williams Carlos Williams in his *Autobiography* mentions Bunting's quick response to his country's need: 'Bunting had been a conscientious objector in the First World War and they had given him some rough treatment. It is worth noting, however, that for the

The Bunting children: Rustam, Roudaba, Bourtai, 1939 (photographed through gauze as a silhouette profile picture).

Second World War he rushed across the United States from California to go to England, as fast as he could, to enlist.'[23]

After spending years trying to make a living and so be able to write poetry, Bunting began a career during World War II which seems the material of novels. Though he had returned to Northumberland by May Day 1939, he still was not in a service in August 1940. The only break in waiting was 'the six solid, stolid lectures' in history from Alexander the Great to the Middle Ages he had given by December 1939 for WEA classes. In August Bunting complained to Zukofsky: 'I am idle;...no nearer job, on waiting lists of army (intelligence), air force (balloons), children's evacuation people...but nothing comes of it' (9 August 1940).[24] From this list he omitted his energetic attempts to become a merchant seaman, a fisherman, or to serve on a minesweeper. Finally accepted as a balloon-man in the Royal Air Force, he trained with a squad of Welshmen, many of whom did not understand English. This may have been where he himself learned Welsh in order to appreciate the sounds of the poetry, especially the lines of Heledd, a Welsh woman whom he ranked among the world's greatest.

For a very short time Bunting was stationed at Hull. Then for a year, during 1940 and 1941, based chiefly at Methill in Fife, Scotland, he lived what the Air Force described as a dangerous life aboard a converted luxury yacht escorting convoys with balloons. But Bunting downplayed this in a note to me as 'not really dangerous. They called it dangerous' (4 July 1973). Actually, the *Golden Hind* was so comfortable it had to be made compulsory to go ashore.

When new methods made his job unnecessary, he volunteered for Persia with a reading knowledge of 'very old, medieval, classical Persian, which he had never heard spoken', and was sent there as an interpreter for a squadron. Years later he still wondered if the right man went to jail in the first court martial for which he acted as interpreter. Amazingly enough, even in this aspect of this life, Pound had an influence. Because of him Bunting had originally learned Persian after he had found a tattered, incomplete book with a newspaper cover marked *Oriental Tales* on the quays of Genoa. Caught up in this early nineteenth century French translation of Firdusi's *Shahnamah*, the epic of Persia, Bunting, Ezra and Dorothy Pound were 'yearning' to find out what happened. Earlier in New York Marian had bought Bunting Steingass's dictionary. So Pound bought Bunting three volumes of Vullers and he seriously

Squadron-Leader Bunting with colleagues in Persia.

set to work learning Persian, 'an easy language' for reading [D].
Since the Luri and Bakhtiari tribesmen still spoke an older Persian,
it was less difficult for Bunting to be in charge of a large group of
Luri workmen than to speak to the Teheranis. To Zukofsky he
wrote:

> My men became the envy of other units. And out of hours (and out of
> bounds) they entertain me now and then as Bakhtiari should, with pipes
> and drums, dancers and singers, sweetmeats and rice and strong drink,
> and a man to fan me all the evening – very welcome in the terrific heat of
> Khuzistan (139° in the shade – and it had been 145° a little earlier). [9
> May 1940].

When their squadron leader volunteered to take a convoy of shells
across the desert for a month-long journey to Tripoli, he wrote to
Zukofsky 'from a conquered city in Italian Africa' about the
nightmare experience he ultimately described in *The Spoils*.

Farther on in the fighting at Wadi Aqarit, Bunting was obliged to
take a commission (as Squadron Leader) which he never wanted,
and set off to Cairo [D]. A year later in Throckley, Northumberland, waiting for reassignment to Persia, Bunting reminisced about
the unbelievable responsibilities which had been his especially
during the Sicilian invasion:

Bunting reading: picture taken in Persia.

I found myself practically in charge of a unit working beyond its
strength...I've even signed documents as Medical Officer!...I planned
operations, interpreted orders from above, ruled everything without
official authority or backing. I even started and regulated a civilian
market (not black but stripy), caught and punished thieves, traced a spy,
instituted liaison with an Italian regiment...[LZ, 23 July 1944]

A story Bunting told me more than once was of the convent of nuns
in Sicily whom he had befriended and who in return promised to
pray for him for the rest of his life.

    At the end of the war Bunting returned to England to implement
his plans to use his earnings to buy a boat in order to live cheaply at
sea again and write. But when the job of Vice-Consul at Isfahan
was offered to him by the Foreign Office, he sold his boat to return
to Persia for supposedly one year. From Isfahan in 1945, he
summarised his career from this new perspective:

...my taste for variety has certainly been gratified in this war. I have been on almost every British front worth being on except Dunkirk, travelled through every rank from Aircraftsman First Class to Squadron-Leader (equals Major, to forestall your question), seen huge chunks of the world that I wouldn't otherwise have visited, been sailor, balloon-man, drill instructor, interpreter, truck driver in the desert, intelligence officer to a busy fighter squadron, recorder of the doings of nomadic tribes, labour manager, and now consul in a more or less crucial post. [LZ, 21 April 1945]

In a turn of events all was settled and a ticket bought for Bourtai, fourteen, to meet Omar Pound in Europe and travel with him to Isfahan to live with her father. But at the last minute Marian cancelled the trip. Though Bourtai realises now that her mother was being realistic about the unrest in the Middle East, at that time her disappointment was doubled. Not only was she not to live in an exotic land with her father who had promised she could study at the Sorbonne, neither was she to attend the University of Chicago whose entrance exams she had passed in a special programme. The second dream faded away when lack of funds forced her to return to school in Eau Claire as a high school sophomore.

In 1946 from a transit camp in Cairo, Bunting was again on his way home to England, writing to Zukofsky:

So my responsibility for telling our two governments what happens in Western Asia – between the Jordan and the Indian border, between the Hadhramand and the Ukraine – is ended at last. So are the pleasant journeys ended, amongst mountain tribes, long trips on horseback, mouflon hunts, banquets with provincial governors and cocktail parties with diplomats...All the tribesmen ask the same question: 'Why are you taking these officers away from us? Who will be left to understand the Kurds and tell the Powers what we need?'...The Bakhtiari sent a note to the British Government asking for my return to Persia.

Reading this later, Bunting wrote modestly: 'I'd rather have all this omitted...It sounds too presumptuous altogether.' But he had written these same stories of life in Persia to others. They had sounded so amazing to his daughter Roudaba that not until much later did she realise that the lavish banquets with the tribesmen in the mountains, the princes he rode with, and the exotic animals he wrote about, the leopard which jumped onto his lap, were not just fantastic stories for her amusement.

In any event Bunting's lament to Zukofsky was premature. In 1946 he accepted a new position as Chief of Political Intelligence. Working at the British Embassy, he wrote again on 5 May 1947 to Zukofsky that the position required 'all the astuteness and tact' he could muster, but he was content to be living in 'one of the most

Photographs taken by Bunting in Persia. Isfahan Majet Shah Mosque, 1947 (top left), with a plaster detail (top right). Mashad, 1948 (below).

civilised countries in the world. One of the pleasantest to live in'.

Two years later Robert Payne in *Journey to Persia* (1951) describes idyllic days visiting Bunting

> spent bathing in this waterfall in the garden of an English poet not far from Shamran...full of dying roses...a red-tiled swimming pool, and the poet was credited with a passionate love of Persia, translated their poetry superbly, knew many Persian dialects and thought the world and ambition well lost as long as he could remain in his garden, with his exquisitely handsome Armenian wife, his books and his pipes. He...was

known for the wisdom of his political judgements,...had...written and rarely published some of the best poetry of our time. He had quelled a German-aided revolt of the Bakhtiari tribesmen almost single-handed, and to that extent he may have altered the course of the war,...I had heard about him in China. Ezra Pound had said once: 'If I was a younger man, I would go to Teheran just to see him.'[25]

The 'exquisitely handsome Armenian wife' Payne met was the young Sima Alladallian whom Bunting had married on 2 December 1948, and then taken to London for a month-long honeymoon to introduce her to his family and country.

When Bunting left the Foreign Office in April 1949, the London *Times* offered him a job as Official Correspondent in Teheran, and for a year he worked there with correspondents of world newspapers. During this time a big breakthrough occurred when Dallam Flynn of Galveston, Texas, contacted Bunting about publishing a collection of his poetry. Finally, in 1950, with a fulsome introduction by Flynn, also known as Dallam Simpson, *Poems 1950* was printed in an edition of about one thousand copies, not all bound.

Bunting described the preface as 'florid, effusive as John Barrymore', and told me he saw only the second copy after someone else corrected the proofs and cut out parts with a penknife. A loyal admirer of Pound's who visited him at St. Elizabeth's Hospital, Flynn made it clear in the introduction that he was fighting the '*suppressing* for nearly two decades' of 'Bunting's magnificent verse. It is appalling that with such verse capable of being written, we must be affronted by false prophets, bards of dubious origin, and writers, who, through nature or necessity, expunge their works in impenetrable nebulae of ignorance and pedantry.'[26] When 'John Kasper and David Horton, publishers of the Square Dollar Series, acquired the unbound copies, [they] reissued them with their own paper covers, probably in the winter of 1951.'[27]

1950 not only marked the year of the first appearance of his collected poems but also the first appearance of Maria Bunting, Sima and Basil's first child. By April, the *Times* job came to an end, and in May he and his family travelled by car to Throckley, Northumberland, not a comfortable trip judging from one photo of a flat tyre being changed. While searching for a new job, Bunting met Peter Russell and Olga Rudge in July, and then in November dined with T. S. Eliot in London, but nothing ever came of this.

He eventually persuaded the *Northern Echo* to hire him as their first foreign correspondent to Italy, and then spent 'six dreary

52   BASIL BUNTING: A LIFE

weeks' in London 'pretending to learn what [he] already knew about newspaper offices, varied by some uninteresting press photography' [LZ, 12 November 1950]. Afterwards he drove with his wife and his daughter to Lucca, Tuscany, only to drive home again in June 1951 when the assignment in Italy ended. But in the meantime the family had found time to visit the Pages at Rapallo in February, an opportunity to relive the happy days of the Twenties and Thirties which must have seemed light years away from the present and the atmosphere of St Elizabeth's Hospital.

About Pound's release Basil Bunting and T. S. Eliot, both disciples, were in strong agreement. But in another area they were not in such accord. Reportedly, in May 1951, Eliot, powerful at Faber & Faber, was not receptive about reprinting a UK edition of Bunting's *Poems* unless the introduction, strongly critical of the British, was omitted. It seems unlikely that Eliot would have been enthusiastic about these lines:

American letters, having indicated such rare and delightful discrimination...are to be commended. Heartily commended! It is not clear that this is just another transatlantic time-lag, though it may very well be. At any rate, it seems ominously apparent at this time, that the island *claqueurs* are catering a seasonal low in clientele.

Occupying, for the moment, Mr Berryman's suzerainty, one attends him:

1. Superciliously confiding to us that England is praising her young poets *beyond recognition*. We don't know which generation Mr Berryman refers to as young...Bunting ignored for two decades, and no other passable British verse being written during the period. Perhaps he means Mr Eliot? But no, one recalls now and again that Eliot was American, is British now only, by virtue of documents of citizenry, an affiliation with Anglo-Catholicism, and a rapport with an assortment of notables, persons of peerage, etcetera (iii-iv).

Although Bunting recognised the weakness of the introduction, out of loyalty he insisted that it remain, and thereby lost any chance of Eliot's patronage, slight as it had been throughout the years. However, according to Clucas, the reason for Eliot's rejection was that Bunting's poetry was 'too Poundian'.[28] Eliot's lack of support notwithstanding, reviewers of the calibre of Hugh Kenner and G. S. Fraser in the United States, Canada, and England took notice of *Poems 1950* in quality journals.

Living frugally in Throckley with his family, Bunting was relieved and pleased when in October he was able to return to Persia as foreign correspondent for the *Times* once more. Increasingly from October to December, Bunting and other foreign correspondents were harrassed by the police, and from December

Bunting with his second wife Sima in Teheran, 1948.

onwards Bunting was under threat of expulsion by Mossadeq.
Terrified by the mobs and riots, many journalists ran away, but
Bunting seemed to thrive on the excitement though he received
threats against his life and was 'shot at once or twice'. Convinced
that hired assassins want the money but not the risk of killing, he
told Jonathan Williams of the time two men with pistols arrived at
the door. His wife merely told them he was not in and they
accepted that, so his afternoon nap was not disturbed. Another time
while he was in the flat of the Reuters correspondent, a hired mob
began shouting for his life outside the Ritz in Teheran. After
watching for a while, he decided to go out to hear what they were
saying. 'And the Reuters man was a bit afraid to go out. I said what
the hell, no one knows what I look like or anything. I went out. I
walked into the crowd and stood amongst them and shouted
DEATH TO MR BUNTING! with the best of them and nobody took

the slightest notice of me' [D]. About thirty years later, when his daughter Roudaba happened to mention this story to an Iranian psychiatrist she was working with in Seattle, the doctor exclaimed that *she* had been in that crowd shouting!

But in April 1952 Mossadeq did finally manage to expel Bunting as a suspicious person – an ex-vice consul, one who knew Persian, and who had a Persian wife – but actually because of his refusal to doctor news that no one else had sufficient information to correct. [LZ, 15 June 1952; 23 March 1953]. After the British authorities enabled Bunting to clear his wife and child whom Mossadeq tried to persuade to remain in Persia, once more they travelled by car to England, Sima pregnant. In June, the month *The Spoils* is dated, they arrived in Throckley to settle permanently in Northumberland. As Bunting described it in a television interview: '...Mossadeq chucked me out and then I reverted to my beginnings. We hadn't any money to buy a house...Nothing. We shared my mother's very small house in Throckley for some time...'[29] Here, in December, their son, Thomas Faramay, was born.

In the years following, when the family was almost destitute, public praises were small comfort:

> 'Dispatches...always been scrupulously fair and objective,' said the *Times* leader writer 'a sound judge of Persian affairs...deep sympathy with the Persian people...devoted his life to the country'. Another time, 'Persia's best friend in the West'. For which my children must starve and I be denied any chance to show sagacity elsewhere. This week we cannot pay the butcher. [LZ, 18 June 1953]

Unable to get a job as an orientalist without a university degree and muzzled by the Official Secrets Act from telling prospective employers of his experience, in September 1953 Bunting found part-time work with the *Manchester Guardian* and did some proof-correcting. Later he made a living by such jobs as proof-reading columns of suburban train times, then seedsmen's catalogues, and finally electoral lists.

One bleak October day in 1953 Roudaba called her father from the States to tell him that his son Rustam, 15, had died that morning at a boarding school in New Hampshire after an eighteen-hour siege of polio; this was the year before the Salk vaccine was discovered. Marian who was summoned once the situation was judged serious rushed to be at his side, but when she called en route from New York, she was given the devastating news of her son's death.

Though Bunting did not know it at the time, Rou and Rusty

together at High Mowing School in New Hampshire had been greatly influenced by him. Because they had been told that their father had gone around New York barefoot, with a long cape, more than once they had dressed themselves flamboyantly as 'poet's children', and gone to New York to act the part. It was not unusual for them to look up other poets' names in the telephone book and then to appear on their doorsteps, Rou in a tee-shirt and long skirt she had made. Rou remembers E. E. Cummings coming to the door and being delighted with the ceramic cat she had made for him – one anatomically correct, scratching his ear. At W. H. Auden's home, after a servant answered the door, Auden appeared, dressed in a suit. Though he was kind enough to the children, he was much more formal. Later at the Zukofskys' birthday party for their small son Paul, the Bunting children were impressed not so much by the fact that Paul could play the violin but that he received a live rabbit.

On another occasion they went into every New York bookshop they could find to ask for Basil Bunting's poems. Their greatest surprise came when a slight, old man just ahead of them asked for Basil Bunting's poems before they did. When they caught up with him on the street, they frightened him until they announced who they were and a delighted Edward Dahlberg introduced himself to Basil's children. Because Rou had liked the Kenneth Patchen writing she had been assigned in school, she wrote to him, not knowing he too was a friend of her father's, and was pleasantly surprised when he wrote back asking if she was Basil Bunting's daughter. All of these memories that Rou still cherishes were not to be shared with Bunting till many years later. The only sharing of that morning was the unfathomable sorrow they both felt. Basil allowed his grief to be known later in one of the most personal of his unpublished poems, 'A Song for Rustam', honouring his dead son.In a BBC interview[30] he admitted that his working hours on the newspaper at this time had a few compensations:

> '...riding home at night on a motor scooter from the bloody newspaper. That was worth doing. In the middle of the night you saw all sorts of creatures on the road that you never see in the daytime. Every kind of owl I got familiar with. Foxes carrying chickens in their mouths and things of that sort. It was very nice in some ways. Of course you were terribly tired. Tiring business being up all night working on the newspaper and then trying to sleep when everybody else is up and about during the day.'

For a change of hours, Bunting transferred to the Newcastle *Evening Chronicle* as a sub-editor on 26 July 1954. 'But that was a great mistake I made. I wanted to see more of my children and I could by working on the *Chronicle* that had reasonable working hours. But they put me on to doing the damned stock exchange report and that sort of thing.'

When Sima and the children were able to visit her family in Persia in October 1956, Bunting remained at his job. Then an old aunt died. Bunting said that she wasn't supposed to have any money, but in fact she had been very friendly with rich relatives, rather remotely related, and had been given quite a lot. 'So I inherited a few thousand pounds from her and bought the house in Wylam.' And then he added wryly: 'I spent the next twenty years trying to pay off the mortgage.'[31]

From the time of the move to Shadingfield, Wylam, in May 1957 until as late as 1966, Bunting was travelling every day to Newcastle to produce the financial page and write articles, with little time for writing poetry. *Nine*'s publication of 'You there' and 'The Thundercloud' in 1956 reveal a rare publication during these rather barren years. Sometime in 1957 Bunting travelled to London and saw Eliot and Bridson, but it seems evident nothing ever came of this trip either. Another gate was shut when in 1962 Margaret de Silver died. She had been a friend who had unobtrusively supported Bunting's talent whenever possible since 1928.

If it had not been for a happy combination of circumstances, the loyalty of friends, especially Jonathan Williams and Louis Zukofsky, and the persistence of Tom Pickard, Basil Bunting might never have left the obscurity of the Newcastle *Evening Chronicle*. When asked in a television interview if he was concerned that his poetry might have never been noticed, Bunting said with equanimity, 'I was quite confident it would be done sometime. If you have practically no readers, but those readers were people like Yeats and Pound, and Eliot, Carlos Williams, well, you're pretty confident some notice will be taken sooner or later.'[32]

However, the story of how it happened is a turning point in his creative life. In 1963 Tom Pickard, an aspiring Newcastle poet, wrote to Jonathan Williams at Jargon Press, North Carolina, about help with his poetry. Williams replied kindly, but directed him to some poets living right there in Newcastle. Bunting's address was included. When Pickard appeared on Bunting's doorstep in December to ask for a contribution to *Eruption*, the magazine he was involved with, Bunting read him *The Spoils* and then gave it to him to publish after a twelve-year silence.[33] Once he began helping

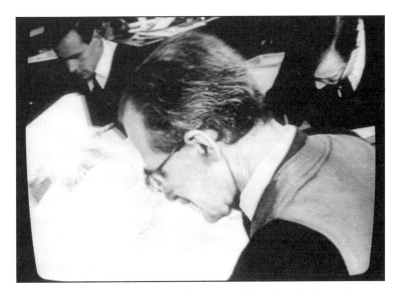

Two pictures from a BBC Television film made in 1966: above, Bunting working at the Evening Chronicle; below, writing 'Briggflatts' on his nightly journey home to Wylam.

Pickard, his own interest in writing was reawakened. By November 1964, Robert Creeley, Donald Hall, and Gael Turnbull were visiting him, and his readings at Morden Tower in Newcastle seemed to have convinced him completely that an audience of

Bunting pictured when he was working on the Evening Chronicle in Newcastle, 1965, before the eye operation which later greatly improved his sight.

'unabashed girls and boys' as well as many older lovers of poetry was out there ready to appreciate his gifts:

> ...a curious experience, reading to these youngsters. They were not hindered by the difficulties that annoy their elders. They took poetry as poetry – a nice noise – without questions about its "meaning". They laughed at the comic bits, they were rapt at the passages of intricate metric that nobody ever took notice of before – not that they understood what was attracting them, but it certainly did attract – and the piece about the sick child [Ode 1:35] made at least one girl cry. I found it all very encouraging. [LZ, 28 July 1964]

A few months later he wrote to Zukofsky: 'Perhaps it is enough to say that between you and Tom Pickard, somehow the old machine has been set to work again, and I have actually been writing. Therefore I send you the first fruits' [LZ, 7 September 1964]. 'A Song for Rustam' was enclosed. Within two years he had completed eight odes and one of his greatest poems, the sonata *Briggflatts*. While commuting to work in Newcastle, Bunting had filled 'two fat notebooks absolutely chocked full, front and back, both sides of the page'. This he had condensed to about seven hundred lines, 'until you get everything as neat and short as you can', before his greatest sonata was finally completed in December 1965 and read for the first time at Morden Tower.

During these months more and more of his poetry was seen in print. Earlier that year Tom Pickard and Gael Turnbull published and distributed *The Spoils*; then in November, Stuart and Deirdre Montgomery of Fulcrum Press published the *First Book of Odes*; in December they brought out *Loquitur*, and in February *Briggflats*. *Agenda*'s Autumn 1966 issue, which contained two new odes, appeared as the first Basil Bunting Special Issue. It seemed Bunting was finally being recognised when he received an Art Council Bursary for 1966, and on 30 August he was able to leave his job on the newspaper to accept a Visiting Lectureship at the University of California, Santa Barbara. Newspapers and journals lauded his work in reviews and by this time all of England could enjoy his readings on television and radio, beginning with the first programme in 1965.

Besides being internationally recognised, other important events occurred in 1966: he met his daughters Bourtai and Roudaba again for the first time in thirty years. Although they had corresponded sporadically throughout this time, they had never been reunited. The summer he arrived in the States he first travelled to Wisconsin where Bourtai and her family lived near her mother. His grandchildren immediately loved their newly found grandfather and his fabulous stories. Bourtai more slowly renewed her acquaintance with a pleasant stranger, a father she had idealised and fantasised about all through her youth.

Earlier he had tried to convince Rou to go to nursing school in England, but Rou had decided on the University of Honolulu. That Christmas Bunting sent Rou a ticket to California for their first reunion. Though Bourtai had been invited also, she was unable to accept. In her last year at the University of Wisconsin, she was trying to balance her family responsibilities and studying by getting up at four in the morning and staying up late at night. When Rou travelled from Hawaii to see Bunting in Santa Barbara, she expected a flamboyant "Poet" – something like the barefoot Poet with swirling cape who had been described to her. To her amazement she met an ordinary looking, quiet, cultured, gentle man with whom, from that time on, she and her family never lost close contact. Later when her father had a cataract removed from one eye, Rou, a nurse, was able to be with him in California for the operation.

Since Bunting's eyesight still prevented him from driving, Maria arrived in California in plenty of time to drive the two of them in Bunting's new secondhand car to Wisconsin in the summer of

1967. It may have been on the way that Bunting was interviewed by
Jonathan Williams for *Descant on Rawthey's Madrigal* in Aspen,
Colorado. With introductions from Mina Loy's daughters,
Williams had been invited to be scholar-in-residence at the Aspen
Institute, and the *Aspen News* took note that Williams was playing
host 'this week to the Northumbrian poet, Basil Bunting, whom he
considers the foremost poet of Great Britain' [22 June 1967: 13].
    Another highlight of that summer was meeting Lorine Nie-
decker, the woman whose poetry he praised so highly. In a letter to
Cid Corman she wrote about the event: 'Basil came! With two
daughters [Bourtai and Maria]...Have you ever met him? His
manner is timid and tender. Withal so kindly. O lovely day for
me.'[34] At the time of Niedecker's death in 1970, Rou remembers
her father, visiting her home in Wisconsin, very angry that so little
notice was taken in either the daily papers or academic publications.
    From Wisconsin Bourtai and her son Ahab, Bunting and Maria
drove on to Montreal's Expo 67 before Maria and Ahab set sail for
Wylam where Ahab lived for a year. Returning to Madison, Bourtai
packed up her four youngest sons and their belongings to travel to
California with Bunting. Leaving with her mother one son who
wished to finish high school in Madison and dropping off another
and his pet monkey in Chicago with his father, Bourtai with her
three youngest sons and Bunting drove across the country in a
holiday spirit. Crossing the Nevada desert, Bunting pretended with
the children that they were in the Sahara with water and dates
rationed. At Isla Vista in Bunting's home close to the Pacific, they
all lived together companionably for several months until Bourtai
found a job in Los Angeles.
    To make up for all the lost years, Bourtai with her family
travelled from Los Angeles to see her father on weekends. One
time he had made kidney stew for them, but he was not sure what
was in it since his cataracts hindered his sight. But to be sure it
would be ready, he had had it cooking on the stove for three days.
After the first cataract operation that summer, he was to have the
second in England the following year. But not before he had
finished a busy schedule in the States with readings at such places
as Harvard and the Guggenheim Museum.
    In June 1968 he was appointed Northern Arts Literary Fellow at
Newcastle and Durham Universities, and in the same year Fulcrum
Press published his *Collected Poems* and Stream recorded *Briggflatts*.
Roger Guedalla's bibliography lists eighteen reviews of the *Poems*,

proof of his rapidly growing reputation.

For a complete biography, someone must chronicle each honour and all his travels; for a briefer biography it is enough to record some highlights between 1969 and 1971: his reading at the Royal Albert Hall International Poetry Festival, his visits to the University of British Columbia and the University of Vancouver, and his stay at the State University of New York at Buffalo. Bourtai and her family met him off the plane in Canada, and both Canadian universities were near Roudaba in Seattle, so that he could visit her family also more frequently during the months when he was there. In 1976 he read in another tour of the States at Harvard, Maine, Yale, Wisconsin, and St Andrew's, as well as in Buffalo, New York, San Francisco, and Davidson, North Carolina. Nearer home, while continuing BBC television and radio interviews and readings, he addressed the Yeats Society in Sligo in 1973.

In 1972 he became President of the Poetry Society and in 1974 President of Northern Arts, and all the while more and more was being written about him with special editions of literary magazines and books coming off the press. His own publications during these years centred on other writers. In 1971 he edited the *Selected Poems* of Ford Madox Ford and in 1976 Joseph Skipsey's *Selected Poems*. One period that seemed to give him leisure and stimulus to work was his return voyage to England from British Columbia in May. Because of the number of his books, this had to be by boat through the Panama Canal. Upon his return to England, when I was more deeply into my dissertation, our correspondence quickened. Bunting wrote that a number of themes he had had in his head 'for at least three years, some longer' had begun to assemble themselves: 'I cannot say more yet, but it seems to me that I shall soon be able to begin work on a sonata, or what is more likely to prove a sonata than not...[23 May 1972]. However, five months later he was less hopeful:

> A whole host of interruptions, trivial at first, but now becoming really serious, have prevented me doing real work for months; and it looks as though I will have to try to find a job again, if anybody will employ me at my age, thus making poetry not far from impossible for a long time to come; and I haven't got a long time to come (though I'm healthy for my age). [23 October 1972]

Although in May he had sent me thirty lines of a sonata that promised to be one of his most beautiful, he published only a few more poems in his lifetime. When the Oxford University Press edition of his *Collected Poems* appeared in 1978 and the Moyer Bell

American edition in 1985, there was little more to add.

His health, usually strong, seemed to fail somewhat in 1979 when he suffered a slight stroke. Colin Simms wrote to me that 'his loneliness, since the departure of most local poets to the South, is more acute. A great tragedy' [27 November 1979]. By early 1980 he was separated from his wife and family and living alone at Blackfell, Washington. But his friends who had left for the South proved they had not forgotten him when they held an eightieth birthday celebration at Warwick University where Tom Pickard, writer-in-residence, Gael Turnbull, and others read with the guest of honour.

His loneliness, however, became more apparent in a letter he wrote to me in May, though at 80 he was still ready for another strenuous transatlantic trip – and more:

> I am to go to a sort of miscellaneous jamboree at Orono, Maine, in August. It is partly concerned with Pound, partly with me...After that, I'll be finished with public reading, except for the two local universities and the Morden Tower, to which I feel some obligations: but first I may possibly read in Paris where my French translator Jacques Darras seems to be arranging something...
>
> I have lived ten years too long. It is cheating the Bible to keep on after three score and ten; and so all my surviving friends of the past have died and I sometimes feel very much alone. MacDiarmid died, Zukofsky died; Tibor Serly gave me the hardest blow, because he was on his way to see me. He telephoned about his journey from London, stepped out of the telephone kiosk and was knocked over by a bus and killed – within a minute of talking to me about our old, dead friends.
>
> Old men talk nonsense and write silly stuff, so I dont write any more...

During the Maine visit that August, Bourtai was able to stay with him, living in the same house as the Hugh Kenners. It was to be the last time she would see him.

By June of 1981, the year Carroll F. Terrell published *Basil Bunting: Man and Poet*, he had moved to Greystead Cottage near Bellingham where he hoped to live for the rest of his life. He wrote to me:

> But first let me call attention to my new address. It signifies that I have at last escaped from Washington, a place I detested, and am just settling in to a little house, pretty nearly where I've wanted to be for many years. I look out over a big garden (not mine but I can use it) to the hills of the dale of the North Tyne, covered with sheep, and lambs too at this season, with a glimpse of the river and quiet all around. Very big trees shelter me from most winds – an enormous ash grows right up against my chimney, and an owl lives in it which never fails to say goodnight to me. I'll miss the children who were the only good things about Washington, since the population of Tarset is only about 30, and no

doubt I'll find shopping awkward, for the nearest shop is six miles away and for anything more than basic needs I'll have to drive 25 miles into Hexham, down an exceedingly twisty road, which makes it nearly an hour's drive. But the place is so lovely nothing of that sort matters...

Best of all was his strong suggestion that this new home might be the place where he could complete the sonata he had sent me a draft of: 'I don't expect to write any more. What a man of my age writes can seldom be any good. Nevertheless in such a splendid place, if there are no nagging worries, something might happen to get down on paper at last – even perhaps "The New Moon".'

When I wrote that I would be in London for four months beginning January 1982 as Assistant Director for the University of Notre Dame's first Junior-Year-in-England programme, he wrote to welcome me. He suggested many things to see in Northumberland and invited me to stay with him for a visit. Tom Pickard in a telephone conversation told me that Bunting had arranged readings so he could meet me in London in case I would not be able to go to him.

In the exceptionally cold winter of 1982 Bunting travelled South to give readings at Coracle Press in a small room crammed with admirers; at Hampstead Library, Keats House, people stood outside in the cold evening drizzle, uselessly hoping to squeeze into an already overcrowded room. At Riverside Studios where crowds were able to be accommodated, Bunting's unassuming son Tom could not get in because he did not have a ticket. When I discovered this and because I knew Tom from his welcome visits to our Notre Dame classes in London, I explained at the door and of course they let him in to hear his father. The Michael Henshaws were his attentive and gracious hosts who had small and large gatherings for him and his friends. Once after a three-hour dinner at a fine French restaurant with two publishers, we walked in and out of bookshops on our way to Foyles. At some places he asked quietly about the sales of his poems. A shop manager who recognised him treated him with deference, getting him a chair so he could browse at a table in a small room. With evident pleasure Bunting looking carefully through books about friends he had known in Paris and Italy and also earlier ones. But the walk to Foyles became too long and taxing, and he had to return to the Henshaws' home by taxi.

The Henshaws accompanied him back to Greystead where he wrote on February 28:

> Since two days after I got home we have been having beautiful weather, bright sunshine and warm enough to do without a fire until evening.

C

There are hundreds and hundreds of crocuses out in the garden besides other flowers...
I was very tired after London. It took almost a week to wear off, but I'm much as usual now. The Henshaws must be tired too. It was very cold the two days they stopped here.
The wild pheasant is back on the garden walk crowing, and the other birds were making quite a noise this morning, though the winter must have killed some of them. I dont see the finches around. I did see two of the peacocks from the farm, a bit bedraggled, but very selfpossessed strutting down the middle of the road, holding up the traffic.

'That infernal cinema crew' were coming again to Greystead on March 10 'to tire me out', he wrote, and one documentary they made, his daughter Rou explained later, was a full-length film seen in cinemas [7 March 1982].

Though after their divorce Basil usually referred to Sima as 'my ex-wife', their continued close relationship was evident. The week before Basil had written:

My ex-wife came up and galvanised me into seeing what we could still do with the car, and she took it down to Bellingham where she managed to persuade the garage, still very busy after the cold winter, to spare the time to mend the windscreen wipers, so that the car is usable, though rattly. Since I hope that it will stay more or less serviceable, I'm going to ask you now to tell me when your next week off comes, so that I can pick you up at Hexham station and bring you to Greystead.

Before I arrived, later in March, Sima had prepared my room comfortably, though, unfortunately, I never met her. However, ever since I had read Basil's letter to Louis Zukofsky about Sima's surreptitiously putting a piece of the Communion Bread in her husband's meal so that he made his Easter Communion in Persia, I had wanted to meet her.

While I was his house guest for a few days, Basil drove me all over the countryside proudly pointing out so much that would help me to absorb the atmosphere of Northumberland. Its distant past was like recent history to him, and in the evenings he could enthrall a listener by telling stories of past and present before the fire which warmed his small cottage.

His deep love of the north was evident as he showed me such places as Hadrian's Wall, nearby Hermitage Castle and Newcastleton, and the little pub in Liddisdale, Scotland. At Hexham Abbey he persuaded someone to open the crypt so we could see the ancient fragments. Each place he knew so well, not only geographically but historically, with all the famous people of each age discussed as if they were intimate friends. He was not strong enough to share everything he spoke of – a walk along the Roman

Wall, Lindisfarne when the tide was out, and Briggflatts. But with the help of his daughter Maria when his car broke down, we covered even more of the area around Hexham. Both father and daughter were able guides to help me enjoy the Saxon history as well as the unique beauty, modern and ancient, within the market town. Although Basil arranged various excursions, more important to me were hearing his stories, his comments about people and poetry, and sharing whatever he wanted to share – from a view of the hills from his window to Ezra Pound's gift of a handwritten Canto from which he unwrapped string and newspaper so carefully.

Whatever the exertion of travelling, it was not enough to keep him from going to Devon to help judge the Arvon International Poetry Competition he wrote about the following March:

> In the South I spent several days with six other poets in Devonshire, as guests of Ted Hughes, finishing the judging of 33,000 poems! Three of them had first of all reduced the number to 1,800 or so by throwing out those they thought the very worst. Adrian Mitchell lightened his share (11,000) by making a private collection of the most preposterous entries. He read us a few of them for fun...I read all my 1800 poems without finding one good one, or more than three or four that were excusable. That was exhausting if you like. One of the judges...spent half a day reading entries aloud in order to tell us why he didnt recommend that one. That might have gone on for ever, if I hadnt made an alliance with Stephen Spender to reverse the procedure and get them to exhibit only the poems they did recommend for the main prizes, and in that way we polished the poems off at a good pace and finished with half a day to spare.
>
> Now I've enough money to be sure of one, probably two years before I get into financial difficulties. But I'm sure I'm a lot older for the experience.

Another birthday celebration, this his eighty-third, gave him simple pleasure, yet his awareness of ageing was poignant: 'Stuart and Deirdre Montgomery had a little party for my birthday; much wine, much laughter, going home at 2.30 a.m. I stayed at the Henshaws' house by Regent's Park, but I have aged enough to prevent me going out into the streets of London even once.'

But never one to dwell on the negative, he continued:

> Your flowers are further on than ours. Our daffodils are only promising to blossom, though we have our usual early profusion of snowdrops, thousands of them, amongst the trees and by the path.
>
> We've a very fine fox about, astonishingly big and astonishingly bold. He often comes to raid our rubbish bins. Sometimes he brings his lady friend with him, so that we could reconstruct what they were up to from their tracks in the snow while there was snow. The fox goes and peeps through the pub window to see who is there, and the vixen goes every night to a house at the Eals where they put out food for her. She is

partial to bread and marmalade. No one will help the Tynedale hunt to get either of those two. We are really proud of the dog-fox, who walks amongst the flocks of an afternoon, scared of no one and nothing. [16 March 1983].

But his love of the Greystead Cottage made it all the harder for him to leave when with very little income he was forced to move at eighty-three. Though his family and friends tried to help him, he was too proud and independent to accept very much. After moving about, staying with friends, living in a winter let in Bellingham and for a short time with his daughter Maria, he was finally relieved that his son-in-law John found him a place of his own, Fox Cottage at Whitley Chapel near Hexham:

> All this year until last week, and almost all the year before, I've been so hassled and worried and confused by being turned out of my pretty cottage at Tarset that I've not had either a calm mind or a trace of energy...For a long time we searched for a new home, I helped by my daughter and son-in-law, my ex-wife and Colin Simms, but there was nothing even tolerable...

He continues angry at the British housing situation, but then he concludes:

> Anyway the upshot is that cottages to let cannot be found, so that after more than a year of searching and disappointment, John, my son-in-law, came up with a plan whereby I might get a mortgage in spite of my age and poverty, and so buy a place of my own. That's what we have done: it's quite a pleasant place, though not a patch on Tarset. I think I will be able to live here comfortably, once it has been paid for, but there were repairs to do before the building society would grant a mortgage, and these have put me badly in debt, which I always dread. So though my worries are much less, they arent over.
>
> Fox Cottage is about eight miles south of Hexham, in a tiny village – no shops at all, but that will be all right once I have a car again, which I expect in a week or so. The cottage stands next door to a well-kept and pleasant old pub. It has no immediate outlook, but as soon as I go out of my door I have pretty wide views, still with forest on the horizon – Slaley forest, oak and other deciduous trees, but open and very windy and comparatively high up. It may be cold in winter. I wish it were on the North Tyne, of course, but these parts (Hexhamshire) are also thought beautiful, and the lanes are narrow and twisting. I shall be a little more cramped than I was, but not badly, and when we can finish furnishing it there will be a bed for visitors. The pub's drinkers park their cars all around me, which is noisy at night, but I'll get used to that in the end.

At eighty-four he was still travelling to London: 'My last trip to London a few months ago tired me beyond reason, so I've no plans of travel even for a few miles (I'll be at this address unless they gaol me for debt) until the worms get me. I keep well, free of rheumatism, but in some ways feeble. My utmost walk must be about a mile, and I wont willingly venture on foot more than half a mile.'

But even in all this hassle and activity, he could still jest in closing: 'And let us have a new Pope please, this one is too conservative' (14 July 1984).

After what was to be his last birthday, Bunting was still worried about debts, but in typical good humour: 'My central heating is effective but costs an awful lot to run. Fortunately people sent me so many bottles of whisky for my birthday that I am thinking of bathing in it. That should warm me up.' After discussing poets and publishers, friends and each member of his family, he adds his usual touch of beauty: 'Last week there were crocuses and such blossoming and we all thought spring had come; but they were just codding us. Inches of snow lying again today. The rooks, which had all come home, escorted by flocks of starlings and a few jackdaws, seem to have gone away again.' And then he began the closing paragraph unusually, with the prophetic, 'Goodbye now...' [19 March 1985].

The next month his daughter Roudaba, who had visited him with her husband and one daughter in 1979 and whose mother had died suddenly in 1982, had a strong feeling that she wanted to visit her father again. Although it was most inconvenient for her family because of the many responsibilities in the spring on their ranch, she flew to England on April 14. It was to prove a very enjoyable time although the little cottage was quite crowded with visitors and Rou had to share a room with Tanya Cossey, a young art student who had been almost a daughter to Bunting for years (and his saki on television). Another good friend, Michael Shayer, arrived on April 15 and slept on the small couch in the living-room with his feet hanging over one end. Maria, his youngest daughter, was in and out during the visit, often taking Rou sightseeing since Bunting had given his car to the Cosseys, afraid that he would injure someone if he kept on driving.

The cottage itself was small and poor with grey cement walls unpainted except for the bedroom Rou and Tanya shared which Tanya had painted white. Shelves of books which covered the living-room walls softened its starkness, but the kitchen/dining-room and bathroom were not so camouflaged. Maria and others who wished to make his life more comfortable were continuously and adamantly refused by this proud man who wished to remain independent to the end. Though Bunting had trouble walking, the group occasionally went to the next door pub for a meal. The week passed pleasantly, and the night before Shayer was to go back south, they all stayed up till the early hours, reminiscing, talking about poets and poetry, drinking and singing ballads, including the bawdy Northumbrian ones Bunting knew so well. These Rou had learned in childhood from her mother who used to sing them while they washed up the dishes together.

The next morning, after both Michael Shayer and Tanya left, Bunting did not feel well but he thought it was the result of the night's drinking. Because his stomach was so upset, he wanted only some lime water; ordinary water, he had always claimed, would only rust your insides. As a nurse practitioner, Rou tried to convince him that in his condition this was not good for him. The next day Bunting, not any better, still refused to see a doctor. To think over a plan of action, Rou took a long walk before asking him if he would see a doctor for her sake since he would not see one for his own, stressing that she was feeling very uncomfortable. He reluctantly agreed and was astonished when the doctor came to the house right away and ordered an ambulance immediately, asking incredulously, 'You mean I'm sick enough to go to hospital?'

Maria and Rou arrived at the Hexham hospital with the ambulance and saw him being placed in Intensive Care, a room with eight beds in a spoke pattern. As soon as he was settled in the cot too short for him to stretch out in, he began half-seriously complaining, 'What's the use of having daughters? One comes all the way from America to put me into hospital!' Although Rou as a nurse practitioner urgently requested to stay the night, the rules of the hospital would not allow this. As they were about to leave, with a loud crash the man next to her father fell out of bed with his bedpan, and Bunting exclaimed, 'See what happens in hospital?' But everyone in good spirits teasingly consoled him with the thought of all the pretty nurses about.

The next day, April 17, after Maria came by for Rou, they stopped at Maria's home to call about their father's condition and to find out if they could bring the lime water he wanted. Relieved when the nurse told them he was fine, they were just going out the door when another call came, about 10 a.m, to tell them that their father was dead. For exercise he had walked down the hall with a nurse and returned to bed, but something had made the nurse, who was leaving, turn back – to find he had just died.

Rou, Maria, and their Auntie Joyce, Basil's only sister, living in Throckley, arrived at the hospital as quickly as possible to see him for the last time. The doctor told Rou that the real cause of death was uncertain but it was most probably a rupture since low blood pressure had indicated internal bleeding; officially it was reported as mesenteric adenitis.

Sima, his ex-wife, deeply grieving, returned immediately from California where she was visiting, but his son Tom, travelling in the Canary Islands, who otherwise called his father almost every week, could not be located. Bourtai in the States was unable to travel to England. And Peggy, the one to whom *Briggflatts* was dedicated, was notified. To the family's amazement calls began pouring in from all over the world – France, Japan, and the United States, for example.

Only four family members, his sister Joyce, his daughters Rou and Maria, and his ex-wife Sima, along with Tanya, and Colin Simms, a close poet-friend who had lived near him for several years, were present for the cremation. When Sima had asked Basil about burial, he had answered impossibly, 'Just put my ashes in the ashbin!' but throughout these past years, others had often suggested Briggflatts to him. So it was then that about twenty friends – many of them poets – respecting the family's wish for privacy stood in the road outside the cemetery near the Quaker meeting house while Basil Bunting's ashes were scattered among the blossoming daffodils in the graveyard at Briggflatts.

CHAPTER 2

Poetics

POETICS AND LITERARY CRITICISM

'There is no excuse for literary criticism' [D]. When Eric Mottram asked Bunting about this earlier pronouncement, he replied:

> It distracts from the work almost always. There are, of course, exceptions. One overstates things as a rule. But there are not very many exceptions. I think that a man who will read *De Vulgari Eloquentia* will have got most of the literary criticism he's ever going to require. [Nothing since Dante.] Well, bits and pieces, but not much.[1]

In general Bunting seems adamant in his stand against criticism and against theorising about poetry, especially in his well-known 'Statement'.[2]

But there Bunting is leading to a favourite topic, reading aloud, suggesting that this is the way the public can cultivate its taste, hear the music, and learn to understand the art: 'Since poetry readings have become popular, [charlatans] have found a new field, and it is not easy for the outsider to distinguish the fraud from the poet. But it is a little less difficult when the poetry is read aloud.'

However, as strongly as most poets, critics, and educators would agree that taste is cultivated by exposure to good art, most, including Bunting, would also agree that it entails something more. In fact, Michael Hamburger, poet-critic, notes that 'the present revival of spoken poetry on the whole has not favoured Bunting's kind of poetry but the kind that conveys instant and obvious "meaning" with little regard for "beauty" '.[3]

As desirable as it would be simply to permeate our culture with good spoken poetry, literary criticism is valuable for an audience which not only 'gets its poetry by ear' but appreciates poetry which requires more than one recital for its complete understanding. Bunting himself implicitly admits this. For every paragraph of his inveighing against the 'wrong kind' of criticism, there are other remarks supporting the 'right kind'. Not only did he discuss criticism, he followed his own principles and actually wrote good criticism about both poetry and music. Most important of all, in his writing he revealed the basic principles of poetry which he himself followed.

One important aspect of Bunting's viewpoint is his subordinating the place of intellect to emotions in art. As early as 1927, when he was music editor for the *Outlook*, he published some principles of criticism which changed only in expression during his lifetime:

> No art depends principally or even largely on its appeal to the intellect, and in the Age of Reason itself Pope was preferred to Young for melody, not for sense; Voltaire's style gained for him more admirers than his doctrines, and Chardin was appreciated not for the realism of his rabbits but for the nobility of his rhythm and design...
>
> ...it may be due to the deficiency of my intellect that it gets but little more from one art than from another. If music speaks first to the emotions, so, it seems to me, do poetry, sculpture, painting, architecture, even the prose art of fiction, whether in the drama or in the novel...All arts are of a party against the intellect, and if music does outrun the others it is by a very short lead.

At this point in his article Bunting admits something essential to his ideas of criticism; an apology, in the strict sense of the word, for his own and for all writing of criticism:

> The principles of criticism must be looked for in a realm that embraces all the arts and where the intellect, however important to the critic as the regulator of his other faculties, plays a limited and subordinate part. This realm is hardly explored at all, and least by the critics who confine their attention to music. It is probable that the principles that may be found in it will be inexpressible in the language of logic. If Beauty and Sublimity escape easy definition how shall their ingredients be tabbed? But until some attempt has been made to describe them criticism must remain more a matter of luck than cunning, of an inborn sympathy than of acquired technique.[4]

Four years later in 'Open Letter to Louis Zukofsky' [LZ, 7 September 1932] published in the Italian newspaper *Il Mare*, Bunting becomes more specific. Admitting that a certain amount of criticism 'for the detection of fraud and adulteration is necessary policework', he adds basic ideas about writing either criticism or poetry. The 'necessary policework...must keep within the rules of evidence: fact, not hearsay; history, not speculation; all the exhibits there alongside their expert analysis'.

In other words, as he later insists repeatedly, both criticism and poetry must be concerned accurately and exactly with the object, the thing itself. Coming closer to his musical concerns, he adds in another letter:

[In good criticism there is] for the poet, technical information as from one good craftsman to another...

For this last Pound's three items quoted by you are a model (Direct treatment: to compose in the sequence of the musical phrase, not in the sequence of the metronome). His wellknown Don'ts are as explicit and concrete. [LZ, 2 October 1932]

In the 'Open Letter' he refuses to accept abstract discussions as good criticism – or as good poetry: 'I NEVER want a philosophy of hats, a metaphysical idea of Hat in the abstract, nor in any case a great deal of talk about hats.' Both in this public letter and in private correspondence, Bunting castigates his friends

flights into darkness, away from the ascertained and reascertainable fact to speculative mysticism; to a region I think devoid of anything permanently valuable.

The mystic purchases a moment of exhilaration with a lifetime of confusion; and the confusion is infectious and destructive. It is confusing and destructive to try and explain anything in terms of anything else, poetry in terms of psychology. (Sept ?th 32)

This tendency towards the vague and abstract away from the specific and concrete is what Bunting is condemning in the 'Open Letter' when he criticises Zukofsky's description of a poem: 'A poem...perfect rest...the desire for what is objectively perfect... the desire for inclusiveness...[Bunting's ellipses] The aspirations of the hatmaker can only faintly affect the hat. The psychology of the poet is not the critic's business. [LZ, 2 October 1932]

Those ideas he brushes aside as having only remote bearing on the poetry itself. Just as Pound a few months later enjoins 'a care for language', for 'accurate registration by language',[5] Bunting, living at this time near him in Rapallo, insists on a 'care for facts'. He concludes by citing Pound's contribution as the synthesis of all that is important to criticism and poetry:

[Pound has] developed a pervading stress on the immediate, the particular, the concrete; distrust of abstractions; shrinking from even the suspicion of verbalism; from the puns and polyvalencies in which mystics delight. It is not unspeculative but sceptical. It will build with facts, declines to soar with inevitably unsteady words. All this is as important to criticism (or to any other department of knowledge or action) as it is to poetry.

Although so many ideas of Pound's are inextricable from Bunting's, they seem to have served chiefly as a catalyst during the few formative years he lived near Pound in Italy. For example, in his 'Date Line' essay completed on 'Jan. 28th, anno XII [1934]', while Bunting was living nearby in Rapallo, Pound mentions five categories of criticism: 'Criticism by discussion', 'by translation', 'by exercise in the style of a given period', 'via music', and 'in a new composition'.[6] Bunting attempted all but one. Interestingly, the one category he did omit, 'via music', was to become the central concern of his poetry.

An example of Bunting's 'Criticism by discussion' which follows the suggestions of Pound in his 1932 Manifesto and his 'Date Line' article is the essay 'The Lion and the Lizard', which Bunting sent from the Canary Islands to Zukofsky in May 1935.[7] By this essay he fulfils Pound's criteria for the best critic, the one who tries to cause an improvement in the art he criticises, and the next best critic, the one who calls attention to the best work. Furthermore, he attempts 'a general ordering and weeding out of what has actually been performed'.[8] More important to the readers of his poetry, throughout the discussion Bunting is revealing his own poetic preferences and practices, especially the kind of music and meaning he is striving for.

The essay which begins with a discussion of the differences between the original *Rubaiyat* of Omar Khayam and Fitzgerald's translation moves to a discussion of the shortcomings of English poetry in general. In the first part he is concerned with specific examples and comparisons, following a method consistent with his earlier advice to Zukofsky. In fact, the first part itself becomes a detailed example of the generalisation which is the basis of the second: 'These notes are not set down to belittle Fitzgerald who was a great poet, a great adapter of a greater poet, but to call attention to certain shortcomings of English poetry in general.'

Bunting first criticises Fitzgerald's continuously exalted tone and unvaried cadence, so unlike Omar's great variety in both areas, and arrives at the conclusion that Fitzgerald removes himself out of the world into 'an unreal rapidly cloying place', 'what d'Annunzio might call a "world of poetry"'. Through an unremitting 'effulgence', Fitzgerald loses and blurs 'the detail, the texture of life'. The conclusion, that 'Life includes splendour, but is not sustainedly splendid', becomes the principle Bunting uses to judge English poetry in general:

> English poets are too often on their dignity, they strive too constantly to be sublime and end by becoming monotonous and empty of lifegiving detail, like hymn-tunes. They have often been the slaves rather than the masters of their metres...This is partly because they have neglected the music of Byrd and Dowland so much more supple rhythmically than English poetry or than the music of classical masters until recently most in favour.

Besides diagnosing the cause of the shortcomings, a neglect of rhythmically supple music, Bunting is explaining what he considers essential to good poetry:

> English poets are commonly too much of a piece to be anything but fragmentary, for life is not of a piece. Their movement, their vowel-successions, their alliterations, have been too commonly splendiferous, until verbal splendour has lost its virtue in English; and when, as recently, they have tried to restore it by the use of contrast, they frequently fail because they will not devote sufficient care and labour to anything much below the sublime; because they do not understand that cacophony is at least as intricate an art as harmony; because they despise or patronize jazz and other popular music;...
> In their debauch of easy magnificence – for it has become more difficult to avoid than to achieve the over-rich – English poets have hazed over sharp outlines and made too free a use of translucent but comparatively empty passives and transitives, forgetting that the world of daylight and full consciousness is, above all, opaque and complex. They have sought yet remoter abstractions even by forced adjectives and conceits, like some of Mr Eliot's, painful to follow. They have often thought more carefully about the impression made by their own personality than about that made by the ostensible object of their verse. 'Ash Wednesday' might serve to demonstrate many of these errors.

That 'the world of daylight and full consciousness is, above all, opaque and complex' is one of Bunting's most explicit public statements about the content of poetry. This concept, a constant in his poetic theory, stated here in the mid-Thirties, could just as well be a comment about 'Villon', 'Chomei at Toyama', 'The Spoils', or *Briggflatts* as about one of the forgotten concepts of English poetry.

Bunting shifts next to another concept, *concern for the object*, connected in those years with Zukofsky and Objectivist poetry. Earlier, Bunting had concluded the discussion of Omar and Fitzgerald by praising the Persian poet's concern for the object:

> [Omar's rhythm] is broken and colloquial or it dances or chatters as Fitzgerald's never does. Omar is not upon his dignity. He is more concerned with the impression made by objects he has made than with that made by his own voice and figure; and those objects are such as the world is full of, not, for the most part, very august, though not necessarily therefore awkward.

Then, closing the second, more general section of the article, Bunting reverts to the same idea, but illustrates what this includes. First, he lists those few who, in his opinion, have 'resolutely "kept their eye on the object" (in Wordsworth's phrase)'. Then he contrasts techniques of Shakespeare with Dante, Homer, and Ferdosi to describe some of the qualities he himself spent his life perfecting:

Shakespeare's talents were much greater than those of any other north European writer, yet he who reads both Shakespeare and Dante must notice how Shakespeare makes three or four casts at an object, three or four approximations, by comparing which, we arrive at his exact meaning. Often the multiplicity is disguised by deft dovetailing of metaphors; nevertheless the drawing, however marvellous the design, is blurred. Whereas Dante says a thing once and exactly. His outlines are sharp and precise.

Similarly he who reads Shakespeare and Homer and Ferdosi must notice how Shakespeare fits his cadence to the mood of the speaker...The epic music, on the other hand, belongs to the object, the matter in hand. Shakespeare's method is admirably suited to the theatre...but it has been applied imitatively and abusively by other poets to kinds far different to the infinite damage of literature.

This essay contains in essence the concerns of Bunting's poetry, both in form and content – an inseparable unity according to Pound: 'A work of art has in it no idea which is inseparable from the form.'[9]

FORM AND MUSIC IN POETRY

For Bunting, form in poetry is associated with music, and as far as his own poetry is concerned he has emphasised the fact that the 'musical analogy is always there for me'.[10] Bunting made his position clear in his 'Statement' by insisting on the necessity of hearing both poetry and music:

> Reading in silence is the source of half the misconceptions that have caused the public to distrust poetry. Without the sound, the reader looks at the lines as he looks at prose, seeking a meaning. Prose exists to convey meaning, and no meaning such as prose conveys can be expressed as well in poetry. This is not poetry's business.

He follows this with a brief description of what he believes is poetry's business:

> Poetry is seeking to make not meaning, but beauty; or if you insist on misusing words, its "meaning" is of another kind, and lies in the relation to one another of lines and patterns of sound, perhaps harmonious, perhaps contrasting and clashing, which the hearer feels rather than understands; lines of sound drawn in the air which stir deep emotions which have not even a name in prose. This needs no explaining to an audience which gets its poetry by ear.

Bunting insists that no theorising about poetry's business is necessary: there is no need of any theory of what gives pleasure through the ear, music or poetry. 'The theoretician will follow the artist and fail to explain him.' And then Bunting, the craftsman who uses words with the utmost care, makes what seems at first an amazing statement: 'The sound, whether it be in the words or notes, is all that matters.' At one time he wrote about his poetry to his daughter Roudaba: 'Poems? Don't try to understand, just listen' [30 August 1966]. And he narrows these statements even more:

> It is perfectly possible to delight an audience by reading poetry of sufficient quality in a language it does not know. I have seen some of Goethe, some of Hafez, produce nearly the same effect they would have produced on an audience familiar with German or Persian.

This complements Pound's idea that '*melopoeia* can be appreciated by a foreigner with a sensitive ear, even though he be ignorant of the language in which the poem is written'.[11]

Without getting involved at this point in the argument of form versus content in music and poetry,[12] it is enough to try to place Bunting's own remarks about this man-made dichotomy in perspective. First of all, Bunting never denies that poetry has meaning; on the contrary, he has stated explicitly: 'Of course my poems have a meaning'.[13] He insists only that the '"meaning" is of another kind'. It is not simply the rational meaning of the words. To him poetry includes so much more that the term "meaning" is inexact, not precise at all. 'Merely intellectual knowledge will make it harder for you to understand the poem because, when you listen to it, you will be distracted by a multitude of irrelevant scraps of knowledge. You will not hear the meaning, which is in the sound' [D]. By this he is attempting to convince simply, without a string of discursive arguments, that his poetry involves much more than an intellectual response.

Spoken poetry is in itself, like music, an intricate composition of pleasurable sounds, tempos, rhythms, motifs, and transitions integrated into an organic whole. Bunting himself describes this: '[Poetry] deals in sounds – long sounds and short sound, heavy beats and light beats, the tone relation of vowels, the relations of consonants to one another which are like instrumental music.' These 'lines of sound drawn in the air' appeal through the senses and the intellect to stir deep emotions which affect the whole human person, a quite indescribably different effect from the merely rational meaning of the words affecting intellectual understanding.

Bunting is being precise when he insists that the term "meaning" in this context is too restrictive to apply to the full effect of the words of a poem. The conclusion of this poet and music critic that 'the sound, whether it be in words or notes, is all that matters' is a valid one.

Bunting never equates music and poetry. He never denies the essential differences between them that Susanne Langer, Wilhelm Ambros, Daniel Webb, Luigi Ronga, Calvin Brown, Clive Bell and so many others[14] insist on: music is pure form inasmuch as it expresses no determinate idea. Non-representational, it is an art of sound with no unambiguous and distinct rendition of feeling, with no appeal to discursive reasoning.

Only if Bunting's statements are understood in a restricted sense do they seem too 'uncompromising' or even 'illogical'.[15] With their full connotations and in the context of other statements, they can be seen for what they are:

> I believe the fundamental thing in poetry is the sound, so that, whatever the meaning may be, whatever your ultimate intention in that direction might be, if you haven't got the sound right, it isn't a poem. And if you have got it right, it'll get across, even to people who don't understand it...But it's not to be taken that I don't think you can add quite a lot to a poem's sound by having something amusing or entertaining or some new observations to make in the course of it.[16]

Another time he added:

> I've never said that poetry consists *only* of sound. I said again and again that the *essential* thing is the sound. Without the sound there isn't any poetry. But having established it and kept it clear that the sound is the essential, the main thing, you can add all sorts of stuff if you want to. You can, if you like, have as elaborate a system of meanings, sub-meanings, and so forth, as Dante had in the *Divina Commedia*.[17]

Gael Turnbull, poet and friend of Bunting, comments on the integration of Bunting's achievement. After noting that the most striking aspect of his poetry is 'continual melodic invention', he concludes: 'it is by the voice I am held. Not sound in any way cultivated for itself, as separate; but spoken and heard. It is the achievement of Bunting's poetry that we "hear" and "apprehend" with no sense of any separation...'[18]

CHAPTER 3

Major Contemporary Influences:
Pound and Zukofsky

T. S. Eliot, Bunting's 'old acquaintance' and critic, acknowledges
essential differences between music and poetry when he defines a
'musical poem' as 'a poem which has a musical pattern of sound
and a musical pattern of the secondary meaning of the words which
compose it'. The composer of 'Preludes' and *Four Quartets* who
characterises each play of Shakespeare's as 'a very complex musical
structure' agrees with Pound and Bunting that 'a poet may gain
much from the study of music', particularly 'the sense of rhythm
and the sense of structure'.[1] More than once, Bunting voiced his
interest in Eliot's belief, so like his own conclusion 'that poetry
should try to take over some of the techniques that [Bunting] only
knew in music'. As Bunting explained to Jonathan Williams:
'...when I discovered Eliot writing poems and calling them
'Preludes', even though the resemblance to say Chopin's Preludes
was slight and superficial, I was extremely interested. He was
obviously thinking on lines not dissimilar from my own' [D]. Years
before he had taken time off from a busy job with the Foreign
Office in Teheran to write to Zukofsky: 'Have you read Eliot's *Four
Quartets*? I did in Cairo on my way here...The verse is exceedingly
skilful – few Eliotisms. I was impressed, am hard to impress
nowadays' [5 May 1947].

Much earlier, Pound had been less impressed than Bunting with
Eliot, and the criticism he directed at him could never have been
directed at Bunting: 'In a recent article Mr Eliot contended, or
seemed to contend, that good *vers libre* was little more than a skilful
evasion of the better known English metres. His article was
defective in that he omitted all consideration of metres depending
on quantity, alliteration, etc; in fact, he wrote as if all metres were
measured by accent.'[2]

Poet-critic Michael Hamburger among others places both Eliot

Ezra Pound

Louis Zukofsky

and Bunting among those 'whose debt to Pound is not in doubt'.[3] Though Bunting admitted his early influence, he noted important differences in their models:

> ...in almost every...respect, Pound's reading was as opposite mine as it could be. All my life the most important English poet for me was Wordsworth, whom Pound despised. He had no use for Spenser with whom I think he is entirely parallel, perhaps because Spenser provided the framework for many generations through his poems and Pound was trying to produce a new framework.[4]

More generally, Hamburger attributes to Pound's range of 'curiosity, invention, and adaptation' and to his 'many styles and his many personae', the 'reason no other English-speaking poet of his time had so much to give to coevals or successors as diverse in practice and outlook as T. S. Eliot, and Robert Duncan, Louis Zukofsky and Robert Creeley, Basil Bunting and Charles Olson...' But the two who should be singled out are Bunting and Zukofsky as the poets who put into practice the 'one decidedly unifying factor in [Pound's] work...his incomparable gift of *melopoeia*,' or, to use his own term, 'a musical mastery and rightness'.[5]

Pound had defined his concept of *melopoeia* during the years of Bunting's discipleship in Rapallo: '*Melopoeia*, wherein the words are charged, over and above their plain meaning, with some musical

property, which directs the bearing or trend of that meaning.' Later
in the essay, he used this property to closely relate poetry with
music: 'In *melopoeia* we find a contrary current, a force tending to
lull, or to distract the reader from the exact sense of the language. It
is poetry on the borders of music and music is perhaps the bridge
between consciousness and the unthinking sentient or even the
insentient universe.'[6]

In the opening paragraphs of 'Vers Libre and Arnold Dol-
metsch', Pound had defined a position about the relationship of
music and poetry which Eliot reprinted almost forty years later with
Pound's approval:

> Poetry is a composition of words set to music. Most other definitions of
> it are indefensible, or metaphysical. The proportion or quality of the
> music may, and does, vary; but poetry withers and "dies out" when it
> leaves music, or at least an imagined music, too far behind it. The
> horrors of modern "readings of poetry" are due to rhetorical recitation.
> Poetry must be read as music and not as oratory. I do not mean that
> words should be jumbled together and made indistinct and unrecognis-
> able in a sort of onomatopoetic paste. I have found few musicians who
> pay the least attention to the poet's own music. They are often, I admit,
> uncritical of his verbal excellence or deficit, ignorant of his "literary"
> value or bathos. But the literary qualities are not the whole of our art.
>
> Poets who are not interested in music are, or become, bad poets. I
> would almost say that poets should never be too long out of touch with
> musicians. Poets who will not study music are defective.[7]

It is difficult to find anything written by Pound about the art of
poetry which does not in some way refer to the art of music. In his
own work he never forgot his cryptic warning: 'Poetry atrophies
when it gets too far from music.'[8]

Although Bunting in his practice and in his public acknowledge-
ments made known his debt to Pound, in the Preface to his *Collected
Poems* he singles out Louis Zukofsky after Pound as the second of
the two living men who taught him much:

> If ever I learned the trick of it, it was mostly from poets long dead whose
> names are obvious:...but two living men also taught me much: Ezra
> Pound and in his sterner, stonier way, Louis Zukofsky.

Only a glance at Zukofsky's *Autobiography* or 'Pericles' in the
second volume of *Bottom: On Shakespeare*,[9] both of which include
music by his wife, would be enough to convince anyone of this
poet's belief in the relatedness of music and poetry. He discusses
this essential relationship in two essays published four years apart.
In the first, 'Poetry: For My Son When He Can Read', he presents
one form of 'the scientific definition of poetry':

...that matters of the 'highest common speech – all that flows from the tops of the heads of illustrious poets down to their lips' – properly embrace the whole art of poetry which is nothing else but the completed action of writing words to be set to music – music being the one art that more than others aims in its reach to speak to all men.[10]

In a letter to Zukofsky, Bunting wrote that he enjoyed reading the essay, but he did not comment at all on the "poetry-music" aspect of his discussion. Instead he rather strongly criticised his friend for supporting 'the contemporary efforts to "reconcile" a scientific outlook with an aesthetic one' [LZ, 21 January 1947].

However, Zukofsky's 'Statement for Poetry', first published in 1950, much more clearly reflects their common interests:

> Any definition of poetry is difficult because the implications of poetry are complex – and that despite the natural, physical simplicity of its best examples. Thus poetry may be defined as an order of words that as movement and tone (rhythm and pitch) approaches in varying degrees the wordless art of music as a kind of mathematical limit.

After illustrating the idea that 'poetry has always been considered more literary than music, though so-called pure music may be literary in a communicative sense', Zukofsky complements Bunting's strongest assertions by adding:

> But music does not depend mainly on the human voice, as poetry does, for rendition. And it is possible in imagination to divorce speech of all graphic elements, to let it become a movement of sounds. It is this musical horizon of poetry (which incidentally poems perhaps never reach) that permits anybody who does not know Greek to listen and get something out of the poetry of Homer, to "tune in" to the human tradition, to its voice which has developed among the sounds of natural things, and thus escape the confines of time and place, as one hardly ever escapes them in studying Homer's grammar. In this sense poetry is international.[11]

Zukofsky returns to these ideas at the end of his 'Statement' in a conclusion which does not merely echo Eliot and Pound, but enlarges their seminal ideas. More than that, it is easy to believe that if this conclusion were a kind of Manifesto such as Pound wrote almost twenty years earlier, it would have been signed by Bunting with gusto:

> No verse is "free", however, if its rhythms inevitably carry the words in contexts that do not falsify the function of words as speech probing the possibilities and attractions of existence. This being the practice of poetry, prosody as such is of secondary interest to the poet. He looks, so to speak, into his ear as he does at the same time into his heart and intellect. His ear is sincere, if his words convey his awareness of the range of differences and subtleties of duration. He does not measure with handbook, and is not a pendulum. He may find it right to count

syllables, or their relative lengths and stresses, or to be sensitive to all
these metrical factors. As a matter of fact, the good poets do all these
things. But they do not impose their count on what is said or made – as
may be judged from the impact of their poems.[12]

If the 'words' of the first sentence were 'spoken words', a
qualification which Zukofsky takes for granted perhaps, this final
paragraph could be considered a summary of Bunting's simpler,
more direct 'Statement' which states in part:

> Poetry, like music, is to be heard. It deals in sound – long sounds and
> short sounds, heavy beats and light beats, the tone relations of vowels,
> the relations of consonants to one another which are like instrumental
> colour in music. Poetry lies dead on the page, until some voice brings it
> to life, just as music, on the stave, is no more than instructions to the
> player...
>   There is no need of any theory for what gives pleasure through the
> ear, music or poetry...The sound, whether it be in words or notes, is all
> that matters.

The words with which Bunting concluded his interview with
Jonathan Williams seems a fitting transition from the discussion of
this background to the consideration of the poetry: 'The best way to
find out about poetry is to read the poems. That way the reader
becomes something of a poet himself: not because he "contributes"
to the poetry, but because he finds himself subject of its energy'
[D].

CHAPTER 4

Odes

'My excellence, if I have one, isn't new or striking...I'd say I remember the musical origins of poetry, the singing side of it, better than anybody else except Ezra and Carlos Williams' [LZ, 6 July 1951].

With a few exceptions in the 'Overdrafts' section of his *Collected Poems* and 'Chomei at Toyama', the origins of all Bunting's poems are, in fact, musical. By calling six of his long poems 'Sonatas', he is immediately identifying this major group in some sense with music. Half of the translations in the 'Overdrafts' section are of Persian poems, originally chanted and accompanied by music and dancing.[1] The translations of works by Latin poets in that section together with the forty-five odes in the First and Second Book of Odes trace their origin, of course, to ancient Greek drama where the ode was choral in quality. Accompanied by music, the chorus of Greek singers used the human voice, 'the first, and certainly the most basic, of all musical instruments', to 'express patterns of sustained pitch and rhythm'.[2] By 'the musical origin' of poetry, Bunting could be referring to the idea that the ode, rooted etymologically in the Greek *aoidein*, 'to sing' or 'to chant', is defined as 'originally a poem intended or adapted to be sung to instrumental accompaniment'.[3] This of course applies not only to Greek but to most early cultures. In Western society it continues to the time of Malherbe who tried unsuccessfully to prevent the dissolution of the 'marriage of music and poetry'.[4]

Although the odes have definite musical origins, recent definitions have emphasised characteristics which overlook this fact; for example: 'in Greek or Latin as in modern poetry, a poem in free verse and structure, frequently addressed to a deity.'[5] Bunting's odes with their emphasis on musical origins are marked in some instances by these general characteristics also; Ode 11 has both a formal dedication and a classic address to 'Narcis'. Generally, however, they do not fit the definition of the formal ode characterised by 'public nature, solemn diction, and stately gravity' without any connection with music.

'My odes are called odes because Horace called his odes,' Bunting said in an interview. 'An ode is essentially a sonnet to be sung, not all of mine are meant to be sung; most of them are.'[6] At this time Bunting was being less precise about Horace. According to one Latin critic, 'the term *odae* which the Greeks did not usually apply to lyrical poetry unless, like Pindar's, it had some affinity with the choruses of tragedy and with epic, was not used to describe Horace's lyrical poetry until some centuries after his death. He himself called them *carmina*, songs.'[7] Originally Bunting too had called his poems 'carmina' in the *Redimiculum Matellarum* (1930). 'Odes' does not appear until *Poems 1950*. Either 'carmina' or 'odes', however, makes the musical foundation for his poetry firm.

Considering Bunting's two books of Odes is a necessary step on the way to appreciating his major works, the sonatas. From the outset it is clear that these brief odes are not comparable to the poet's longer, more important poems. Some seem to have been written as technical exercises in which Pound, Zukofsky, and others were involved. Many are stepping stones thematically and technically to later, more mature work. Others are high points in the career of a poet who is never satisfied to remain at a certain stage of development. Bunting answered an interviewer's question about his early poems by saying: 'Some of them I'm quite detached from. Others I can see the beginnings of things I afterwards elaborated and [they] became more intimately connected with me.'[8]

To assess Bunting's advancement chronologically through the odes, a reader can simply read each book in turn since the odes are arranged according to dates. Bunting himself perfected the chronology in each edition of the *Collected Poems* since 1968, immediately removing 'They Say Etna' from the 1950 edition. In the Note to the Fulcrum edition he explains: 'I have taken my chance to insert a couplet in the First Book of Odes and promote 'The Orotava Road' from limbo to its chronological place amongst them, which has obliged me to renumber many' [158].

To the Preface of the 1978 edition of his *Collected Poems* (Oxford University Press) he added a note which he dated 1977: 'A new edition of this book has given me a chance to put right a few words and stops the compositor got wrong, and to add four short new poems. A fifth seems better lost.' What he did was change the positions of two odes in the First Book of Odes, making 'Search under every veil' first and 'See! Their verses are laid' second, and add to the Second Book of Odes, 'All the cants they peddle', 'Stones trip Coquet Burn', and 'At Briggflatts Meetinghouse'. To 'Overdrafts' he added 'You can't grip years, Postume'. The fifth new one, 'better lost', may have been 'Snow's on the fellside, look! How deep' (1977), published in *Agenda* (Spring 1978) in the Basil Bunting Special Issue but not in the *Collected Poems*. A third one published in that *Agenda* and uncollected was a translation of Manuchehri, 'You, with my enemy, strolling down the street', but that is dated 1949.

Finally, in the first American edition (1985), he wrote one last ode to the Preface: 'There is one solitary short poem that I have added to the collected volume.' Prophetically, that was a revised 'Now we've no hope of going back' ('Perche no spero'). In the introduction Jonathan Williams writes: 'The one addition...is 'Perche no spero'. Jennifer Moyer and Britt Bell, the publishers, spent an afternoon with BB at Whitley Chapel only ten days before his death, and they have heeded his wishes: just the *one* extra poem' [7].

Since Bunting's chronological development is easily seen through the organisation of the odes, it is more logical to briefly discuss some of these short poems in a way that leads to the more important discussion of the longer works. In the odes details of craftsmanship are worked out and themes are introduced which recur with increasing significance in the longer poems.

As Bunting has insisted, the important aspect of his poetry is the music. However, it is through his subject matter that he makes a statement about the primacy of human values in life, whether as a member of society, as an artist, or as an individual involved usually in love and friendship or in thoughts of mortality. These thematic concerns become broader and deeper in the sonatas. For discussion purposes Bunting's odes can be grouped around these themes: love in its broadest sense, society and art. Each of these encompasses a wide range of variations and several odes combine themes (I-12, 25, 26, 34, 37; II-2, 3, 6, 9). In a category by itself are the poems about mortality which begin and end his Books of Odes and which will be discussed at the end of this chapter.

One of the best love poems and the earliest collected poem in which Bunting analyses and identifies an emotional state through the depiction of nature is Ode I-3. Dedicated to Peggy Mullett, this is a poem for which Yeats had a 'particular fancy' (LZ, 9 September 1953):

I am agog for foam. Tumultuous come
with teeming sweetness to the bitter shore
tidelong unrinsed and midday parched and numb
with expectation. If the bright sky bore
with endless utterance of a single blue
unphrased, its restless immobility
infects the soul, which must decline into
an anguished and exact sterility
and waste away: then how much more the sea
trembling with alteration must perfect
our loneliness by its hostility.
The dear companionship of its elect
deepens our envy. Its indifference
haunts us to suicide. Strong memories
of sprayblown days exasperate impatience
to brief rebellion and emphasise
the casual impotence we sicken of.
But when mad waves spring, braceletted with foam,
towards us in the angriness of love
crying a strange name, tossing as they come
repeated invitations in the gay
exuberance of unexplained desire,
we can forget the sad splendour and play
at wilfulness until the gods require
renewed inevitable hopeless calm
and the foam dies and we again subside
into our catalepsy, dreaming foam,
while the dry shore awaits another tide.

In this poem the movement of all the formal elements such as
rhythm, measure, and sound work together as an intricate unit to
produce a movement paralleling the movement from low tide to
high tide to low tide again. By these means Bunting identifies all
the movements of a fluctuating emotional state with the movements
of the sea and the resulting conditions of the shore. Long periods of
cataleptic anticipation and 'inevitable hopeless calm' are mitigated
by brief periods of 'playing/ at wilfulness'. Employing a Bergsonian
time device, Bunting has the first section encompassing the period
of numb expectancy continue for seventeen lines. Alternating end-
rhymes emphasise a rhythmic pulse imitative of the ebb and flow
of the waves and the restless thoughts of the speaker. Just before
this period ends, the rhymes become imperfect ('indifference'/
'impatience'), highlighting the exasperation which 'Strong memo-
ries/ of sprayblown days' is urging to 'brief rebellion'. An
emotionally brief period follows whose brevity is underlined by its
description of only six lines which reaches the climax of 'mad
waves...braceletted with foam,...tossing as they come/ repeated

invitations in the gay/ exuberance of unexplained desire'. All the elements of the ode then combine to bring about the lowest point of activity of the sea and of the mind:

> ...until the gods require
> renewed inevitable hopeless calm
> and the foam dies and we again subside
> into our catalepsy,

But here Bunting moves back to the speaker's actual emotional condition, the one which began the ode ('dreaming foam'). He deftly contrasts this with its longed-for opposite in the last line, 'while the dry shore awaits another tide', through the assonance of 'dry' and 'tide', two antithetical words which link the two states. At the same time the duration of 'while' and the spondaic 'dry shore' create the slowed life rhythm of the actual state of the cataleptic persona.

Among the odes concerned with love, 'O, it is godlike to sit self-possessed' [II-7] deserves special mention and will be discussed in the next chapter on translations. The satire and style of *'Personal Column'* [I-6] mask the sensitiveness revealed in the poignant translation of Hafez' poem, 'You leave', I-28, or the mature gentleness revealed in 'Birthday Greetings' which Bunting associated with a young Bakhtiari girl in Persia. 'Southwind, tell her' [I-29] sings a contemporary version of the anonymous sixteenth century song, 'O western wind, when wilt thou blow', and the music of 'Dear be still!' [I-9] revolves about the skilful use of spondees which underline the power of the 'headlong desires' he is trying to educate his beloved to let 'time lengthen slowly'. Bunting's note on Ode I-33 aptly describes this poem dedicated to Anne de Silver: 'The cool breeze of a pure, uncomprehending rendering of Handel's best known aria', again the association with music.

The same delicacy appears in the music and meaning of 'Stones trip Coquet burn' (1970), a poem about the upper waters of the Coquet River in Northumberland. Not primarily a love poem, it has been explained by Bunting: 'It's only when the lines are put together that it turns into something erotic. And that's only because you feel this poem and attribute feeling to the river.'[9] Seamlessly, Bunting fuses the image of the burn and a coquette in delicate lines that describe the action of both while imitating the sound of the water:

> in midgy shimmer
> she dares me chase
> under a bridge,

giggles, ceramic
huddle of notes,

While readers can be charmed by this, Bunting had a lifelong goal
that this ode only hints at:

> ...all my life, since I was a youngster, I wanted to do the 'O fons
> bandusiae' and I can't even get the first line. Like nearly all of the great
> poets, Horace depended on sound and the 'O fons Bandusiae' creates
> throughout, but especially in the first lines, the actual sound of the
> running water of a stream. You might be able to create a spring in
> English, perhaps if you were very skilful and able, but it wouldn't bear
> any resemblance, however unique, to Horace's sounds.[10]

> > [O fons Bandusiae, splendidior vitro,
> > dulci digne mero non sine floribus,
> >   cras donaberis haedo,
> >   cui frons turgida cornibus.]

As varied as this sampling proves the love poems to be, those
focusing on society as a theme have an even greater variety. Of the
two odes in dialect, 'Gin the Goodwife Stint' [I-14] and 'The
Complaint of the Morpethshire Farmer' [I-18], the second is so
consistently published as representative of Bunting's work that he
has exclaimed he is as tired of it as Yeats was of 'The Lake Isle of
Innisfree' [LZ, 10 November 1964]:

> On the up-platform at Morpeth station
> in the market-day throng
> I overheard a Morpethshire farmer
> muttering this song:

> Must ye bide, my good stone house,
> to keep a townsman dry?
> To hear the flurry of the grouse
> but not the lowing of the kye?
>   ...

> Where are ye, my seven score sheep?
> Feeding on other braes!
> My brand has faded from your fleece,
> another has its place.

> The fold beneath the rowan
> where ye were dipt before,
> its cowpit walls are overgrown,
> ye would na heed them more.
>   ...

> Canada's a bare land
> for the north wind and the snow.
> Northumberland's a bare land
> for men have made it so.

Sheep and cattle are poor men's food,
grouse is sport for the rich;
heather grows where the sweet grass might grow
for the cost of cleaning the ditch.
A liner lying in the Clyde
will take me to Quebec.
My sons'll see the land I am leaving
as barren as her deck.

Pound who included these two odes next to selections of e.e. cummings in his anthology, *From Confucius to Cummings*, comments in his notes:

> The stylistic reform, or the change in language, was a means not an end. After the war of 1914-18 there was definitely an extension of subject matter. This anthology cannot analyse the results, it is a lead up, but the poetry of the last forty years definitely breeds a discontent with a great deal that had been accepted in 1900. Of the poets who had appeared in the 1920s it has been asserted that Cummings and Bunting show a deeper concern with basic human problems in relation to the state of the times..., Bunting in more glum sobriety.[11]

These early odes of Bunting's in the Northumberland dialect are comparable with the early poems of D. H. Lawrence in the Nottinghamshire dialect which Pound praised highly. In a review of Lawrence's *Love Poems and Others*, he wrote: '...when Mr Lawrence ceases to discuss his own disagreeable sensations, when he writes low-life narrative, as he does in 'Whether or Not' and in 'Violets', there is no English poet under forty who can get within shot of him.'[12] He went on to quote dialect which Lawrence – and Bunting – could use so effectively. Although both D. H. Lawrence and Bunting are faithful to local speech patterns, Bunting's dialect poems seem closer to the traditional form and compressed language of the ballad. Kenneth Cox, for one, sees in the 'sparseness and purity of Mr Bunting's line, especially manifest in his earlier work, the tempered and taciturn spirit of the border ballads', and he regards his compression of language as a compression of emotion, 'as of speech through compressed lips'. In this way, he believes, Bunting keeps his poetry close 'to the feeling which engendered it and to the object described'. Cox sees not only these 'ballads', but all Bunting's poetry 'in the stark tradition he adorns, close to the state of inarticulateness'.[13]

Cox supplies the doctrine and poetry of Wordsworth as an interesting connection between the border ballads in their northern tradition and Bunting's poetry. This is strengthened by Bunting's acknowledgment of Wordsworth's influence. Cox makes the Wordsworthian doctrine explained in the Preface to the second edition of *Lyrical Ballads* a link in this 'stark tradition': '...choose incidents and situations from common life,...relate or describe them,...in a selection of language really used by men...'[14] In a casual sketch of his background entitled 'the Education of X', Bunting credits Wordsworth for showing him when he was 'a small kid...what [poetry] was' [LZ, August 1953], and the Lucy poems, remarkable for their simplicity and their ballad qualities, seem to be favourites of his:

> [Wordsworth] attempted in Lucy, etc. the simplicity which is commonly recommended as the nearest road to the sublime, and sometimes came within sight of the distant peak: and he attempted the Lucretian manner, not without successful pages. [LZ, 3 November 1948]

Bunting unfalteringly approaches the simplicity he admires in Wordsworth as 'the nearest road to the sublime', not only by means of the compression of speech in the dialect poems, but in the simple colloquial utterance he strives for in all his poetry. This ability to condense real speech into simple, naturally rhythmic patterns is the result of a lifetime's work.

To some extent like Wordsworth, and to a greater extent like D. H. Lawrence, Bunting sees the radical dichotomy between urban and rural life. Like his contemporary, he blames a materialistic society for changing lives which need to be in touch with the soil at least to some degree in order to be in touch truthfully with life.[15]

However, although he expresses these values in his poetry, he never attempts primarily to reform society through his art.[16] Bunting's stance towards those trapped in an urban culture is usually that of an observer, as in 'As appleblossom to crocus' [I-25]. This is true even when he speaks in the first person through a persona, for example, in 'Two hundred and seven paces' [I-26].

In the strong eighteen-line Ode I-31, Bunting uses Latin in an epigraph to root the present situation in the past as part of the universal situation of men and women in society: 'O ubi campi!' At one reading Bunting made sure his hearers appreciated the irony of the 'O ubi campi' (fruitful fields) used in an ode about the American Dustbowl farmers of the Thirties. Unlike the ruined Morpethshire farmer headed for Winnipeg, the alternative for the farmer addressed in this ode is 'a city job or relief – or doss-and-grub'. The ironic tone seems directed not so much towards the farmer as towards those responsible for the man's plight:

> The soil sandy and the plow light, neither
> virgin land nor near by the market town,
> cropping one staple without forethought, steer
> stedfastly ruinward year in year out,

> grudging the labour and cost of manure,
> drudging not for gain but fewer dollars loss
> yet certain to make a bad bargain by
> misjudging the run of prices. How glad
> you will be when the state takes your farm for
> arrears of taxes! No more cold daybreaks
> saffron under the barbed wire the east wind
> thrums, nor wet noons, nor starpinned nights! The choir
> of gnats is near a full-close. The windward
> copse stops muttering inwardly its prose
> bucolics. You will find a city job
> or relief – or doss-and-grub – resigned to
> anything except your own numb toil, the
> seasonal plod to spoil the land, alone.

This ode is interesting technically as a study in the use of Horatian contrasts in mood, vocabulary, and description.

Through the influence of Pound, but more from Bunting's own travels, society as a theme broadly includes farflung cultures; for example, the Far East in 'Vestiges' [I-20], the Near East in the Samangan ode, I-32,[17] and in 'Under sand clay. Dig, wait' [II-5], and the Spanish culture of the Canary Islands in 'The Orotava Road' [I-30], and also in 'All you Spanish ladies' [II-8]. Bunting enjoyed remarking that a grandfather in the Canaries wrote to him that 'The Orotava Road' is the closest thing to what he remembered of the old days – before the tourists discovered the place. Each of these has a music and form to fit its meaning and mood. Among these, 'Vestiges', important as a transition to the chapter on translations and adaptations, will be discussed in detail later.

One of the most outstanding poems about society is Ode I-35. Not specific geographically, it belongs to any place or people whose suffering awakens the same kind of guilt and compassion Bunting describes:

> Search under every veil
> for the pale eyes, pale
> lips of a sick child,
> in each doorway glimpse
> her reluctant limbs
> for whom no kindness is,
> to whom caress and kiss
> come nightly more amiss,
> whose hand no gentle hand
> touches, whose eyes withstand
> compassion. Say: Done, past
> help, preordained waste.
> Say: We know by the dead

they mourn, their bloodshed,
the maimed who are the free.
We willed it, we.
Say: Who am I to doubt?
But every vein cries out.

Bunting comments on this poem in a letter to Zukofsky: '...the
change of weight in the middle of 'Search under every veil' is very
deliberate: up till then I have only a stock sentimental poem which I
attempt to raise suddenly onto another level altogether. The fact
that you don't grumble at the sentimental beginning is quite
possibly due to what is thus reflected back from the end, which I
think I couldn't have got in the same light movement [LZ, 28 July
1949].

A link between the odes concerned with society and those
concerned with art are the few that combine themes. Many of those
about society and all those with combined themes carry graded
tones of irony which some critics see as characteristic of the ode in
the twentieth century. Whether the use of irony is especially
modern is debatable, but it is a characteristic means Bunting uses
to express his views of society at times. One example is the bitingly
satiric 'The Passport Officer' [I-23], in which the impersonal
official is compared to a dog who 'scrutinises the lamppost', 'sets
his seal on it', and 'moves onto the next'. At other times Bunting
uses irony to express his vision of the relationship of the poet and
society. In Ode I-11 dedicated 'To a Poet who advised me to
preserve my fragments and false starts', the controlled disdain is a
match for Alexander Pope's 'Sporus'. The dignified tone coupled
with the less than elegant diction of

> ...in the damp dustbins amongst the peel
> tobacco-ash and ends spittoon lickings litter
> of labels dry corks breakages and a great deal
> of miscellaneous garbage...

is reminiscent of Yeats's

> A mound of refuse or the sweeping of a street,
> Old kettles, old bottles, and a broken can,
> Old iron, old bones, old rags.[18]

Through a montage technique, 'An arles, an arles for my hiring'
[I-12] depicts with ironic humour the decline of a poet who is
finally 'cadging for drinks at the streetcorners'. Its tone is much less
sarcastic than 'What the Chairman Told Tom' (II-6), an ode
Bunting labelled a joke.[19] Although 'Tom' is specifically Tom
Pickard, Bunting's disciple, the character represents any unrecog-
nised poet struggling against powerful but insensitive philistines.

None of these poems, however, reaches the level of bitterness of
Ode I-37, 'On the Fly-Leaf of Pound's Cantos'. Whether or not it
is because of its intensity, this ode ranks among his best:

> There are the Alps. What is there to say about them?
> They don't make sense. Fatal glaciers, crags cranks climb,
> jumbled boulder and weed, pasture and boulder, scree,
> *et l'on entend,* maybe, *le refrain joyeux et leger.*
> Who knows what the ice will have scraped on the rock it is smoothing?
> There they are, you will have to go a long way round
> if you want to avoid them.
> It takes some getting used to. There are the Alps,
> fools! Sit down and wait for them to crumble!

Without the title, the ode is simply a lively commentary on the
Alps; with it the poem is one of the greatest compliments from one
contemporary poet to another. The ode is dated 1949, that is,
during the time of Pound's commitment to St Elizabeth's Hospital,
which makes the tribute all the more valuable and explains
somewhat the exasperation of the last line. The forthrightness and
indignation echoes Pound's tone, heard so often in his letters and
in some of his writings.

Both this ode and Ode I-3 use the same opening device, a stark
brief sentence, to gain the reader's attention: 'I am agog for foam'
and 'There are the Alps'. Here, however, this blunt statement
occurs in some form three times, as if, unbelievably, he must point
out the obvious and unavoidable fact before the viewer.

Besides the interest which the tone and the balance of short and
long sentences provide, there are the unexpected areas of
onomatopoetic dissonance in phrases such as "crags cranks climb"
and in the contrast of sound and meaning of verbs within the
movement of 'Who knows what the ice will have scraped on the
rock it is smoothing?'

A later ode (1969) echoes almost the same tone as 'On the
Flyleaf of Pound's Cantos' in the opening stanza:

> All the cants they peddle
> bellow entangled,
> teeth for knots and
> each other's ankles,
> to become stipendiary
> in any wallow;
> crow or weasel
> each to his fellow.

For background Bunting writes in his Notes: 'Whoever has been
conned, however briefly, into visiting a "poet's conference" will
need no explanation of this ode.' But what is notable is not the

exasperated and biting tone in the first stanza but the contrast
created by the shift in the second. A mellower – but not soft –
Bunting concedes:

> Yet even these,
> even these might
> listen as crags
> listen to light
> and pause, uncertain
> of the next beat,
> each dancer alone
> with his foolhardy feet.

Besides introducing rhyme to contrast the tone and pattern of
this stanza with the first one, he underscores the meaning with
imitative rhythm; for example, the irregular lines 'and pause,
uncertain/ of the next beat' blend into the regular dance rhythm,
and rhyme, of 'each dancer alone/with his foolhardy feet'. These
last lines carry faint traces of Yeats's dance and dancer. In his last
years Yeats spoke more of the association of music and poetry with
dance: 'Poetry and music are twin sisters, born of the dance. They
have to keep very close together or else they will get lost.'[20]

Bunting's few odes concerned with art have a singular beauty
none of the others has. 'Nothing' [I-15], published in *Poetry*[21] as
'The Word' with I-16 as 'Appendix: Iron', was described by
Zukofsky as an 'adaptation of classical quantitative measure in
English'.[22] The patterns of long and short syllables are evident
though much more difficult to analyse in English lines:

> Celebrate man's craft
> and the word spoken in shapeless night, the
> sharp tool paring away
> waste and the forms
> cut out of mystery!

Further, the strong stresses and even the alliteration in some lines
echo the Anglo-Saxon verse:

> and hewn hills and bristling forests,
> steadfast corn in its season

More than any other, this ode looks forward to *Briggflatts* in tone,
theme, and technique.

Ode I.16, separated now from 'The Word', is an instance of a
modern poet's effective use of industrial imagery:

> Molten pool, incandescent spilth of
> deep cauldrons – and brighter nothing is –
> cast and cold, your blazes extinct and
> no turmoil nor peril left you,
> rusty ingot, bleak paralysed blob!

Bunting's note to Ode I.36 clears up any misconceptions about the meaning of the poem:

> A friend's misunderstanding obliges me to declare that the implausible optics of this poem are not intended as an argument for the existence of God, but only suggest that the result of a successful work of art is more than the sum of its meanings and differs from them in kind.

It is evident why Thomas Cole spoke of the ode as 'Yeatsian'[23] and perhaps just as easy to see the influence of the Book of Revelation and St John's Gospel:

> See! Their verses are laid
> as mosaic gold to gold
> gold to lapiz lazuli
> white marble to porphyry
> stone shouldering stone, the dice
> polished alike, there is
> no cement seen and no gap
> between stones as the frieze strides
> to the impending apse:
> the rays of many glories
> forced to its focus forming
> a glory neither of stone
> nor metal, neither of words
> nor verses, but of the light
> shining upon no substance;
> a glory not made
> for which all else was made.

After Zukofsky had read this, Bunting answered his comments:

> The words that bother you in 'See their verses are laid': 'impending' is weak, but I couldn't find what's wanted – what's the word for quarter of the solid formed by the rotation of an ellipse on its axis, and has it an adjective? 'shouldering' probably has for you moral echoes which haven't worried me. I meant it physically, in which sense it is exact. Neatness: the civil service air of an embassy overcoming my natural untidiness? Energy? Of a kind. Both ['Search under every veil' and 'See! Their verses are laid'] are attempts to concentrate a lot of weight behind one punch. The first is artful – makes a feint to deceive the reader: the other 'comes out fighting'. There's nothing more to it. One could easily have said as much in a page and a half. [28 July 1949]

Needless to say, whatever 'one could easily have said' would have completely lost the powerful impact of this brief ode.

Ode I.34 combines the three themes of love, society, and art in a poem which Cole as early as 1951 singled out as 'an excellent example of Bunting's lyric quality'.[24]

To Violet, with prewar poems.

> These tracings from a world that's dead
> take for my dust-smothered pyramid.

Count the sharp study and long toil
as pavements laid for worms to soil.
You without knowing it might tread
the grass where my foundation's laid,
your, or another's, house be built
where my weathered stones lie spilt,
and this unread memento be
the only lasting part of me.

Cole's comment that in Ode I.34 'rime is used to fine advantage,
making one wish that Bunting had used it more often'[25] overlooks
the deeper influence of Malherbe, after Horace, Bunting's 'other
first spur' (LZ, 'June the New Moonth, 1953').[26] To Bunting,
Malherbe was

> the man who never forgot music for a moment and who, for all his
> determination to eat more toads than the next fellow, ate 'em with such
> a clean melody and so little mumbo-jumbo that he stands inspection still
> without any allowances for period, etc. [LZ, 6 August 1953]

This French poet who tried to preserve 'the marriage of music
and poetry' by writing his odes always within a musical framework
recognised a musical foundation as inseparable from the ode.
'From the welter of metrical forms, Malherbe chose the ten-line
strophe of five-syllable lines,...and by increasing the number of
syllables to eight, Malherbe transformed it into an instrument of
incomparable harmony.'[27] By using Malherbe's ode form, Bunting
achieves a degree of this harmony in Ode I.34.

When Ode I.34 was published, Bunting made a comparison
between a gun and a work of art which points out qualities he was
striving to incorporate in his odes:

> What do I 'feel with a machine-gun?' Well, it depends on the gun. I
> criticise a machine by nearly the same criteria as I do a work of art. A
> Lee-Enfield rifle, a Hotchkiss machine-gun, have nothing superfluous
> nor fussy about them. They are utterly simple – having reached that
> simplicity via complication and sophistication galore. The kind of people
> who, if they had literary minds at all, would like euphuism or trickiness,
> prefer Lewis guns or Remington or Ross rifles. My machine-gun is a
> Hotchkiss and I feel toward it something similar in kind to what I feel
> for Egyptian sculpture [...] I think Holbein or Bach or Praxiteles, as well
> as Alexander, would have appreciated a Hotchkiss gun; whereas a lot of
> our machines might *merely* have astonished them. [22 September 1941]

This kind of simplicity which he holds out as a goal to himself is
the outstanding quality of Ode I.20. As an "adaptation" this poem
could easily be grouped with those in the next chapter. However, its
brevity, its unique source, and Bunting's own categorisation
prompt its discussion here.

Like Eliot's notes for *The Waste Land*, Bunting's note about 'Vestiges' [I.20] is presumably written tongue-in-cheek for all those who wish to chase after the references and allusions which he scorns in his 'Statement' on poetry. Nevertheless, the information about the Jengiz-Khan – Chang Chun correspondence in E. Bretschneider's *Medieval Researches from Eastern Asiatic Sources*[28] deepens the reader's awareness of the poet's background and is valuable for a full appreciation of the poem. From pages of details in Bretschneider's book and from his own imagination and background, Bunting has chosen single items which he piles up to create a realistic montage of 'vestiges'.

Part I balances Part II with a simplicity reminiscent of oriental art. In Part I the personae of the poem describe in pithy phrases their present poor conditions, shifting to remembrances of the past which impinge on the present:

> Salt grass silent of hooves, the lake stinks,
> we take a few small fish from the streams,
> our children are scabby, chivvied by flies,
> we cannot read the tombs in the eastern prairie.
>   who slew the Franks, who
>   swam the Yellow River.

> The lice have left Temuchin's tent. His ghost
> cries under north wind, having spent
> strength in life: life lost, lacks means of death,
> voice-tost; the horde indistinguishable;
> worn name weak in fool's jaws.

> We built no temples. Our cities' woven hair
> mildewed and frayed. Records of Islam and Chin,
> battles, swift riders, ambush,
> tale of the slain, and the name Jengiz.

Between the mention of 'the name Jengiz' and the introduction of tall Chutsai, sitting under a tree, Bunting builds a bridge between present and past with a one-line stanza, 'Wild geese of Yen, peacocks of the Windy Shore.' The scene of ancient Peking is suggested with the simplicity of oriental art by means of two details which reveal the strength, pride, and grandeur of that ancient civilisation.

In the next stanza Bunting brings to life what is essential in Bretschneider's history about Chutsai, 'an ingenious statesman' recognised by his height and 'splendid beard', a former prisoner who rose to the highest position in the empire. In this vignette Chutsai, who administered the taxes on the land north of the Yellow River, calculates wisely a specific business deal, underlining

the ageless greed of men and the regard of a wise administrator for
the people.[29] The simplicity of the ending parallels that same
quality in ancient governing:

> Tall Chutsai sat under the phoenix tree.
> – That Baghdad banker contracts to
> double the revenue, him collecting.
> Four times might be exacted, but
> such taxation impoverishes the people.
> No litigation. The laws were simple.

Bretschneider admires the correspondence between Jengiz and
Chang Chun for creditable reasons:

> The translation of these letters will enable the reader to form a
> judgment of the character and mode of thought of those illustrious men.
> Chinghiz, in his simplicity, professes such sound principles of governing
> people, and his words express such profound truths, that they would be
> valid even in our days and for our countries in Europe. On the other
> side, Ch'ang Ch'un inspires sympathy by his modesty, candour, and
> sincerity. He seems to have been endowed with high intelligence,
> knowing well his time and human nature.[30]

In Part II of the ode the vestiges of this correspondence are as
strong and yet as delicate as calligraphic writing. Bunting strips
down pages of the letters, written in formal, classical Chinese style,
to their utmost simplicity:

> Jengiz to Chang Chun: China
> is fat, but I am lean
> eating soldier's food,
> lacking learning.
> In seven years
> I brought most of the world under one law.
> The Lords of Cathay
> hesitate and fall.
> Amidst these disorders
> I distrust my talents.
> To cross a river
> boats and rudders,
> to keep the empire in order
> poets and sages,
> but I have not found nine for a cabinet,
> not three.
> I have fasted and washed. Come.
>
> Chang: I am old
> not wise nor virtuous,
> nor likely to be much use.
> My appearance is parched, my body weak.
> I set out at once.

From all the details about Liu Chung Lu and the escort of

twenty Mongols for the three-year journey, the golden tablet with
the Khan's order that the Taoist master should be treated as the
Emperor himself, and finally Chang's reluctance to travel with girls
for the Khan's harem, Bunting chooses only the telling few:

> And to Liu Chung Lu, Jengiz:
> Get an escort and a good cart,
> and the girls can be sent on
> separately if he insists.

By selecting details and arranging them within a broad historical
framework, Bunting creates a double and even a triple perspective
in Part I. He shifts this perspective to focus on the close-up of
specific details in the correspondence in Part II. The chronological
time of the first three stanzas of the poem is so indefinite that it can
include both eras immediately following the Jengiz Khan Empire
and the present when 'litigation' is all-important and laws are
anything but 'simple'. This multiple perspective enlarges Bunting's
theme beyond the limits of his source.

Poetically, Bunting reinforces the contrasts of vestiges of the past
and the present by speaking in at least three voices in Part I, and
then contrasting these with the extreme simplicity of the two voices
of the correspondents in Part II. Speaking in the first person plural,
the reminiscing voice of the persona of the first three stanzas
describes matter of factly, yet with an overtone of sadness, the
present conditions. The past quickly intrudes in the restless form of
the 'life lost', 'voice-tost' ghost of Temuchin. Bunting underscores
the mournful tone through long vowels and dipthongs and open
syllables ('hooves', 'tomb', 'few', 'who', 'who slew', 'who', 'cries',
'flies', 'prairie') which lengthen the lines:

> We cannot read the tombs in the eastern prairie,
> who slew the Franks, who
> swam the Yellow River.

Bunting counterpoints the slower movement with a quickened
rhythm suggestive of the restlessness of Temuchin's ghost,
paralleling in the present the restlessness of the poverty-stricken
descendants of his people. The internal rhyme of 'name' 'slain'
necessitates a dramatic pause before the word 'Jengiz', the signal
for the shift to the perspective of the more distant past.

The voice of an anonymous narrator bridges the eras in the
single one-line stanza and then in a more ordinary tone sets the
stage for the new scene: 'Tall Chutsai sat under the phoenix tree.'
The interesting detail of the phoenix tree which Iranians assure me
is well known as an actual tree and as a metaphor places Chutsai in

the Near East as definitely as does his comment about the 'Baghdad banker'. Its metaphorical meaning, 'a single time', 'a unique time', elevates the period of the Jengiz Khan Empire to a unique era of government.

The thoughts of Chutsai in a third voice record in direct, economical terms a proposed tax plan, its possible extension, and its logical bad outcome. By leaving the counsellor's judgment implicit, Bunting underlines its obvious justice at the same time he furthers the economy of the poetry.

With his single line, 'No litigation. The laws were simple', the anonymous commentator provides, first, a smooth distancing to bring the reader back to himself to encourage a personal judgment; second, a finished ending to Part I; and third, a dramatic transition to Part II. The chief voices in the second half of the poem are, of course, those of the two correspondents. Bunting's choice of details outlines the uncomplicated wisdom and way of life of the two men, representatives of different kinds of power: one with the soldier's talents to create a new empire, another with the poet's and sage's power to help keep the empire in order. In a few rhythmic phrases Bunting delineates the essential character of each man. Neither downplays his worth with a false humility, yet each knows his limitations. Without embellishment Bunting has Jengiz summarise his successes:

> In seven years
> I brought most of the world under one law.

Perhaps it is too much to expect the reader to recognise the writing of Chutsai in the Khan's letters, though the simple rhythm of his brief statements and his straightforward manner of speech echo Chutsai's style in Part I. Bunting more easily brings out the basis for Jengiz Khan's powerful leadership through each detail he selects to represent the lengthy correspondence. Further, because he selects only a few details from his letters and Chang's, Bunting does not intend to rewrite the historical correspondence as poetry, but to create vestiges of it which fit into the whole structure of his poem:

> Jengiz to Chang Chun: China
> is fat, but I am lean
> eating soldier's food,
> lacking learning.
> In seven years
> I brought most of the world under one law.
> The Lords of Cathay
> hesitate and fall.
> Amidst these disorders

I distrust my talents.
To cross a river
boats and rudders,
to keep the empire in order
poets and sages,
but I have not found nine for a cabinet,
not three.
I have fasted and washed. Come.

The culmination of the section, the single word, 'Come', is at once inviting and commanding. Bunting balances Chang's courteously humble description of himself by the simple, composed acceptance of the "invitation-command": 'I set out at once.' Whether or not the reader knows that his acceptance cost three years of arduous travel is not important for Bunting's purpose, to point up the basic simplicity and order in this flourishing culture. Again, according to his poetic intent, he has transformed the historical correspondence into telling vestiges of a past civilisation:

Chang: I am old
not wise nor virtuous,
nor likely to be of much use.
My appearance is parched, my body weak.
I set out at once.

Finally, in four short lines, Bunting rounds out the picture of the wise ruler who gives indisputable orders to subordinates, yet leaves them free to arrange details methodically and expeditiously:

And to Liu Chung Lu, Jengiz:
Get an escort and a good cart,
and the girls can be sent on
separately if he insists.

Although Bunting insists that the poet remain anonymous in the poem,[31] the details he has chosen to include and the structuring of parts to emphasise their interdependent meanings make this not simply an artefact which is independent of its sources, but a poem with a highly personal vision. Bunting has incorporated historical and imagined details within a broad perspective to create an independent artefact which has its own original structure and which presents its own special vision. The vestiges of the Jengiz-Chang correspondence point to the essential factors in a civilisation strong enough to last through Jengiz Khan's lifetime and even after his grandson's, Kublai's. The poet creates his poem with indivisible form and content which highlight the essential factors which made this possible – simplicity and disciplined order. Deliberately, Bunting has contrasted the strength and human appeal of even the vestiges of this ancient civilisation with the poverty and degradation of succeeding ones which could include the present. He suggests this contrast through a montage of details which in their turn become vestiges of a different sort from those of the correspondence. The single details combine to suggest all that is left of this civilisation years later through the neglect of values which made it great: 'grass silent of hooves', stinking lake, scabby children 'chivvied by flies', lice, and 'cities' woven hair mildewed and frayed'. Restless ghosts of former times and undecipherable legends on tombs are the only vestiges these people in their turn can faintly recognise. The interlocking parts of the poem – contrasting perspectives and voices, rhythms and images – reinforce the interlocking structure of vestiges in this profound poem.

Though it is too late now to ask Bunting if he intended this, the theme of mortality gives the two Books of Odes a framework. This theme is not one that overshadows the other themes of love, art, and society, but one that gives the whole a shape, something the poet was seeking in all his work.

To open the First Book a youthful Bunting depicts the endless tedium of life without death in his first ode, 'Weeping oaks grieve, chestnuts raise', originally titled 'Sad Spring'. Here in union with all of mourning nature, he feels sad that creation is being perpetuated, 'immortalities never changing' on land and on water. With a world-weary tone he describes life as a sea of sameness, a 'merciless reiteration of years', and mourns that we 'descry no death', that 'spring/ is everlasting/ resurrection'. It is hard to believe this youthful ennui, especially for readers who know that at this time he is 24, poor but hale and hearty, and enjoying life with Pound and Yeats in Rapallo. Even if he is looking back at the chestnut trees of Paris, it still seems a pose and more an ode preserved for the melody of some of its lines: 'Weeping oaks grieve, chestnuts raise/ mournful candles' and

> Weary on the sea
> for sight of land
> gazing past the coming wave we
> see the same wave.

Barbara Lesch notes the chiasmus here: weary/sea, see/wave, which strengthens its musicality.[32] In a classical sense the first stanza can be a strophe, the second an answering antistrophe, and the third, a parodoxical epode, but this may attribute to the ode a stateliness that it does not quite live up to.

How different this first ode is from the final one, written when Bunting was 80 and added to his *Collected Poems* when he was 85.

But long before, he had mentioned death several times in his earlier
poems, for example, in I-4, 'Empty death' and in the powerful
'Nothing', I-15:

> ...the word
> ranks and enumerates...
> mimes...
> ...
> life of man's own body
> and death...
>> The sound thins into melody,
> discourse narrowing, craft
> falling, design
> petering out.
> Ears heavy to breeze of speech and
> thud of the ictus.

In this carefully shaped ode the design which began in the first
stark line, 'Nothing', comes full circle in the final line where death
has stilled 'thought's intricate polyphonic/score dovetail[ed] with
the tread/sensuous things/keep in our consciousness'. A clear
statement about poetry and his view of life, this ode is one which
smoothly synthesises music and meaning. The more it is read, the
more its beauty can be appreciated.

In the Second Book he prepares his readers for the clear
mortality theme of the final odes. Written at 65, 'You idiot! What
makes you think decay', II-4, reveals his disgust with ageing, yet
also his hope for compassionate sexual love. Another, more
sanguine prospect mediates between the beginning and end of '*At
Briggflatts meetinghouse*', II-11; the forceful spondaic opening of
'Boasts time mocks cumber Rome' softens to the poignant music of

> Yet for a little longer here
> stone and oak shelter
>
> silence while we ask nothing
> but silence.

And then in a complete reversal from the ennui of 'Weeping oaks
grieve, chestnuts raise/mournful candles', the poet, now 75, ends
with Lear-like wisdom about the possibilities of beauty and joy in a
fleeting life, 'Look how clouds dance/under the wind's wing, and
leaves/delight in transience'. This is all the more remarkable in
light of what Bunting wrote when he sent it to me:

> I've written almost nothing for a long time. You will easily imagine that
> inflation on the scale we are enduring leaves no peace to a man whose
> income is fixed and very small. More and more has to be done without. I
> never know two months in advance how we shall live. That is not a
> circumstance favourable to reflection, let alone steady craftsmanship.

But I'll put a little bit into the envelope that I concocted for the tercentenary of Briggflatts meeting house, which is being celebrated this spring. It is not easy to write "religious" poetry without falling into a dozen traps: but perhaps I have avoided most of them. [11 May 1975]

Dated 1977 and published in *Agenda* (Spring 1978) as 'Per che no spero', the last ode Bunting wrote was improved and dated 1980 before it was added to the final 1985 American edition of the *Collected Poems*. Bunting corrected that title to make the Italian phrase 'Perche no spero' an epigraph, and he used the first line, 'Now we've no hope of going back', as the title in the Table of Contents. On television he introduced this last ode as words a man might speak to his yacht, but the metaphor has deep overtones which make this poem a powerful final ode:

> Now we've no hope of going back,
> cutter, to that grey quay
> where we moored twice and twice unwillingly
> cast off our cables to put out at the slack
> when the sea's laugh was choked to a mutter
> and the leach lifted hesitantly with a stutter
> and sulky clack,
>
> how desolate the swatchways look,
> cutter, and the chart's stained,
> stiff, old, wrinkled and uncertain,
> seeming to contradict the pilot book.
> On naked banks a few birds strut
> to watch the ebb sluice through the narrow gut
> loud as a brook.
>
> Soon, while that northwest squall wrings out its cloud,
> cutter, we'll heave to
> free of the sands and let the half moon do
> as it pleases, hanging there in the port shrouds
> like a riding light. We have no course to set,
> only to drift too long, watch too glumly, and wait,
> wait.

Bunting's insistence on the necessity of hearing a poem should be remembered here, and Bunting himself should be heard reading this ode. The energy in his voice and the emphases on some words counterpointed with pauses, especially in the last lines, dismiss any possible sentimentality. Surprisingly, Bunting returns to the rhyme of some of the early odes in these seven-line stanzas. But the pattern (abbacca) by which the first, fourth, and seventh lines knit the couplets of lines 2 and 3, and 5 and 6 is much more skilful: 'that grey quay'/'unwillingly'; 'heave to'/'moon do'. Threaded through the ode are internal rhymes and echoes of rhyme: 'loud', 'cloud', 'shrouds'; and 'cutter', 'mutter', 'stutter', 'strut', 'gut'. The stiff-lipped apostrophe, 'cutter', creates a refrain in every second line. Only this much pattern for this formal leave-taking. Spondees disrupt the rhythm at dramatic points for emphasis: 'the chart's stained,/stiff, old, wrinkled and uncertain' and 'that northwest squall wrings out its cloud'. Pointing out combinations of onomatapoeia, assonance, and alliteration – 'when the sea's laugh was choked to a mutter/and the leach lifted hesitantly with a stutter/and sulky clack' – barely suggests the power of the music.

More than the music alone, the metaphor adds a strength that is masterful. Though Bunting was reticent about his personal life, by being specific about 'twice and twice' he may be alluding to his marriages when at 80 he writes stoically: 'Now we've no hope of going back,/cutter, to that grey quay/where we moored twice and twice unwillingly/cast off our cable to put out at the slack'. He allows us to see 'how desolate the swatchways look,/...and the charts,/stained, stiff, old, wrinkled and uncertain,/seeming to contradict the pilot book'. By apostrophising the cutter, he creates the needed companionship for the final voyage which he foresees and resigns himself to, 'glumly'. When Bunting read this, he emphasised a pause before each 'too' in the second last line which further solemnised the ending. Abbreviating the last line of the 1977 version by omitting the last phrase, the unnecessary 'like the proud', is a fine revision; in every line of the ode the indomitable pride of the persona speaks.

That Bunting added only 'Perche no spero' to his last edition of his *Collected Poems* indicates, of course, that he valued it as one worth preserving. But although this is his final ode, it reveals only one aspect of his view of mortality. For Bunting's full view, this ode must be read with the other poems about mortality which he wrote during his last years – not only the ode '*At Briggflatts meeting-house*', but the overdrafts 'You can't grip years, Postume' (*Eheu fugaces*) and 'Snow's deep on the fellside. Look'.

Though 'You can't grip years, Postume' is a translation of Horace and therefore belongs more correctly in the chapter on translations, it is an important late contribution to Bunting's view of the transience of life. He thought very highly of it, as he wrote to me: 'The only [Latin poem] worth keeping is the *Eheu fugaces*, and I'm not certain that you have even seen that' (23 February 1973). In a completely different tone from his last ode Bunting's persona eyes morality and death with Horatian equanimity, the *aequa mens*. Unlike the Persian translations, 'When the sword of sixty comes nigh his head' (Firdosi), written when he was 35, and 'All the teeth ever I had are worn down and fallen out' (Rudaki), written when he was 48, this ode translation, written when he was 71, seems more likely to reflect his own attitude at this time of his life: 'You can't grip years...nor tame death'. The 'Coda' of *Briggflatts* is heard in 'we'll go aboard.../to cross, kings some, some/penniless plowmen', and the strong refrain of 'Nothing...' is heard in

> For nothing we keep out of war
> or from screaming spindrift
> or wrap ourselves against autumn
> for nothing, seeing
> we must stare at that dark,...

One critic of Horace, J. B. Leishman quoting Willi, writes of Horace's 'continuous awareness of death. In ode after ode a similar interweaving of different "philosophies" and attitudes may be observed' – 'Epicurean moderation and Epicurean-Ciceronian equanimity with Platonic grandeur of measure, with Roman-Stoical virtus...'[33] All this Bunting captures, musically, in this poem, especially in these last stanzas:

> We must let earth go and home,
> wives too, and your trim trees,
> yours for a moment, save one
> sprig of black cypress.

> Better men will empty
> bottles we locked away,
> wine puddle our table,
> fit wine for a pope.

To appreciate Bunting's melody and craftsmanship here, consider a translation in the correct Alcaic metre:

> Land, home, and wife so dear to your heart shall then
> be all relinquished; nor of the trees you tend
>   shall any save that hateful cypress
> follow its briefly-installed possessor.

> A worthier heir shall open the Caecuban
> a hundred keys now guard, and with vintage
>   surpassing those that crown the pontiffs'
> liberal feasting shall drench the pavements.[34]

Though completed later, 1977, another Horatian overdraft, 'Snow's on the fellside, look! How deep',[35] expresses the same equanimity, with even more energy in places:

> We'll thaw out. Logs, logs for the hearth;
> and don't spare my good whisky. No water, please.
> Forget the weather. Elm and ash
> will stop signalling

when this gale drops.
Why reckon? Why forecast? Pocket
whatever today brings,
and don't turn up your nose, it's childish,
at making love and dancing.
When you've my bare scalp, if you must, be glum.

Love and dancing contrast with ageing and glumness, but the tone and proportion are clearly on the side of equanimity and wholehearted living. Though this did not measure up to Bunting's standards for his *Collected Poems*, it along with the others on mortality helps put 'Now we've no hope' in perspective.

Mortality is strongly prevalent in many other longer works: *The Spoils*, for a vivid example; also *Chomei at Toyama*; and *Briggflatts* with its slowworm theme, for another. Bunting corrected me, however, when I suggested that the final stoic expression of the sonata is the underlying pain of inevitable death: 'The pain, yes – not of death, but of wrong unrighted or unrightable' [4 July 1973]. This suggests the complicated interweaving of this theme with others in the longer poems.

But the longer poems and overdrafts aside, it is here in the First and Second Book of Odes that Bunting's theme of mortality acts as an uncomplicated framework to shape the two books of shorter works. This is not to imply that Bunting went about it like Yeats who not only shaped each book of poetry but played off one book against the other to create an impressive design of his whole collection. Bunting did not like that kind of precise pattern in poetry or music, so it seems natural he would never structure his books of odes quite so formally either. Nevertheless, his lifelong concern for shape and pattern and the evident correspondence between the themes of the first and last odes, together with recurrences throughout, give the Books a shape and loose pattern based on this theme of mortality.

Through the odes Bunting demonstrates his idea that 'Poetry is a craft which you learn by trying... Unless you work very hard for it you won't get anywhere.'[36] Although the overall quality of the odes is uneven, the chronological development is steady as the difference between the first collected ode dated 1924 and the last one completed in 1980 proves. The themes throughout are generally 'what men [and women] experience in common life'.[37] Bunting strongly believes 'you can't write about anything unless you've experienced it; you're either confused in your subject matter or else you get it all wrong'. However, Bunting has not set out to make a poem of his experience in each ode: 'You set out to make a shape of sounds: musical sounds. You set out to make something that is agreeable to have around.'[38] Through the odes and also through the translations and adaptations he continuously refined his ability to create agreeable musical shapes which he combines to their best advantage in the sonatas.

CHAPTER 5

Translations and Adaptations

'If ever I learned the trick of [writing poetry], it was mostly from poets long dead whose names are obvious...' ('Preface'). One method Bunting used to learn the 'trick' of it was writing translations and adaptations. He groups most of these in 'Overdrafts', an appendix to his *Collected Poems*, although he includes the best in the main sections of the book. The variety, works of Latin, Italian, Persian, Chinese, and Japanese writers, witness to his background and interests.

Bunting clearly learned from Pound's advice to young poets about translating. As early as 1913 Pound had advocated a training programme for prospective poets which included reading poetry, 'preferably in a foreign language', to 'fill the candidate's mind with the finest cadences he can discover' and translating this poetry: 'Translation is likewise good training, if you find that your original matter "wobbles" when you try to rewrite it. The meaning of the poem to be translated can not "wobble".' In 1912 Pound had written 'As for "adaptations"; one finds that all the old masters of painting recommend to their pupils that they begin by copying masterwork, and proceed to their own composition.'[1] Through his early translations Bunting was embarking on just such a programme. His exasperated ending of Catullus' lyric poem, LXIV, indicates he was translating this more as an exercise than anything else: '– and why Catullus bothered to write pages and pages of this drivel mystifies me.'

In even the most exact paraphrase of a foreign work, Bunting creates something more than a literal translation. Pound's ideas in 'A Retrospect' throw light on Bunting's goals:

> My pawing over the ancients and semi-ancients has been one struggle to find out what has been done, once for all,...and to find out what remains for us to do, and plenty does remain, for if we still feel the same emotions as those which launched the thousand ships, it is quite certain that we come on those feelings differently, through different nuances, by different intellectual gradations...No good poetry is written in a

> manner twenty years old, for to write in such a manner shows
> conclusively that the writer thinks from books, convention and cliché,
> and not from life, yet a man feeling the divorce of life and his art may
> naturally try to resurrect a forgotten mode if he finds in that mode some
> leaven, or if he thinks he sees in it some element lacking in
> contemporary art which might unite that art again to its sustenance,
> life.[2]

From this struggle to discover the best way to 'unite that art again to
its sustenance, life', Bunting's translations emerge.

During the mid-Thirties Pound from Rapallo kept 'nagging'[3] W.
H. Rouse in letter after letter about his translation of Homer. This
correspondence has a close connection with Bunting. In March
1935, Pound wrote to T. S. Eliot: 'Re translatin': ole Rouse is
getting stubborn, won't even pay any attention to Aurora's
manicuring or Telemachus' feet. Damn. And he might have been a
useful stimulus to Bunt. and Bin. [Binyon].'[4] What Pound was
trying to convince Rouse to work for, Bunting too was trying to
accomplish in his translations:

1. Real speech in the English version
2. Fidelity to the original
   a. meaning
   b. atmosphere
No need of keeping verbal literality for phrases which sing and run
naturally in the original.[5]

As important as this background is to understanding Bunting's
poetry, the most essential ideas regarding his translations are his
own. In the *Criterion* review of E. Stuart Bates's *Modern Translation*,
Bunting unequivocably states his position.[6] He deals with *Modern
Translation* in one succinct paragraph which concludes: 'Closing
Mr Bates's book, one may repeat his introductory statement: the
subject of modern translation "does not appear to have yet been
dealt with".' He discusses his own position by first tracing
Dryden's idea that

> [some] translations [are] meant to stand by themselves, works in their
> own language equivalent to their original but not compelled to lean on
> its authority, claiming the independence and accepting the responsibility
> inseparable from a life of their own.

Bunting then distinguishes between a crib, which translates
'sentence by sentence; Dryden, effect by effect'; and Chaucer who
'translates nothing less than the whole poem'. He backs his
preference for Chaucer's model by holding that the greatest poems
result from that kind of translating which 'long and deeply
influence literature and are therefore best worth discussing'. In this
line he places the translations of Fitzgerald and Pound, explaining

their merits in detail and comparing their methods. He admires not only an idiomatic language, but 'an idiom in sequence of ideas', something he believes Pound lacks, and *'familiar* comprehension' rather than 'academic lucidity'. 'As to the morality of tampering with texts,' Bunting claims that 'the question does not arise when the main purpose is to make an English poem, not to explain a foreign one: and between these two aims no middle course seems to prosper.'

LATIN POEMS

The only hint outside the poems themselves that Bunting gives his reader to this background of ideas is his note to the 'Overdrafts': 'It would be gratuitous to assume that a mistranslation is unintentional.' Besides his general ideas about translation, his meticulous concern for technique would preclude any such assumption. The painstaking care with which he translated Zukofsky's tribute to Pound into Latin is an index of his concern for precision. However, even here in 'Verse and Version', if he must choose between clarity of meaning and sound, his choice is a foregone conclusion:

First your poem: I am no hand at Italian and intended sending it to Monotti, but in the meantime tried what I could do with it in Latin, which seemed to me more suited than modern Italian (not Dante's) to the monumental terseness, especially when dealing in relatives without antecedents – this? Italian reader inquires Which? So I showed my poem to Ezra and he seems to intend to print it, and that will be all right,...provided I haven't made any egregious errors, which is quite possible, and I am not certain Ezra would detect them though he knows more Latin than I do.

But since Latin is in some ways more precise than our own lingo, there were places where I was in doubt and may have got your meaning a few shades out, shades not delicate as the difference of pale pink and paler, but properly Cimmerian catastrophic indigoes. In the second stanza, what tense is *put?* I have made it present, rejecting past or perfect not from any ability to penetrate the ambiguity of English, but because *superimponunt* sounds better than *superimponebant* or *superimposuerunt.* And in the last line of the poem is *every kindness* object or subject? Before happening for every kindness happens? I have made it nominative. If ablative, then *'prius quam pro omnibus mitioris'.* Or maybe omitting *'pro'*...

As for the difference of *verba* and *dicta, tristitiam* and *maestitiam,* I chose by the noise they make; though I rejected *luctus* as being too definitely funereal. *Dicta* perhaps connects with *mens* as well as *ora. Id* for *this* rather than *istud* because I conceived you to be avoiding rather than courting emphasis on the pronoun: the *horum* of line 5 being plural is not likely to cause confusion. *Its* in line 8 may refer either to *sorrow* or to *this*: so might *eius*, though I think it would be more natural to take it with *id.* The dislocation of *omnia* in line 12 avoids the ugliness of -*que quam* and of course is not, in Latin, an inversion, that is, a *per*version. The only other liberty with your word order is *tristitiam* before *superimponunt*, which is more natural in Latin, makes a better rhythm, and avoids the possible ambiguity that might arise from setting *tristitiam* and *eius* together. Punctuation supplied, concession to the deadness of the dead language. [LZ, September 1932]

The completed poem shows the results of this careful attention to details:

In that this happening 　　　is not unkind it put to 　　shame every kindness	quia id quod accidit 　　　non est immitis pudebat omnia 　　mitiora.
mind, mouths, their words, 　　people, put sorrow 　　　　on 　　its body	mens, ora, dicta horum, 　　hominesque, tristitiam superimponunt 　　eius membra.
before sorrow it came 　　and before every kindness, happening for every sorrow 　　before every kindness	prius quam tristitia accidit, 　　omnisque prius quam mitiora; accidit pro omnibus tristitiis 　　prius quan omnia mitiora.
(Louis Zukofsky)	(Basil Bunting)

Bunting's attention to technique has precedent in the writings of the Latin poets themselves. Commenting at length on the 'Law of Iambic Shortening' operative in Lucretius, an editor of *De Rerum Natura* concludes that 'metrical convenience or necessity is the determining factor'.[7] Bunting's modern translation of Lucretius' invocation to Venus, the opening lines of *De Rerum Natura*, follows this principle of musical necessity overriding all else. This is more easily seen in a comparison of Bunting's work with those of others. In this comparison other factors just discussed as important to Bunting are highlighted also. For example, even though one translator prefaces his work with strong statements against the 'mechanical and pedantic accuracy of grammar and syntax', and argues for 'the throbbing reality of the great living Roman', and for the 'higher accuracy: the accuracy of the imagination, at once interpretative and creative', in the final analysis he is describing Bunting's work better than his own. In Bunting's version twenty-five lines of the original are condensed to eighteen. Phrases translated as 'Makest to teem the many voyaged main/ And fruitful lands',[8] Bunting with simple directness translates as 'you fill rich earth and buoyant sea with your presence'. The difference in diction makes it difficult to believe these translations were made within a few years of each other.

In a translation ten years later than Bunting's, lines are rendered unmusically and archaically; for example, 'Each kind of living creature is conceived/ Then riseth and beholdeth the sun's light.'[9] Bunting translates this as 'for every living thing achieves its life through you,/ rises and sees the sun'. Instead of such a translation as 'Before thee, Goddess, and thy coming on,/ Flee stormy wind and massy cloud away',[10] Bunting writes directly, 'For you the sky is clear,/ the tempests still'. Years of work will eliminate such congestions as the *-ts st-* in 'tempests still' and the heaviness of 'untrammelled allrenewing southwind'. With these exceptions the invocation is smooth and rhythmical, reminiscent both in tone and content of Chaucer's 'Prologue' to *The Canterbury Tales.*

Besides the translation of Lucretius' invocation, Bunting made at least one attempt to translate Catullus which he thought worth preserving, LXIV. The classical scholar, L. P. Wilkinson, notes that Catullus wrote this epyllion, 'the Peleus and Thetis', under the influence of late Greek poets and that, peculiarly, this influence marked a period of decadence in Roman poetry before its period of maturity.[11] Bunting, like Catullus, may have wished to try his hand at 'a poem distinctly epic in character, partly as giving scope to a greater variety of powers',[12] since this was written about the same time that Bunting was working on the Persian epic, Firdosi's *Shahnamah*, which both Pound and Bunting were trying to get published.[13] Whatever may have been the reason, Bunting did manage to capture the predominant alliteration of *p*'s in the first line of Catullus' poem, *s*'s in the second, and *f*'s in the third:

> Peliaco quondam prognatae vertice pinus
> dicuntur liquidas Neptuni nasse per undas
> Phasidos ad fluctus et fines Aeeteos,

> Once, so they say, pinetrees seeded on Pelion's peak swam
> over the clear sea waves to the surf on the beaches of Phasis
> when the gamesome fleece-filchers, pith of Argos, picked for a foray,

In fact, by transferring 'Phasis' from the third to the second line, he was able to reproduce the *as* sound repeated three times in the original second line. It does not seem that Bunting was attempting the quantitative Latin verse in the hexameters of the original, so difficult to approach in English, but rather to translate the excitement and richness of vocabulary into modern speech. Although Bunting cuts short his translation of 'this drivel' in disgust, the portion he has translated holds its own among more recent attempts. For example, he had compressed twenty-eight lines of the original into only twenty lines. In his favour are the directness and sweeping rhythms of such lines as 'The Lady of Citadels shaped them a light hull for darting to windward/ and laid the cutaway keel with her own hands and wedded the timbers.'

However, in spite of successful attempts at compression and simplicity, Bunting's overdraft in general is as overloaded with epithets as the original: 'you, heroes, brood of the gods, born in the prime season,/ thoroughbreds sprung of thoroughbred dams' and 'you, bridegroom/ acclaimed with many pinebrands, pillar of Thessaly, fool for luck, Peleus'. Repetition of a proper name in the second last line is effective for dramatic emphasis: 'to whom Jove the godbegetter, Jove himself yielded his mistress'; however, repetition of two names, Thetis and Peleus, in each line of a three-line sentence adds neither to the rhythm or the overall sound, and little to the sense:

> Forthwith, thus the tale runs, love of Thetis flamed up in Peleus
> And Thetis took Peleus spite of the briefness of man's lifetime;
> even her father himself deemed Peleus worthy of Thetis.

Bunting's greatest tribute to Catullus is 'O, it is godlike to sit selfpossessed', II-7, with the epigraph '*Ille mi par esse deo videtur*'. These first five lines of the Latin lyric LI are themselves translations of the first lines of Sappho's poem which Catullus used in his poem to Lesbia. Bunting's note to me (4 July 1973) that here he meant to suggest 'some distant kinship with the Sapphic stanza' is singularly appropriate:

> O it is godlike to sit selfpossessed
> when her chin rises and she turns to smile;
> but my tongue thickens, my ears ring,
> what I see is hazy.
>
> I tremble. Walls sink in night, voices
> unmeaning as wind. She only
> a clear note, dazzle of light, fills
> furlongs and hours
>
> so that my limbs stir without will, lame,
> I a ghost, powerless,
> treading air, drowning, sucked
> back into dark
>
> unless, rafted on light or music,
> drawn into her radiance, I dissolve
> when her chin rises and she turns to smile.
> O, it is godlike!

The final line, 'O, it is godlike!' is quite clearly echoing the final line of the Sapphic stanza: − × × / - -.

In *The Catullan Revolution*, Kenneth Quinn asserts that the polymetric poems of Catullus prepared the way for the Odes and Epodes of Horace. According to Quinn, it is fashionable to disparage both poets for their preoccupation with metre. Besides metre, 'structural tightness' and language[14] occupied the attention of both poets. Bunting's interest in the work of these men parallels his concern with technique. The influence of Horace, the third Latin poet represented in the 'Overdrafts', is the only one Bunting acknowledges in his 'Preface'.

Two translated Odes, 13 in Book III and 12 in Book I, bear the stamp of Bunting's own craftsmanship. The first one, III-13, was for Horace a metrical experiment on a theme from Sappho in the pure Ionic metre.[15] Bunting has experimented in his translation also. For the usual sixteen-syllable first line of each stanza, he has substituted a shorter first line of six or seven syllables followed by a caesura-like pause which introduces the indented second line. Together this approximates the sixteen syllables of the original. In each stanza the second line sweeps into the third which is invariably twelve syllables. Instead of three-line stanzas, Bunting ends his stanzas with a fourth line of 12-14 syllables. David Gordon sees Bunting deftly experimenting with the *ionic a minore* metre: × × / / | × × / /. Even without a discussion of the specific patterns of short and long syllables which give classical poetry its particular characteristic, Bunting's experimentation is evident:

> Yes, it's slow, docked of amours,
>   docked of the doubtless efficacious
> bottled makeshift, gin; but who'd risk being bored stiff
> every night listening to father's silly sarcasms?
>
> If your workbox is mislaid
>   blame Cytherea's lad...Minerva
> 's not at all pleased that your seam's dropped for a fair sight
> of that goodlooking athlete's glistening wet shoulders
>
> when he's been swimming and stands
>   towelling himself in full view
> of the house. Ah! but you should see him on horseback!
> or in track-shorts! He's a first-class middleweight pug.
>
> He can shoot straight from the butts,
>   straight from precarious cover, waistdeep
> in the damp sedge, having stayed motionless daylong
> when the driven tiger appears suddenly at arms'-length.

For this experiment Bunting has no less an authority than

Wilkinson who claims that in 'rendering the Horatian stanza-poems we must choose or invent some stanza that recalls the movement of the original. Horatian stanzas progress; they cannot be represented by a pair of couplets.' He concludes that 'there is no easy way of reproducing that effect'.[16]

It does not seem that Bunting was working to exactly reproduce the Ionic metre of this Ode, although the feel of it does come through in much of the poem:

's not at all pleased that your seam's dropped for a fair sight

If the licence of using a pause for a beat, as is usual in music, is granted, then this next phrase becomes Ionic:

; but who'd risk be ing bored stiff

just as it is heard in

He can shoot straight from the butts,

and more briefly in 'of the house. Ah!' Since the 'Ah!' is added to the original text, it may well be to strengthen the echo of the Ionic metre just as neatly as the line 'in the damp sedge, having stayed motionless daylong' does.

By compressing the original twenty lines of the second translated Ode, I-13, Bunting is experimenting with another style of translation which communicates the contrasting emotions quickly and forcefully. For a more literal and linear version, a reader could go to Joseph P. Clancy's translation,[17] but for a vivid sense of the 'sick/badtempered, silly' speaker who 'on tenterhooks' begs 'Dulcie' to 'Please stop gushing' about her new lover, he can turn to Bunting's compressed lines:

> Please stop gushing about his pink
> neck smooth arms and so forth, Dulcie; it makes me sick,
> badtempered, silly: makes me blush.
> Dribbling sweat on my chops proves I'm on tenterhooks.
> – White skin bruised in a boozing bout,
> ungovernable cub certain to bite out a
> permanent memorandum on
> those lips. Take my advice, better not count on your
> tough guy's mumbling your pretty mouth
> always. Only the thrice blest are in love for life,
> we others are divorced at heart
> soon, soon torn apart by wretched bickerings.

The surprising seriousness of the ending of this ode shows where in practice Bunting's open admiration of Horace's 'trick' of association and contrast was leading. Wilkinson comments that the 'element of surprise plays a large part in some of the odes of Horace which lull a reader into security' in one mood only to awaken him suddenly by an unexpected introduction of another. He believes that Horace was among those who exploited contrasts, and that 'indeed he loved contrasts for their own sake'.[18] Besides affecting his choice of odes to translate, Bunting's own love of contrasts, influenced by Horace, is most evident in his sonatas.

'You can't grip years, Postume' (*Eheu fugaces*), a translation of Ode II-14, differs from the other Horatian odes in tone. It is not the voice of an amused or jealous and sarcastic observer, but the reflective tone of a mature and thoughtful persona who speaks with urbane acceptance of the inevitability of death which strips one of everything. The rhythms reflect a far steadier and wiser outlook than that of the younger mercurial persona 'on tenterhooks' in Ode 13 for example. This persona can face the inevitable prospect of death with an equanimity reflected in one sentence which goes on steadily for twelve lines through three strophes, and then in a second sentence which carries the reader smoothly through two more sections:

> You can't grip years, Postume,
> that ripple away nor hold back
> wrinkles and, soon now, age,
> nor can you tame death,
>
> not if you paid three hundred
> bulls every day that goes by
> to Pluto, who has no tears,
> who has dyked up
>
> giants where we'll go aboard,
> we who feed on the soil,
> to cross, kings some, some
> penniless plowmen.
>
> For nothing we keep out of war
> or from screaming spindrift
> or wrap ourselves against autumn,
> for nothing, seeing
>
> we must stare at that dark, slow
> drift and watch the damned
> toil, while all they build
> tumbles back on them.

The finality of the situation is underlined in the direct one-strophe sentences which conclude the ode, already cited in the previous chapter in the discussion on mortality.

In 1948 Bunting chided Zukofsky for forgetting the 'more permanent values' Horace represented, and suggested that

> Horace works wonders with a word order which was crabbed even to his contemporaries, as one may see by reading Lucretius and Ovid on either side of him in time. It is not right to banish such effects, which have their place, one I think too much neglected now, even though we and especially I follow Yeats's example of plain diction and plain syntax. [LZ, 3 November 1948]

Included in what Bunting considers 'permanent values' is certainly the economy and restraint which is characteristic of the writing of Horace, the use of relatively simple vocabulary, abrupt transition, and intentional paradox. All of these values which add to the musical quality of the poetry are also true of Bunting's work. Further, each one has the ability to express the everyday, the commonplace, so as to make it his own through a metrical art which can be appreciated only by 'those who read him aloud'. Written about Horace's poetry, these comments are as easily applicable to Bunting's as this longer quotation is:

> [Those who read him aloud] will observe for themselves in their favourite passages the reinforcement of the leading thought by the emphasis of the rhythm, the symmetrical responsions and nice interlockings of words and phrases, the...not obtrusive alliteration, the real or fancied adaptation of sound to sense in softly musical, splendidly sonorous, or picturesquely descriptive lines. This kind of criticism may easily pass into the fantastic. It is better suited to the living voice than to cold print.[19]

ITALIAN ADAPTATION

Besides working with Latin in his efforts to refine his style, Bunting experimented with translating the Italian of Machiavelli. However unintentionally, Bunting has added to the statesman's reputation as a poet and literary stylist by translating his prose report of 'A Description of the Method Used by Duke Valentino in Killing Vitellozzo Vitelli, Oliverotto da Fermo and Others' as a contemporary poem, 'How Duke Valentine Contrived'. Ezra Pound admired it enough to include it in his *Active Anthology*[20] and Bunting collected it as the final poem in the 'Overdrafts' section.

As a translation of Bunting's, it is unique – a colloquial but almost literal version of the prose. By this colloquialism and by typography, he emphasises the poetic qualities of the work. According to Gilbert, a modern critic and translator of the Italian statesman, 'Machiavelli subtly exploited the possibilities, including the colloquial qualities, of Florentine speech; such is his command of word order that through inversion he can get emphasis without appearing to use resources not at the command of any normal speaker.'[21] These are exactly the qualities that Bunting has translated into his twentieth-century poetic version.

If this poem, completed in 1933, was a technical exercise at all, it must have convinced Pound that Bunting had created the 'new thing' that the older craftsman demanded in a translation. Goodwin, who is not always complimentary to Bunting, admits that rather than the more superficial tricks of style that 'quite unintelligent and minor poets' could learn from Pound, 'the less superficial aspects of style, such as the handling of colloquial rhythms which are less teachable', were learned by only a few poets willing to devote 'intense study' to Pound's work; 'one who did, with limited success, was Basil Bunting'.[22] Through colloquial rhythms and diction, Bunting presents insights and nuances which he forces the reader to consider by writing Machiavelli's prose as poetry.

A selection of Gilbert's prose translation, curiously close to Bunting's poetic one, gives a norm for comparison:

> And though Vitellozzo was very reluctant, and the death of his brother had taught him that one ought not to injure a prince and then trust him, nonetheless persuaded by Paulo Orsini, whom the Duke had bribed with gifts and promises, he agreed to wait for him.[23]

> Vitellozzo
> was uneasy, he had learned from his brother's death
> not to trust a prince he had once offended,
> but Orsini argued
> and the Duke sent presents
> and rotten promises
> till he consented.

A prose paragraph of description becomes free verse in Bunting's translation. The prose version begins with this sentence:

> Fano and Sinigaglia are two cities of the Marches situated on the shore of the Adriatic Sea, fifteen miles apart, so that he who goes toward Sinigaglia has on his right hand the mountains, the bases of which sometimes are so close to the sea that between them and the water there is very little space, and where they give most room, the distance does not reach two miles.

Bunting's poem economically presents each detail in relief:

> Fano and Sinigaglia are towns of the Marches
> fifteen miles apart on the Adriatic.

> Going to Sinigaglia you have the mountains on your right,
> very close to the sea in some places,
> nowhere two miles away.

Details such as the colour of a man's clothing or the slight wink of a conspirator which only an eyewitness could report with authority are accentuated in the poetic version:

> Vitellozzo,
> unarmed, in a tunic with green facings,
> as glum as though he knew what was going to happen,
> was
> (considering his courage and the luck he had had in the past)
>   rather admirable...
>
> The Duke noticed, and tipped a wink to the Rev. Michael
> who was responsible for Liverotto...

The quality of Machiavelli's writing that Bunting captures best, the imperturbable, matter-of-fact tone recounting bribery, treachery, and murder by strangulation, creates an understatement laced with sardonic humour:

> Night fell, the rioting abated,
> and the Duke thought it opportune
> to put an end to Vitellozzo and Liverotto,
> and had them led out to a suitable place and strangled.
> Neither said anything worthy of the occasion...

Bunting puts aside the temptation to end the piece dramatically in order to finish appropriately on a low key:

> Pagolo and the Duke of Gravina Orsini
> were left alive until the Pope sent word
> he had taken Cardinal Orsino, Archbishop of Florence,
> together with Mr James da Santa Croce:
> upon which, on the eighteenth of January, at Castel della Pieve,
> they were strangled in the same manner.

Gilbert comments on the only possibility of an excellent translation in his introduction to his own work:

> The hope to naturalise in his own idiom the stylistic qualities and the spirit of a great work is the translator's will-o'-the-wisp. So seldom does it happen, that the man who believes he has accomplished it is likely to be a victim of self-delusion...But we can suppose translations equivalent to their prototypes only when we imagine that translators are stylists with the power of the geniuses they interpret...[24]

In his version of Machiavelli's report, Bunting is working to present a contemporary view of a shrewd statesman's personality and an episode that seems almost immediate, but he himself downplays the overdraft as an 'adaptation' and 'a pretty raw one'.[25] For all its narrative interest and understated humour, one cannot help being grateful he did not continue in this "prose-poem" mode. Its linear progression with its dramatic necessity of straightforward narration does not allow for Bunting's stronger poetic gift of building more leisurely through a process of incrementation, through repetition and contrasts of sounds, rhythms, themes, and visual and aural motifs. This is the kind of poetry for which translations of Persian poetry prepared him further.

PERSIAN TRANSLATIONS

The sampling in the *Collected Poems*, the few translations published in such periodicals as *Nine*, and those sent to Zukofsky indicate the variety of Persian poetry that Bunting translated: qasidas, ghazals, a qit'a, rubai, and large parts of Firdosi's epic, the *Shahnamah*, *The Epic of Kings*. The poets whose works he chose to translate were among the best: Manuchehri, Onsuri, Rudaki, Sa'di, Hafez, and Firdosi. A story by Obaid-e Zakani, *The Pious Cat*, was published posthumously. His knowledge of Persian literature was not merely classical, as this list suggests. In a letter to Zukofsky he explained:

> It is no boast to say that I am more widely read in Persian than most of the Orientalists in the British and European universities, especially in early poets – Ferdosi, Rudaki, Manuchehri, Farrukhi, etc. whose work is fundamental to a real understanding of Persian literature in the same way that the work of Homer and Aeschylus is fundamental to an understanding of Greek. Lacking it, many Orientalists have lacked proportion in their enthusiasm and run after secondary poets. Hafez, for example, interpreted exclusively in the light of Naser-e Khosro or Khanqani, is less interesting and far less compelling than the real Hafez who never, I think, ceased to listen to the echo of Manuchehri and Onsuri. [LZ, 29 October 1953][26]

Besides this scholarly background, Bunting's familiarity with modern Persian, literary and colloquial, as his household language and as that spoken as a member of British Intelligence dealing with tribesmen, as a diplomat and consul, and as a journalist for *The Times* and Persian newspapers – all this gives his translations an authority and rich immediacy translations by purely literary scholars lack.

It is difficult to appreciate Bunting's work in this area without some slight background in Persian literature. Bunting takes for granted that his reader understands a fundamental idea: because the themes and various structures of Persian poetry were so fixed by tradition, the outlet for the poet's ingenuity was in perfecting the meaning and rhythm within the framework and themes he chose. For example, in the *qasida*,[27] a lyric of at least twelve lines generally, each unit (*bayt* or distich) is composed of two balanced halves (*misra*) corresponding to each other in metre and parallel in theme. The *qasida* is in monorhyme introduced in the opening *bayt*, the only unit in which both halves are rhymed. All the remaining *bayts* repeat this rhyme, but only at the end of the unit. Since the poetry was originally to be sung or recited, the monorhyme could be made acceptable to the ear, although it seems wearisome to the eye. To compose a *qasida* tests the poet's skill in adapting the metre to the theme and rhyming ingeniously.

The half-lines are connected by one thought, or in certain cases by one thought and its underlying argument. Connections can also be the result of merely formal measures, such as parallelisms, the harmony of common images, etc. Rarely are thoughts grouped together grammatically over two or more *bayts*. Since each *bayt* is to some extent independent, the logical connections of the poem are not so clear and obvious as in Western poetry. In Bunting's translation of seven *bayts* from a *qasida* of Manuchehri's many of these characteristics are retained:

> Shall I sulk because my love has a double heart?
> Happy is he whose she is singlehearted!
> She has found me a new torment for every instant
> and I am, whatever she does, content, content.
> If she has bleached my cheek with her love, say: Bleach!
> Is not pale saffron prized above poppy red?
> If she has stooped my shoulders, say to them: Stoop!
> Must not a harp be bent when they string it to sing?
> If she has kindled fire in my heart, say: Kindle!
> Only a kindled candle sends forth light.
> If tears rain from my eyes, say: Let them rain!
> Spring rains make fair gardens. And if then
> she has cast me into the shadow of exile, say:
> Those who seek fortune afar find it the first.[28]

In his first *bayt* the question and comment are sides of one thought; here even the monorhyme introduced in each half of the first *bayt* is echoed. The introductory general thought of the stanza supported by the cluster of parallel clauses which are themselves filled with parallelisms illustrate the explanation of Jan Rypka, a renowned critic of Persian poetry:

> Persian poetry is seen more as filigree work, full of finely-wrought details, with no strictly logical sequence of verses...The Persian is led far more by imagination than by logic, both regarding description and

abstract speculation. Instead of developing one idea from another, he strews them about in apparently haphazard fashion, yet always with the remainder in mind. [However, the verse] is inferior if there is no progress.[29]

Bunting's advice to Zukofsky (21 April 1945) to examine Upham Pope's beautifully illustrated book of Persian art, especially the pictures of the miniatures and the tile ceilings of domed mosques, is good advice to anyone who would like to see a graphic design of a Persian poem.[30]

Bunting's translation accentuates the contrast between the long-suffering lover and the tormenting beloved, the basic framework of the *qasida*, through internal rhyme in both halves of the introductory *bayt*, 'I' / 'my love' and 'Happy' / 'he' / 'she'. Within this *bayt* he found English equivalents, 'a double heart' / 'singlehearted', which not only echo the monorhyme of the original through two syllables, '-le heart', but which punctuate the emotional contrast between the shunned possibility of 'sulking' in the first line and the impossibility of being 'happy' in the second.

He begins a series of *bayts* with the initial word 'If', interlocking them further by beginning the second part of each second half-*bayt* with 'say'. The parts of these half-*bayts* are connected to one another by the repetition of the key word of the first part, in the second part: for example,

If she has kindled fire in my heart, say: Kindle!

And more than once this key word is repeated in the next half-*bayt* with a twist of meaning:

Only a kindled candle sends forth light.

In this instance Bunting has heightened the key word further through alliteration and imperfect internal rhyme.

As interesting as the technical accomplishments are in this *qasida*, it is difficult to forget the poem is a translation. It never completely fulfils Bunting's own criteria: 'a translation in English equivalent to [its] original but not compelled to lean on its authority...'[31] Some of this is traceable to lines dependent on unfamiliar ideas and customs, acceptable in another time and culture, but difficult for us to respond to; for example, a man exclaiming that his beloved 'bleached my cheek with her love', or 'tears rain from my eyes'. However, in most translations Bunting is able to make us accept naturally, almost without noticing, unfamiliar ideas or figures of speech:

The singer is weary of his broken voice,
One drone for the bulbul alike and the lion's grousing.

or

> Alas for flowery, musky, sappy thirty
> and the sharp Persian sword!
> The pheasant strutting about the briar,
> pomegranate-blossom and cypress sprig!

(Firdosi)

In Manuchehri's *qasida* Bunting does not quite transform the combination of unfamiliar ideas and modes of speech and images into a poem 'claiming independence and accepting the responsibility inseparable from a life of its own'.

Another *qasida* that reinforces the idea of the 'filigree' connections of Persian poetry is Rudaki's famous 'Lament in Old Age' which Bunting translated in 1948 as 'A Qasida by Abu'abdulla Ja'far bin Mahmud Rudaki of Samarkand' (2 December 1948). He first wrote to Zukofsky in praise of this poet in August that year, connecting his poetry with music in his train of thought:

> Rudaki's qasidas have given me great delight, especially the wonderful one about all his teeth falling out. One must certainly add his name to the list of the world's very great poets, even though the remains are so few and fragmentary. I will perhaps send you a prose translation if I ever finish it. I have taken a great liking also to Persian classical music and wish I could get some records of it. [2 August 1948]

A few months later he added that his translation was of interest 'in so far as it gives some idea of the way a Khorassani mind worked in 950 a.d., I mean in my English. Rudaki's Persian is delightful' [2 December 1948]. In the same letter he included a copy of the *qasida* with these brief but enlightening notes inserted after the title:

> (Monorhyme – every second line – with a good deal of internal rhyming and alliteration. The vocabulary exceedingly simple, the main effects being got by the cross-beat of ictus and stress in an elaborate quantitative measure.)

To the Western mind the connections from line to line and within lines in this *qasida* are less obvious than in the preceding one by Manuchehri, but more delightful in their variety. Bunting's translation of the first part of the sixty-four line Rudaki poem illustrates this:

> All the teeth ever I had are worn down and fallen out.
> They were not rotten teeth, they shone like a lamp,
> a row of silvery-white pearls set in coral;
> they were as the morning star and as drops of rain.
> There are none left now, all of them wore out and fell out.

Was it ill-luck, ill-luck, a malign conjunction?
It was no fault of stars, nor yet length of years.
I will tell you what it was: it was God's decree.

It would be unusual for a modern Western poet to compare his teeth to shining lamps, silvery-white pearls set in coral, the morning star, and drops of rain, yet by piling up these images in extremely simple and forceful statements, Bunting convinces us in the opening lines that this lament for teeth 'worn down and fallen out', is a universal and deeply felt one. He reinforces the lamenting quality through a skilful use of incrementation and parallelism by echoing six times throughout the poem the unornamented half-line: 'The days are past when...', for example:

The days are past when his face was good to look on,
. . . .
The days are past when she was glad and gay
. . . .
the days are past when he managed affairs of princes,
the days are past when all wrote down his verses,
the days are past when he was the Poet of Khorassan.

In a section such as

a cure for pain
and then again a pain that supplants the cure.
In a certain time it makes new things old,
in a certain time makes new what was worn threadbare.
Many a broken desert has been gay garden,
many gay gardens grow where there used to be desert.

Bunting proves his adeptness at handling the intricate interlockings in *bayts* which continuously add to the theme, but the passage itself is too general to provide him with the raw material he needs to build vivid, concrete images.

The most general explanation of the *ghazal*, another lyric form, which has something of the character of the European sonnet, is that although it follows the *qasida* in structure and rhythms, it seems more a Persian outgrowth of the fixed Arabic erotic prelude of the *qasida*. The *qasida* begins with the interest-arousing lament that at the place of the poet's desert rendezvous he found only a cold fire; from there on he speaks of the real purpose (*qasida*) of the poem – eulogy, paean, description, etc. In distinction to this Arabic court poetry form, the *ghazal* ('whisperings', 'a lovers' exchange'), more radically Persian, from the cultural life of the town, speaks chiefly of love, human or mystical, although anything might be added to the subject matter that stirred the emotions.

Of all the types of Persian poetry Bunting translated, the most numerous are the *ghazal*; and these are works of the greatest writers of the form, Manuchehri, Sa'di, and Hafez. Bunting's translation of 'A Ghazal of Sa'di's'[32] reveals its more personal nature, as well as the less important tradition of including the name of the poet in the last few lines so that even if a *ravi*, a professional singer, presented the poem, the poet himself would receive his just recognition.

Writing to Zukofsky, Bunting commented:

> I'll type out my last translation, one of the most famous poems in the language in mediaeval times, imitated by Hafez, but now less heard of, one of the finest of Sa'di's long lines in Persian. This prevents the translation being line for line, but doesn't prevent it being almost literal. [28 July 1949]

> Last night without sight of you my brain was ablaze.
> My tears trickled and fell plip on the ground. That I with
> sighing might bring my life to a close they would name
> you and again and again speak your name till
> with night's coming all eyes closed save mine whose every
> hair pierced my scalp as a lancet. That was
> not wine I drank far from your sight but my heart's
> blood gushing into the cup. Wall and door wherever
> I turned my eyes scored and decorated with shapes
> of you. To dream of Laila Majnun prayed for
> sleep. My senses came and went but neither your
> face saw I nor would your fantom go from me.
> Now like aloes my heart burned, now smoked as a censer.
> Where was the morning gone that used on other nights
> to breathe till the horizon paled? Sa'di!
> Has then the chain of the Pleiades broken
> tonight that every night is hung on the sky's neck?

> (Sa'di)

With only a little effort Westerners should be able to appreciate that it is 'by art concealed behind apparent simplicity that Sa'di demonstrates calculated deliberation',[33] an art Bunting would be strongly attracted to.

By not using the end-stopped lines of the Persian form, Bunting adds to the emotional effect of uncontrollable lovesickness. Onomatopoetically, *plip* is unsuccessful, adding nothing to an otherwise good line, and the image in 'all eyes closed save mine whose every/ hair pierced my scalp like a lancet' is not clear. Neither belongs in a poem with lines translated as vividly as

> Wall and door wherever
> I turned my eyes scored and decorated with shapes
> of you. To dream of Laila Majnun prayed for

sleep. My senses came and went but neither your
face saw I nor would your fantom go from me.

By not translating the images into more familiar, Western terms,
Bunting preserves the richness of Sa'di's at the same time that he
broadens his reader's enjoyment in such Eastern contrasts as 'Now
like aloes my heart burned, now smoked like a censer' and in the
oriental ending:

> Has then the chain of the Pleiades broken
> tonight that every night is hung on the sky's neck?

Even though Bunting includes only one *qasida* of Manuchehri's in
his *Collected Poems*, he translated several of his *ghazals*, two of which
were published in *Nine*.[34] Bunting praises no other Persian poet as
he does Manuchehri:

> Manuchehri? Haven't I ever pestered you with him? If one puts Homer
> and Firdosi carefully in one place and then looks for the three or four
> greatest poets remaining I don't see how anyone who has the luck to
> read him can omit Manuchehri. His variety is enormous and everything
> he did he did better than anyone else. You want the directness of some
> Catullus? Go to Manuchehri. You want the swiftness of Anacreon?
> Manuchehri. The elaborate music of Spenser? Go to Manuchehri. The
> formal, full dress ode with every circumstance of solemnity and
> splendor? Not Pindar, Manuchehri. Satire direct and overwhelming,
> Manuchehri all alone – no competitor. He was a younger contemporary
> of Firdosi, and like him went to the Ghaznavi Court – I think probably
> after Firdosi had left it, for most of Manuchehri is addressed not to
> Mahmud but his successor. But at that time one man might well have
> heard both of them, to say nothing of Unsuri and Farrukhi, both also
> very great poets. I do not know where else at any time a man could have
> had such an experience. I think Manuchehri began by imitating the
> great Arabic poet then still recent, Al-Motanabbi, and found he could
> do it standing on his head. So first he set himself difficult technical
> problems and solved them, then he began inventing new forms, finally
> he found he could say what was in him without any elaboration at all and
> have a great poem. [28 July 1949]

It could well be his great admiration for the poet that kept
Bunting from collecting poems he felt were inadequate translations. A hint of that occurs in a letter which included a translation
of Manuchehri's *ghazal*, 'Night is hard by. I am vexed and bothered
by sleep':

> I am going to enclose...a literal version of one of Manuchehri's ghazals.
> The last couplet is very famous and has been quoted or imitated by
> nearly every notable ghazal writer in Persian history.
>
> > We, men of wine are we, meat are we, music...
> > Well, then! wine have we, meat have we, music...

E

> But the characteristic of the original is vigour, which has evaporated in the translation and I dont know how to get it back. [28 May 1949]

After this letter though, Bunting made only the slightest changes in punctuation, capitalisation, and in the omission of words, and clarified the meaning of only one line before the *ghazal* was published in *Nine* (August 1950). The changes, too slight to vitalise the poem as Bunting wished to do, left the overall effect the same, a translation which hints strongly at the vigour of the original.

Another poem of Manuchehri's appears only in his private correspondence:

> So! I have been reading Manuchehri: bloody fine poet too. The bird that preens its feathers many times a day, going over and over them 'like a petty clerk who has made a mistake in his accounts'. And the sonority of his musammats. And the wonderful transitions. And his observation of deer and flowers and camel drivers and girls. The tulips that 'are a row of parrots asleep with their head under their wings'. The names of ancient Arab poets, in a satire –
>
> Amru'l Qais and Labid and Akhtal and blind A'sha and Qais
> who keened over the bones of dead encampments and fallen tents,
> as we mourn for the ruins of poetry and broken rhymes –
> Bu Nuvas and Bu Haddad and Bu Malik bin al Bashar,
> Bu Duvaid and Bu Duraid and Ibn Ahmad. Do you hear
> him who sang 'She has warned us', who sang 'The honest sword',
> who sang 'Love has exhausted' – ?
> Bu'l Ata and Bu'l Abbas and Bu Sulaik and Bu'l Mathil,
> and the bard of Lavaih and the Harper of Herat.
> Where are the wise Afghans, Shuhaid and Rudaki,
> and Bu Shakur of Balkh and Bu'l Fath of Bust likewise.
> Bid them come and see our noble century
> and read our poetry and despair...
>
> [May Day, 1939]

Here, in my opinion, is one of Bunting's best Persian-based poems. Only one rough note, 'likewise', detracts from the otherwise continuously fluid rhythm of the long lines –

> who keened over the bones of dead encampments and fallen tents,
> as we mourn for the ruins of poetry and broken rhymes –

The series of names which at first seem impossible to incorporate into a mellifluous line, actually enhance the poem through their incantatory effect, if the reader is careful to keep each vowel distinct. With attention to the sound of each *a* pronounced as a long Italian *a* and each *i* as long *e*, the reader can appreciate the music of such a line as 'Bu Duvaid and Bu Duraid and Ibn Ahmad. Do you hear'. The ending, reminiscent of Shelley's *Ozymandias*, capitalises on the accumulation of verb phrases, 'Bid them come and see our noble century/ and read our poetry', in order to build to the final single word, 'despair', an effective satirical anticlimax.

'You, with my enemy, strolling down the street', another translation of Manuchehri from 1949, which he published in *Agenda* (Spring 1978) was prudently not included in his final 1985 *Collected Poems*. Though the tone is vigorous, only one contrast redeems it somewhat, the images in 'Plainly, your love is flooding his brook:/the day is gone when it trickled into mine.'

Another poet whose translated *ghazals* Bunting did not publish in his *Collected Poems* is Hafez, the one who after Sa'di brought the form and its musical language to its perfection. Bunting's translation of one famous *ghazal*, 'If that Shirazian beauty would lay hands on my heart', bears comparison with all those which both Kritzeck and Arberry present for comparative study in their books. Since Bunting wrote the Persian phonetically for this one along with another *ghazal*, 'She said: "You have been out to see the spectacle of the new moon" ',[35] it was possible for Iranians whom I asked to compare Bunting's translation with the others mentioned above to evaluate his as one which to them presents most aptly to readers in the twentieth century the tone, mood, and vocabulary of the originals.[36] With these phonetic versions and the English translations Bunting sent valuable notes on content and form.

I will comment further about the *ghazal* insofar as it includes music, singing, and dancing interludes in my discussion of *Briggflatts*.

The one poem of Hafez's which Bunting did publish in his *Collected Poems* (as Ode I-28) he first wrote to Zukofsky in four continuous lines with the heading, '(Hafez, a rubay)', and the ending note, '(which is nearly a blues)' [29 September 1935]. 'Epigrammatic in character, severe and Gregorian in effect', the *rubai* is emphatically Persian, probably originating in Rudaki's poetry. Its form which Bunting purposefully modifies is four half-lines of which line 1, 2, and 4 are in monorhyme; line 3 usually outside the rhyme pattern marks an anticipatory pause before the climactic last line. Two or three long syllables invariably introduce the *rubai*, a fine detail which Bunting retains in his translation. Bunting's poem gains its powerful effect by giving the impression of being 'unstudied and spontaneous', yet terse in its revelation of the poet's true feelings:

> You leave
> nobody else
> without a bed

you make
everybody else
thoroughly at home

I'm
the only one
hanged
in your
halter

you've driven
nobody else mad
but me.

By dividing the four lines of the *rubai* into fourteen, Bunting has carefully arranged them for rhetorical and rhythmical emphasis. Although he has translated all three invariably long, introductory beats of the *rubai*, through the typography he has emphasised the first two to gain the keening effect of the Persian *ghazal* singer and to set the modern blues atmosphere. By beginning each section with an echo of the first line, he strengthens the first suggestion of the blues at the same time he underlines the tension between the antagonists ('You leave', 'you make', 'I'm', 'you've driven').

The contrast of the syncopation of the second line in each section, interesting in itself rhythmically, becomes a kind of bridge to the last line, especially in the first, second and fourth sections. In each case he varies the rhythm of the concluding line ('without a bed', 'thoroughly at home', 'halter', 'but me'). Further, he prepares for this by the slight variation in each of the second lines in order to build to the climax of the final line of the poem ('nobody else', 'everybody else', 'the only one', 'nobody else'). By dividing the original lines, Bunting has played the similarities of each fragment against its variations. The following schema shows this more clearly:

You leave	you make	I'm	you've driven
nobody else	everybody else	the only one	nobody else mad
without a bed	thoroughly at home	hanged	but me.
		in your	
		halter	

After reading only two sections, one is aware of the variety of parallelisms; the third section, varied enough to break any suggestion of monotony, prepares by its alliteration and emphatic single-word lines for the climax. This depends on single words alliterated (mad/me) to complete this 'blues'.

A justification for Bunting's not attributing this poem to Hafez is that his version has such different visual and aural effects it becomes a new poem. The fragmentation of lines emphasising in an original way content, rhythm and sound creates a poem Hafez would be hard put to recognise. Besides, the new form expresses a universal sentiment found in too many poems and blues lyrics to be attributed solely to Hafez. Bunting's reply to my question about his having created in effect a new poem was 'If I'd thought there was very much of Hafez left in the product, I'd have put it with the other translations' [23 May 1972].

The *rubai* was, of course, the form used by Omar Khayyam in his great *Rubaiat*, a copy of which Bunting carried with him, along with a pocket edition of Dante, during his war years in the East. Long before that time [30 August 1933], Bunting had sent a copy of a *rubai* of Khayyam's to Zukofsky, but only the phonetic Persian and no translation is included:

asrár-i-jihán chunánki dar dáftur-i-mást

gúftan nátavan, ki an vabál sár-i-mást.

chun níst darín márdum [xxxx]-i-daña ahlé

nátavan gúftan haránchi dar khátir-i-mást.

umr-i-khayyám

Unfortunately I never asked Bunting for a translation, so the only line he sent during a discussion was the translation of the third line in which an Iranian friend had supplied 'mast' for the crossed-out word for me: '[Mast] means "drunk", which is a term of praise with Khayyam and would never be applied to "mardum-e ahle", learned men, a term of abuse. The sense of the lines is: "Since amongst these learned men there's not one real person." '

Written in Persian, the rhyme scheme becomes apparent if the lines are examined from right to left:

اسرار جهان چنانکه در دفتر ماست

گفتن نتوان، بآدم وبال سر ماست

مرد سینه ملئی مردم رانه اهل

نتوان گفتن هرآنکه در خاطر ماست

Bunting has a great deal to say in his letters by way of introduction to the *qit'a*, the 'fragment', 'attributed, perhaps wrongly, to Sa'di', which he published among his 'Overdrafts'. A poem is a *qit'a* if the opening verse, the *bayt* which introduces the monorhyme in both halves of the first unit, is absent. Its theme is arbitrary – philosophical, ethical, meditative – and often based on personal experiences. Bunting introduces his *qit'a* to Zukofsky by filling in the background of the poet who he believes is its true author, Unsuri:

> The most important of Unsuri's poems are lost – they were romances, the first to exist in any language unless we count the Greek novels – but there are a good many qasidas left, and, I think, a powerful short poem which is printed amongst the poems "attributed" to Sa'di. I will try to translate it for you. [28 July 1949]

When he sent it to his friend, he added the note: 'Attributed to Sa'di: But, I think, possibly by the much earlier and greater poet Unsuri. Unsuri wrote "Vamiq and Azra' (or translated it from Pahlevi) and may have been the first to write a "Laila and Majnun". Sa'di wrote neither' [6 August 1949].

> This I write, mix ink with tears,
> and have written of grief before, but never so grievously,
> to tell Azra Vamiq's pain,
> to tell Laila Majnun's plight,
> to tell you my own
> unfinished story.
> Take it. Seek no excuse.
> How sweetly you will sing what I so sadly write.

In pencil at the end of the poem, he wrote enthusiastically: 'This last poem is song in fullest sense: hope my rendering would be singable. Last line a bit Jacobean, lute cadences all ready for it.'

Zukofsky's suggesting a punctuation mark for clarity primed Bunting to reveal his knowledge of Persian poetry and his ideas about its origin:

> You're right, no doubt, about the comma after Azra and Laila in the little Unsuri piece. Too familiar myself, I thought that 'everybody' was familiar with the names and the outline of the story of Laila and Majnun, and that that would explain the preceding verse about Vamiq and Azra. I even thought you had referred to it in your first long work...Laila's parents refused to let her marry him and he went mad, the stereotype of the lovers who go mad all through romantic poetry in Europe as well as the East. Nearly all the main romantic themes seem to come from a group of now lost Pahlevi poems of the fifth and sixth century, of which Vamiq and Azra is one, Xosro and Shirin another, Vis and Ramin the most closely preserved in its Persian version: and Laila and Majnun may or may not have been another: as a source of the romantic subjects it should, by analogy, be one, but it is barely possible that Nezami of Ganjeh invented it in the twelfth century. [5 September 1949]

Although Bunting translated long sections of Firdosi's epic, the *Shahnamah*, and dreamed of the leisure necessary to complete the long poem, it is only through his correspondence that this work is discovered. Even though Pound sent some of the epic to Eliot to try to publish, in a letter to Otto Bird he commented: 'Bunt'n gone off on Persian, but don't seem to do anything but Firdusi, whem he can't put into English that is of any *interest*. More the fault of subject matter than of anything else in isolation.'[37] The only poetry of Firdosi's that Bunting includes in his collection is the lyrical ode, 'When the sword of sixty comes nigh his head'.

In 1951 Bunting explained to Pound one of his purposes, during that lean time at least, in translating Persian poetry:

> But I'm not hoping for honour and glory, nor expecting to make a living, nor even hoping for translation good enough to approve of: just texts and cribs so that a chap who wants to get at the stuff can. So that another generation may not have quite as many cursed vexations as ours when it sets out to acquire knowledge.[38]

For another generation, in the 'Foreword' to Omar Pound's *Arabic and Persian Poetry*, Bunting expressed his matured thoughts more fully:

> Persian poetry has suffered badly, Arabic poetry rather less, from neoplatonic dons determined to find an arbitrary mysticism in everything...
> There are difficulties in the way of a more satisfactory account of Persian poetry. Hafez, for instance, depends almost entirely on his mastery of sound and literary allusion, neither translatable. Minuchihri's enormous vigour and variety expresses itself often in patterns as intricate as those of a Persian carpet. Even dons are put off by the vast size of Sa'di's *Divan*, and fail to find the key poems...
> There is at least as much variety in either of these literatures as in any European tongue...
> Sooner or later we must absorb Islam if our own culture is not to die of anemia. It will not be done by futile attempts to trace Maulavi symbols back to Plotinus or by reproducing in bad English verse the platitudes common to poetry everywhere. Omar Pound has detected something that Moslem poetry has in common with some of ours. He makes it credible. He makes it a pleasure. By such steps, though they may be short and few, we can at least begin our Hajj.[39]

Omar Pound, who advises his readers that 'Basil Bunting's translations of Rudaki's lament in his old age...and one of his quatrains "Came to me...Who?..." are superb',[40] would be one of the first to admit that Bunting's earlier attempts paved the way for his later, smoothly modern translations.

Bunting would surely be the first to enjoy the fact that *The Pious Cat*, his delightful translation of a children's story by Obaid-e Zakani was his last poem published, posthumously. His 'Post Script' gives clear, slyly humorous directions for reading:

> You must call him Obeyed, like the English word 'he obeyed the law': *obeyed a zaw-kaw-nee*, and save most of your breath for the *nee*. He wrote

this story about six hundred years ago, and Persian children still read it at school, or they used to, twenty years since. Any story that lasts as long as that is worth listening to, I think. Perhaps not everything in it is true, but bits of it are very true indeed.

The date '1939-1977' reveals how long ago he began work on this story whose 'deep wisdom.../and learned science and politic guile/ and rime and rhetoric and style' cannot help but delight children of all ages. To the ears of modern Westerners, echoes of Gilbert and Sullivan and other English writers may sound louder than those of Obaid-e Zakani. These reverberate not only in 'rimes and rhetoric and style', but in the disguised subjects of satire which any human being under any modern government or in (or out of) any religion – Christian, Muslim or whatever – can appreciate. Here Basil is able to vent his lifelong frustration with bureaucracy, hypocrisy, and unthinking, gullible human beings in a creative way which allows everyone to laugh at them in relief. Although it cannot be seriously considered as one of his greatest poems, this spirited translation published in 1986 nicely balances the serious, reflective tone of some of his last poems.

JAPANESE ADAPTATION

Bunting rightly believed that *Chomei at Toyama* was 'a poem which whatever its worth or worthlessness in itself, might have a useful influence: showing, for instance, that poetry can be intelligible and still be poetry: a fact that came to be doubted,' he believed, 'by the generation that took most of its ideas indirectly from Eliot.'[41]

The poem has its basis in a prose work of Kamono Chōmei, *Hojoki*, 'Life in a dwelling one *jo* [ten feet] square', 'the most delicate contribution to the prose of the times'.[42] 'The times' (1153-1216) so nearly parallel to those in which Bunting was living were the late Heian and early Kamakura Periods when the military caste held power and the science of war was taking preference over intellectual matters. However, in his work Chomei describes a series of natural calamities rather than the fighting that also ravaged the country.[43]

Bunting introduced his readers to Chomei in a brief biography written for *Poetry* (August 1933), the issue in which extracts of the poem were published:

> Kamo-no-Chomei, i.e. Chomei of Kamo, flourished somewhat over a hundred years before Dante. He belonged to the minor Japanese nobility, and held various offices in the civil service. He applied for a fat

job in a Shinto temple, was turned down, and the next day announced his conversion to Buddhism.

He got sick of public life and retired to a kind of mixture of hermitage and country cottage at Toyama on Mount Hino, and there, when he was getting old, he wrote his celebrated *Ho-Jo-Ki*, of which my poem is, in the main, a condensation.

Both works, the prose and the poetry, open with the author's view of the mutability of life which underlies all that seems permanent – cities and populations. As illustrations of the changes that men must endure, both works give vivid descriptions of the Great Fire that ravaged the capital of Japan, Kyoto, in 1177, the great whirlwind of 1180, the transfer of the capital that same year and then its relocation to its original site in 1180, the famine of 1181-82, and the earthquake of 1185. Besides these specific hardships, both describe the general precarious circumstances of everyday life for the majority of people. All this instability and unrest motivates Chomei, as he leads his reader to believe, to retire from the world as a hermit. Step by step, the lines trace his progress from the ancestral home he inherited before he was thirty to a small cottage which he left before he was fifty for a ten foot square hut on Mount Hino. The rest is a description of the simple pleasures of the hermitage informed by philosophical attitudes towards the impermanence of all things. In a tribute to Bunting, Sam Hamill who studied Zen in Kyoto, singles out *Chomei* as great poetry and comments on its philosophical attitudes as 'representative of the blend of Confucianism and primitive Buddhism that permeated twelfth century Japanese culture. And it reflects both the stern self-discipline of the Confucian and the gentle compassion of the Taoist-Shinto-Buddhist.'[44]

Preserving the design of the whole was something Bunting had to fight for with his editors. Just as critics of Chomei have recognised that it is the systematic design which elevates *Hojoki* above others in the genre *zuihitsu* (fugitive essay),[45] Bunting appreciated the balance which he transferred to his poetic version. In January 1933 he tried hard to convince Morton Dauwen Zabel, associate editor of *Poetry*, that printing extracts only would ruin the design of the whole:

First: re Chomei, I'll wait and see the extracts you suggest before making a definite answer...of course I'd best like it to be printed whole, since to me it seems to depend in a high degree on the general design: the balance of the calamities and consolations pivoted on the little central satire, the transmogrification of the house throughout, the earth, air, fire and water, pieces, first physical then spiritual make up an elaborate design, which I've tried not to underline so that it might be felt rather than pedantically counted up. Also the old boy's superficial religion breaking down to anchor it in its proper place.[46]

A few months later Bunting reluctantly acquiesced to its fragmentation, a wise move perhaps in the light of the Honourable Mention he received in *Poetry*'s annual awards:[47]

> All right, you must do as you think best in all the circumstances. I hate to see *Chomei* cut up, because I think it depends mainly on the balance of parts throughout and the picking out of four somewhat "poetical" bits rather misrepresents the very simpatico ole Jap.[48]

The *Poetry* notes that Bunting included in this letter explains further his idea of the overall design:

> The *Ho-Jo-Ki* is in prose, but the careful proportion and balance of the parts, the leit-motif of the House running through it, and some other indications, suggest that he intended a poem, more or less elegiac; but had not time, nor possibly energy, at his then age, to work out what would have been for Japan an entirely new form, nor to condense his material sufficiently. This I have attempted to do for him.[49]

By teaching that Chomei followed the *yugen*, the 'lonesome' school of poetry, scholars in Japan give some support to Bunting's judgment.[50]

The design Bunting was trying to save is essential to the balanced form of the whole. In general, the first part of the poem, the series of calamities affecting society, balances the last part, the personal, simple life of Chomei as a hermit. Between these parts is a section which serves as a fulcrum and transition. In a letter Bunting made sure I understood that 'the real balancing point of the Hojoki is the bit that begins "A poor man living amongst the rich" to "if he doesnt he passes for mad" ' [4 July 1973]. *Poetry*'s omission of the entire section as well as many lines about Chomei's moves disconnects the two large divisions, social calamities and personal poverty, disrupting the unity of the whole.

But even before this omission, the editors had fragmented the careful design in the series of calamities by their omission of the entire whirlwind and removal of the capital sections. Within this first large part, the design includes two natural catastrophes before and two after the moving of the capital. In this way the four calamities caused by an element in nature – fire, air, water, or earth – are balanced on either side of one in which the sufferings and loss is caused by purely human whim: 'Nothing compelled the change nor was it an easy matter'. The three locations of the capital are themselves carefully balanced: from Kyoto to the new location, then back to Kyoto. Though each of the natural calamities depends on one natural element in particular, Bunting is as careful as Chomei to bring in echoes of the other three throughout the descriptions; for example,

> As the wind veered
> flames spread out in the shape of an open fan.

The design of the first part also includes a transition between large populations and groupings of houses in the city and Chomei and his series of individual dwellings by describing the unstable everyday circumstances surrounding the ordinary man and his home. By omitting this section also, *Poetry* further disrupted the balance of the whole. In addition, through their omission, they transformed into a final comment a passage of two lines which is in fact only the connecting link between the large calamities and the balancing point, the section about the precarious existence of a poor man's life and dwelling:

> This is the unstable world and
> we in it unstable and our houses.

Since the section following these lines is the balancing point of the poem and leads smoothly to the second half about Chomei's life as a poor man, what seems a slight transformation really interrupts the continuity of the entire design.

After the central passage about the poor man in society, the poem continues with the description of Chomei's progressive moves from Kyoto to his hut and his life as a hermit. Divesting himself of most unsettling concerns of men illustrated in the first part, the hermit draws consolations from the very natural elements which earlier in the poem caused suffering and death – earth, air, fire, and water. These examples are outstanding in their simple beauty:

> A shower at dawn
> sings
> like the hillbreeze in the leaves.
> . . .
>
> I rake my ashes.
>
> > *Chattering fire,*
> > *soon kindled, soon burned out,*
> > *fit wife for an old man!*

Human beings with their disturbing concerns are kept at a distance. To highlight this distance, Bunting mentions no particular names; all is vague and unspecific:

And I hear Soanso's dead
back in Kyoto.
I have as much room as I need.
I know myself and mankind.
. . . .
I dont want to be bothered.
(You will make me editor
of the Imperial Anthology?
I dont want to be bothered.)

In contrast to this, Bunting designates specifically each thing that contributes to his pleasure; for example,

The view from the summit: sky bent over Kyoto,
picnic villages, Fushimi and Toba:
a very economical way of enjoying yourself.
Thought runs along the crest, climbs Sumiyama;
beyond Kasatori it visits the great church,
goes on pilgrimage to Ishiyama (no need to foot it!)
. . .

one zest and equal, chewing tsubana buds,
one zest and equal, persimmon, pricklypear,
ears of sweetcorn pilfered from Valley Farm.

Physical consolations are elevated by being combined with the consolations Chomei receives from poetry and music, from his 'books above the window,/ lute and mandolin near at hand':

Be limber, my fingers, I am going to play *Autumn Wind*
to the pines, I am going to play *Hastening Brook*
to the water. I am no player
but there's nobody listening,
I do it for my own amusement.

Chomei's lately adopted religion is more a veneer over the whole picture of an egocentric life rather than something deeply permeating it. Bunting makes this as unmistakable in his poetry as in his note to the poem:

I cannot take his Buddhism solemnly considering the manner of his conversion, the nature of his anthology [poems composed at the moment of conversion by Buddhist proselytes], and his whole urbane, sceptical and ironical temper. If this annoys anybody I cannot help it.

By his image Bunting broadens Chomei's attitude to one easily recognisable by the East or West:

no one will be shocked if I neglect the rite.
There's a Lent of commandments kept
where there's no way to break them.

By typography alone Bunting is able to accentuate Chomei's ironic stance:

> I have renounced the world;
> have a saintly
> appearance.

Underlying this balance of calamities and consolations, physical
and spiritual, is the deeper irony that Bunting emphasises to enrich
the design of the whole. According to Bunting, this balance 'is
pivoted on a little central satire'.[51] The little central satire he speaks
of is rooted in the central section about the poor man which
introduces Chomei's unsatisfying moves to smaller and smaller
dwellings, apparently towards a greater degree of the detachment
counselled by Buddha, but in reality towards a greater, un-
hampered enjoyment of simple pleasures.

Bunting capitalises though on the old man's honesty with himself
and others to keep his persona throughout the poem a 'very
simpatico ole Jap'. In fact, a distinctly original aspect of Bunting's
version is his creation of a unique persona, basically the historical
writer of the prose work, but one with a much less placid
temperament who speaks in a wide range of tones. Appropriately,
the elegiac tone pervades the poem, but through his courteous but
more colloquial diction, and by means of short, more direct lines
which state opinion baldly without apologies or explanations,
Bunting creates a persona who expresses himself with a much
greater range of feelings: humour, belligerence, haughtiness,
melancholy, compassion, condescension, and resignation:

> My hands and feet will not loiter
> when I am not looking.
> I will not overwork them.
> Besides, it's good for my health.
> . . .
>
> I am out of place in the capital,
> people take me for a beggar,
> as you would be out of place in this sort of life,
> you are so – I regret it – so welded to your vulgarity.

After a description of a child's death:

> His father howled shamelessly – an officer.
> I was not abashed at his crying.

And:

> Oh! There's nothing to complain about.

One level of satire is based on the honest old man's admission of
a goal in life not quite in line with the highest ascetic practices of
his new religion. But beneath this is yet another, deeper irony

which Bunting allows his reader to discover with only unobtrusive hints from him. The greatest irony which underlies the situation of the whole poem is that neither an absence of great sufferings nor a wealth of simple consolations gives Chomei the complete happiness he seeks:

> Hankering, vexation and apathy,
> keeping a carriage wont cure it.
>
> Keeping a man in livery
> wont cure it. Keeping a private fortress
> wont cure it. These things satisfy no craving.

The same note of sadness and dissatisfaction runs beneath the descriptions of the consolations:

> easy to take it down and carry it away
> when I get bored with this place.
> . . .
> I do not enjoy being poor,
> I've a passionate nature.
> My tongue
> clacked a few prayers.

Bunting deepens the final irony of these last lines of the poem through the 'leitmotif of the House' which includes 'the transmogrification of the house' he mentions. Within the first few lines he introduces this leitmotif:

> Eaves formal on the zenith,
> lofty city, Kyoto,

and continues repeating it to the end:

> Oh! There's nothing to complain about.
> Buddha says: 'None of the world is good.'
> I am fond of my hut...

By means of this recurrent motif which he sees as an indication of an intended elegy, he tightens the structural design of the whole. Furthermore, he is able to use it as a basis about transience and permanence, sufferings and happiness, life and death. Immediately after the lines about the eaves of Kyoto, Bunting adds the description of 'house-breakers' who in this case are building bungalows. From this first suggestion of the transience of man's dwellings on earth until the last lines written from a hut which in many ways foreshadows the grave, Chomei's final 'dwelling', Bunting continuously combines the mention of houses with the description or suggestion of death. This basic theme of the transience of all things converts even the innocent-looking

epigraph of the poem to a subtly artistic summary of his thought:
'(Kamo-no-Chomei, born at Kamo 1154, died at Toyama on
Mount Hino, 24th June 1216)'.

In the first part of the poem the destruction of lives is often
combined with the destruction of buildings:

> Some choked, some burned, some barely escaped.
> Sixteen great officials lost houses and
> very many poor.
> . . .
>
> Not a house stood. Some were felled whole,
> some in splinters; some had left
> great beams upright in the ground
> and round about
> lay rooves scattered where the wind flung them.
> . . .
>
> Lamed some, wounded some.
> This cyclone turned southwest.
>
> Massacre without cause.
> . . .
>
>   Dead stank
> on the curb, lay so thick...
> . . .
>
> That winter my fuel was the walls of my own house.

In the rest of the poem Bunting connects the leitmotif of the
House with the transience of life much more delicately. In the
second half of the poem the death of the grandmother begins the
chain of Chomei's moves which ends when he reaches his smallest
dwelling. This one foreshadows the grave with its suggestions of
clay and 'barrow':

> I have filled the frames with clay,
> set hinges at the corners;
> easy to take it down and carry it away
> when I get bored with this place.
> Two barrowloads of junk
> and the cost of a man to shove the barrow,
> no trouble at all.

In the final section whose setting is this ten-foot hut, Bunting
skilfully rounds out our conception of his persona at the same time
that he less directly and vividly speaks of death. It is almost as if
Chomei is unable to speak directly of his own mortality and death,
though he is reminded of it by everything in his past experiences
and present surroundings:

> Toyama, snug in the creepers!
> Toyama, deep in the dense gully, open

westward whence the dead ride out of Eden
squatting on blue clouds of wistaria.
(Its scent drifts west to Amida.)

Even though the connection of Chomei's thoughts with death here
is explicit, Bunting's notes at the end of his poem in *Poetry* give
further support to my idea:

> *Amida*: in the more or less polytheistic Buddhism of medieval Japan,
> Amida presides over the earthly paradise, where the souls of decent
> dead men repose for awhile. He was reverenced about as widely as Mary
> is by Catholics, and Chomei, probably attracted by the poetic qualities
> of the Amida myth, professed a special devotion for him.[52]

Nature, poetry, and music never cease recalling to Chomei the
evanescence of all and the end, death.

> Summer? Cuckoo's *Follow, follow* – to
> harvest Purgatory hill!
> Fall? The nightgrasshopper will
> shrill *Fickle life*!

Bunting enlarges the Japanese image of the cuckoo's promise to
guide one on the road of death by combining it with the Dantean
image which suggest Chomei's reluctance to follow. Besides the
sounds of the insects which seem to him to sing of the
impermanence of life, even the songs he plays for his 'own
amusement' underline his constant recollection of the temporality
of all things: *Autumn Wind* and *Hastening Brook*. The single line, 'A
ripple of white water after a boat', epitomises the complete thought
of Mansei's poem which Bunting merely hints at:

> To what shall I compare
> This world?
> To the white wake behind
> A ship that has rowed away
> at dawn![53]

Bunting deliberately underscores the central satire by adding
lines of a poet Chomei only mentions but does not quote:

> *Somehow or other*
> *We scuttle through a lifetime.*
> *Somehow or other*
> *neither palace nor straw-hut*
> *is quite satisfactory.*

Bunting's note for *Poetry* shows better than those condensed for
his *Collected Poems* that he was aware of other specific works of
Chomei:

> He wrote: *Tales of the Four Seasons*; *Notes With No Title* (critical essays);
> and a quantity of poems; edited an anthology of poems composed at the

moment of conversion by Buddhist proselytes (one suspects irony); and was for a while secretary to the editors of the imperial anthology.[54]

In one of these works, *Mumyosho*, a section headed 'The Modern Style' ('*Kindai Katei*'), Chomei, 'himself one of the most original poets among [his] contemporaries', reports the views of his Master, Shun'e, in the form of answers to questions. In a reply which points to Bunting's own writing, Chomei's Master explains that 'the qualities deemed essential to the style are the overtones that do not appear in the words alone and an atmosphere that is not visible in the configuration of the poem'. After illustrating his belief that 'these virtues will be present of themselves' in every simple, exact description, he concludes:

> It is only when many meanings are compressed into a single word, when the depths of feeling are exhausted yet not expressed, when an unseen world hovers in the atmosphere of the poem, when the mean and common words are used to express the elegant, when a poetic conception of rare beauty is developed to the fullest extent in a style of surface simplicity – only then, when the conception is exalted to the highest, and 'the words are too few', will the poem, by expressing one's feelings in this way, have the power of moving Heaven and Earth...[55]

Insofar as it is appropriate to the style and subject matter, Bunting's persona, *Chomei at Toyama*, reaches towards a high degree of this compression and simplicity which Chomei also strove for in his writing. Bunting himself gives strength to the assertion; after reading this quotation, he wrote to me: 'I congratulate you on finding this magnificent passage from the Shun-e' [4 July 1973]. Although almost every passage is an example, the following is especially noteworthy:

> My jacket's wistaria flax,
> my blanket hemp,
> berries and young greens
> my food.
>
> (Let it be quite understood,
> all this is merely personal.
> I am not preaching the simple life
> to those who enjoy being rich.)
>
> I am shifting rivermist, not to be trusted.

Bunting wrote in *Poetry* (1933) that Chomei 'was as modern as, say, Cummings', and in his 'redaction and interpretation'[56] he succeeded in writing an 'adaption'[57] that speaks to us in the twentieth century as simply and easily as Chomei's did to those in the thirteenth. The questions Chomei was asking are some of the most fundamental. A prose translation of the *Hojoki* begins:

The flow of the river is ceaseless, and its water is never the same. The bubbles that float in the pools, now vanishing, now forming, are not of long duration: so in the world are man and his dwellings.

...of those I used to know, a bare one or two in twenty remain. They die in the morning, they are born in the evening, like foam on the water.

Whence does he come, where does he go, man that is born and dies?...Which will be the first to go, the master or his dwelling? One might just as well ask this of the dew on the morning-glory. The dew may fall and the flower remain – remain, only to be withered by the morning sun. The flower may fade before the dew evaporates, but though it does not evaporate, it waits not the evening.[58]

Bunting condenses this simply:

> Swirl sleeping in the waterfall!
> On motionless pools scum appearing
>   disappearing!
>
> . . .
>
> In the town where I was known
> the young men stare at me.
> A few faces I know remain.
>
> Whence comes man at his birth? or where
> does death lead him? Whom do you mourn?
> Whose steps wake your delight?
> Dewy hibiscus dries: though dew
> outlasts the petals.

Hugh Kenner admires this 'writing that confines itself to discovering what are the essentials of the job in hand and setting them down'. He sees that 'lofty city Kyoto/wealthy, without antiquities'

> precisely defines a quality: but six words are apt to be overlooked if one assumes a point to be unimportant unless dilated into witty rhetoric. Mr Auden would have fashioned this distich into a whole chorus.[59]

It is this kind of writing that enables Bunting through his redaction to condense the material of the original so that the design of the work could be brought out in relief.

As a slight concession to his readers, Bunting comments that Chomei's 'Kyoto had a number of curiously detailed parallels with New York and Chicago',[60] which, he had previously explained to Harriet Monroe, were not his invention and which he did not feel called upon to disguise.[61] Bunting's version emphasises these parallels by translating 'Sixth Ward' as 'Sixth Avenue', or sentences such as 'Along the banks of the Kamo River there was not even room for horses and cattle to pass' as

> Dead stank
> on the curb, lay so thick on
> Riverside Drive a car couldnt pass.

Bunting modernises sentences so that a city-dweller anywhere in the world today can empathise with the speaker. He translates

> If a man's house stands in a crowded place and a fire breaks out in the neighbourhood, he cannot escape danger. If it stands in a remote situation, he must put up with the nuisance of going back and forth to the city, and there is always a danger of robbers.

as

> If he lives in an alley of rotting frame houses
> he dreads a fire.
> If he commutes he loses time
> and leaves his house daily to be plundered by gunmen.

Thomas Cole, editor of *Imagi*, admires Bunting's use of the 'double image' with which he 'ironically parallels...the decay and destruction of the ancient Japanese capital Kyoto with, prophetically, present-day New York City. However, he sees this quite narrowly as a technique which allows Bunting to rail against the ultimate decadence which follows bad government and the overcrowded conditions in great capitals'.[62]

A more recent critic, Anthony Suter, offers a more transcendent view:

> Bunting takes an ancient subject – the reflections of Chomei, a twelfth-century Japanese poet, on the disasters that occur during his lifetime – to emphasise the eternal nature of the sufferings of man and the intimate relation of his fate to the cosmic cycle of events.[63]

To my mind, Suter's idea must be combined with Cole's to correctly describe another of Bunting's contributions to Chomei's thought. Besides making the formal intention of the work clearer by bringing out in relief the underlying design, Bunting makes the universality that is only implied in the prose vividly realised in the poetry. Through the 'double image' Bunting associates many more eras and cultures than those he or an individual reader may think of. Though he wrote this before World War II and the wars in Korea and Vietnam, by bringing us up shortly to modern times through names and images or by including a metaphor which associates the Renaissance with the subject matter, he forces us to enlarge the scope of the poem to include all eras and cultures.

Suter goes a step further than the others in judging that Chomei represents a turning point in Bunting's work. He sees it as the first poem chronologically that stands entirely on its own: 'from there on, with the exception of *The Well of Lycopolis* (1935), literature or other source material is no longer required for understanding'.[64] It is certainly true that the enjoyment *Chomei at Toyama* provides on one level does not depend on its prose source; however, some knowledge of the original would prevent a critic from such an inept evaluation as this:

> In long poems such as *Chomei at Toyama*, Bunting sets down data from various sources, without comment and without transition passages, in the hope that an "ideogram" will result.[65]

Bunting had known stronger criticism long before Goodwin's however. In a letter to Harriet Monroe, he wrote candidly:

> Re Chomei: Ezra likes it and so does Yeats, but Eliot speaks ill of it because I haven't been in Japan, which seems irrelevant, and because he says it echoes Pound, which, if true, would be a count against it. But Pound supposes it to contain echoes of Eliot. I'm not aware of echoing anybody. Except Chomei: his book was in prose and four to five times as long as my poem. But I think everything relevant in Chomei has been got into the poem.[66]

Pound, nevertheless, besides urging the editors of *Poetry* to print the poem,[67] gave his wholehearted approval through the agency of Eliot at Faber & Faber when he included it without abbreviation in his *Active Anthology* (1933). At a reading in London, on 1 February 1982, Bunting commented unpretentiously that the poem is written in 'an upside-down quantitative verse'. However it is described, in my opinion it is one of Bunting's best long poems after *Briggflatts*.

In most of the translations and adaptations Bunting is experimenting with technique, trying to learn 'the trick of it' from Latin and Persian master poets – Lucretius, Catullus, Horace, Hafez, Sa'di, and Manuchehri. In his adaptation of Machiavelli's work, reminiscent of Pound's Canto IX, he successfully transforms a diplomatic report into a poem, but neither its unvaried techniques nor its borrowed material allow it to be compared favourably with any sonata, even the shortest. The work that Bunting transforms into the most successful adaptation is Chomei's *Hojoki*. Besides passages that look forward to *Briggflatts*, the tone and themes of *Chomei at Toyama* fit in with those in Bunting's own collected works. Awareness of the brevity of life, the beauty of nature and art, the vagaries of fortune, the instability of all of this in view of the inevitability of death are themes that Bunting will develop most fully in his sonatas.

CHAPTER 6

Early Sonatas

No clear line divides the translations and adaptations from the early
sonatas insofar as both depend to a greater or lesser degree on the
works of other poets. *Villon, Attis: Or, Something Missing,* and *The
Well of Lycopolis* should be read against a background of the poetry
of Villon, Catullus, Lucretius, Cino da Pistoia, and the sonnet of
Milton's to his 'late espoused Saint'. However, *Aus dem zweiten
Reich* (1931) and his last sonatas *The Spoils* (1951) and *Briggflatts*
(1965), except for a line or two, are independent of any other
poetry. The one characteristic that does set this group of six long
poems apart from the rest is not their dependence or independence
but their sonata form.

Bunting explained to Jonathan Williams that he had reached the
conclusion early 'that poetry should try to take over some of the
new techniques that [he] only knew in music'. Discovering this idea
in 'Preludes' interested Bunting in Eliot's poetry, even though
Bunting saw that 'the resemblance to...Chopin's Preludes was
slight and superficial'. Nevertheless, he realised that Eliot was
'obviously thinking on lines not dissimilar from [his] own'. Bunting,
however, favoured the sonata rather than the prelude or any other
musical form:

> I had thought all along that the sonata was the more likely one to be of
> use. But I got off on the wrong foot trying to imitate Beethoven's
> sonatas, using extremely violent contrasts in tone and speed which don't
> actually carry well onto the page, and I had to puzzle about that for
> awhile before I discovered it was better to go back to a simpler way of
> dealing with the two themes and to take the early or mid-eighteenth-
> century composers of sonatas – John Christian Bach and Scarlatti – as
> models to imitate. [D]

Actually the term "sonata" is used with a certain looseness in
discussions of music. One of its broadest definitions is a
composition contrasting three or four, sometimes two, movements
in different rhythms and at different speeds and in different keys,

with a return in the last movement to the initial key. As general as this definition is, it does not include the majority of Scarlatti's sonatas which are one-movement sonatas. Complicating matters further, the musical term "sonata form" generally signifies the work just described, one in several movements; specifically though, it designates the structure of a single movement of a sonata, usually the first.

Another aspect of the sonata which makes it difficult to discuss is that because of its long evolution pieces quite unlike in form are all labelled "sonata". The sonatas of Beethoven that Bunting found unsuitable to imitate belong to a period later than that of Johann Christian Bach (1735-1782) and Domenico Scarlatti (1685-1757). By Beethoven's time (1770-1827) the sonata had passed through many transitional stages and had developed into the form most familiar to listeners today.

The sonatas of Beethoven, besides presenting much greater dramatic contrasts than Bach's and Scarlatti's, organized these contrasts within a fairly rigid framework. It is not difficult for musical theorists to describe the structure of Beethoven's sonatas in general terms. On the other hand, the only generalisation about the Scarlatti sonatas that scholars agree on is that they are almost always one-movement sonatas in binary form, that is, divided roughly into halves.

The typical freedom of the sonata during his time was capitalised on by the prolific Scarlatti to such an extent that Ralph Kirkpatrick can write hundreds of pages in his definitive work, *Domenico Scarlatti*, preparing the reader for his generalised description of the Scarlatti sonata, only to spend the rest of his book carefully discussing specific departures from this basic definition. In other words, the Scarlatti sonata, along with others written during this period, has an imitable freedom the later classical sonata lacks.

This freedom is evident also in the works of Johann Christian Bach, the "London" or "English" Bach. He contributed to the growth of the sonata by emphasising thematic contrasts and by demonstrating the dramatic possibilities in the transition sections, rather than allowing them to remain merely ornamental. These characteristics are recognisable ones in each of Bunting's sonatas.

That Bunting was attracted to the form of the sonata which allows freedom to accommodate a variety of contrasts and associations is not surprising; that further he finds in the music of J.C. Bach and Scarlatti the models best suited to his poetry is even more fitting. The sonata form of the Baroque Period still retained traces of characteristics of earlier one-movement pieces. These earlier pieces fall into almost any number of short sections in contrasting styles. For example, a work of Buxtehude falls into thirteen sections, alternately slow and quick. This, of course, is a forerunner of both the sonata and the dance suite which are 'so similar in origin and parallel in development' that some music authorities suggest they be studied together. Both forms evolved to accommodate contrasting sections, movements, or compositions within one form. Many examples in this process can be cited: Bach's *Art of the Fugue* which Bunting mentions as a kind of model for his poetry (LZ, 18 June 1953) and Corelli's *Concerti Grossi*, another favourite of Bunting's, are among the best known. In the twentieth century Kirkpatrick paired most of the Scarlatti sonatas, since in his opinion they were written to be combined. Bunting mentioned to me an even earlier linking as an influence on his work:

> [Scarlatti's] sonatas are...single, except a few written late in his career, but it was an obvious development to link two or three or four of them together in an age that was making so much of the dance suite. Something very like that had already happened in J. C. Bach and others. The dance suite origin is made plain by the final movements, mostly minuets, rondos, etc. The thematic links in the earlier dance suites were attenuated or dropped: but 19th century composers often brought them back again in their sonatas. I wanted something not rigid, but capable of a kind of hidden continuity, and a string of movements made like Scarlatti's but unobtrusively linked seemed what was wanted. [23 May 1972]

Although the musical analogy is always in his mind, Bunting has insisted more than once that his is no slavish imitation of a model. To him that kind of precision suggests an artist who is 'controlled by the model instead of controlling it'. Bunting's freedom parallels that of the pre-classical composers:

> Music has suggested certain forms and certain details to me, but I have not tried to be consistent about it. Rather, I've felt the spirit of a form, or of a procedure, without trying to reproduce it in any way that could be demonstrated on a blackboard. (There's no one-one relationship between my movements and any of Scarlatti's). You could say the same about the detail of sound. Eliot – and Kipling – show prodigious skill in fitting words to a prearranged pattern, very admirable: yet they don't do it without losing some suppleness...Critical notions are in control from the outside so that the poem is constrained to fit them, as though it had never been conceived in the form it wears...My matter is born of the form – or the form of the matter, if you care to think that I just conceive things musically. There's no fitting, at least consciously. Whatever you

think I am saying is something I could not have said in any other way. [23 May 1972]

Each of his sonatas proves the truth of this statement.

VILLON

Villon (1925), Bunting's first collected sonata, was not published until 1930. That year it appeared in his first book of poems, *Redimiculum Matellarum*, and in *Poetry* (October 1930) where Ezra Pound had sent it months earlier. Pound thought so highly of it he also included it in *Profile* (1931) and in his *Active Anthology* (1933). In November 1931 *Poetry* announced that *Villon* had won the annual Lyric Prize of fifty dollars. Special attention was called to 'the song in the first section' which they reprinted with the note that it 'interprets, without directly translating, the lyric manner of the old French poet and his feeling about life and death'.[1]

Bunting has said that he writes of nothing he has not experienced.[2] To add proof in this case, Kenneth Cox in his 'Commentary on Basil Bunting's *Villon*' adds details to the background of Bunting's prison experiences which parallel Villon's, experiences which give the poem a stronger authority and sincerity.[3] Bunting dislikes talking about this time and this reticence is evident in 'Crime and Punishment', a review of three books on this subject in the *Outlook* [LIX, 4 July 1927] Bunting merely remarks that one book is 'a poor journalistic write-up of English prisons, full of irrelevancies and inaccuracies'. 'It is difficult,' he concludes, 'to believe that the author is really as ignorant, prejudiced, and sensational as he appears in his work.' Neither statement reveals his strong authority for such judgments.

His most candid remarks about his own prison experiences are in a review of Conrad's *The Rover* in *The Transatlantic Review* [August 1924]. Although the pertinent paragraph is long, it provides an important introduction to *Villon*:

> I read *Romance* for the first time in the solitude of an English prison. The Book of Kings, Isaiah's harsh splendour and the voluptuous majesty of the Song of Solomon had tempered my weariness for several months...*Romance* was a real book, a book written by a man and not by the heavy finger of God. In that emptiness, where no new thing ever enters, it took possession of my eyes and ears. My cell grew full of aromatic bales, fading into the shadows of Don Ramon's warehouse; Thomas Castro walked with me around the patch of rotting cabbage-stalks that was our exercise ground; even Seraphina visited me occasionally, keeping modestly to the dark places, an indistinct but

sympathetic form. It was all amazingly concrete. I *saw* that warehouse; I saw the bay and its town, the hovels, the cathedral, the palace: I watched the hanging of the pirates at Kingston; and when I came to the long trial at the end of the book I heard the rustle of the public and the muttering of the turnkeys to one another.

In the poem the ramifications of the prison theme which reach much further than physical imprisonment exemplify the encompassing movement evident throughout the poem. In this same way the words spoken do not belong to only one speaker, but sometimes are attributable to both Villon and the contemporary poet, and even go beyond the past and present to include the future. This encompassing movement underlies the dominant contrast upon which Bunting builds his entire sonata. Throughout the parts Bunting shifts from particulars to broad universal statements which culminate in lines at the end of the poem decrying his unsuccessful attempt to resolve all "unnoted harmonies" into song:

> How can I sing with my love in my bosom?
> Unclean, immature and unseasonable salmon.

According to Bunting, Pound scratched out about half the poem with a blue pencil, sighing at Part III, 'I don't know what you young men are up to.'[4] What remains is sometimes obscure but a strong promise of good poetry from a young man of twenty-five.

In the barest terms the dominant contract or chief opposition in the sonata is between art and life, imagination and reality.[5] Bunting begins by associating life and reality with the kind of truth which is provable by the intellect and senses and ends by associating it with death and impermanence. With art and imagination he associates the unreal, the fantastic and illogical – all that supports life to make it bearable, all that enlarges and beautifies it and which survives beyond individual human lives. This permanence is associated with art and imagination until finally, in the resolution of the themes, Bunting attempts to make art and imagination subsume and elevate all points of opposition in the poem.

The constant grouping and regrouping of subjects has the kind of intricacy and precarious stability of a steadily shifting kaleidoscope design. In Part I the dominant contrast between real life and art in the first half is opposed in the second half to the conflict between death, impermanence, and human desire for some kind of permanence. The persona is caught between denying art as 'lies' and calling on art to help him endure reality as it helped Villon. He employs art, imitating Villon, to scornfully remind human beings that they are mortal and impermanent, that it is art, the work of imagination, which is enduring.

Appropriately, the contrasts are underlined in each part by a variety of techniques. After setting up the contrast between the 'anatomised' poetry of Villon and the real message of the dead man. Bunting describes in the first half of Part I the individual situation of two men in prison, Villon and the poet-narrator, using contrasting rhythms and verse forms to express his feelings. For example, the first line, 'He whom we anatomised' is basically iambic tetrameter, Villon's characteristic ballade metre. But counterpointing the iambic metre is the cadenced rhythm dependent on two strong stresses, 'He' and 'anatomised'. By leading climactically to this last word, the rhythm emphasises the irony of attempting to analyse Villon's poetry through any superficial method.

The next two lines are a quotation from an anatomising critic, Clement Marot, a contemporary of Ronsard who also figures in the poem in this camp:

'whose words we gathered as pleasant flowers
and thought on his wit and how neatly he described things'

Bunting incorporates this quotation to provide a contrast to the regular iambic and to make more dramatic the abrupt single-word line, 'speaks'. This one-stress "bob" suddenly shifts the tone from the mockingly satiric to the serious, alerting the reader to a change in atmosphere. 'Speaks' acts as a pivot between the free, light lines preceding and the serious, heavy lines following:

to us, hatching marrow,
broody all night over the bones of a deadman.

The stress pattern of the lines in the stanza, 2, 4, 4, 1, 3, 4, diagrams the action of the climactic pivot or "bob", but Bunting's greater skill lies in his ability either to loosen the lines with unstressed syllables or to tighten them by paring them to even one word. He proves his skill in the first half of Part I in which his cadenced verse is fleshed out by the music of his vowel gradations, alliteration, assonance, and intricate crossed rhyme ('mockery' – 'have CY GIST' – 'over me').

The second half of Part I, the serious parody of Villon's introduction to his *'Ballade des Dames du Temps Jadis'*, contrasts effectively with the first half: unrhymed free verse now shifts to rhymed octosyllabic quatrains. Anthony Suter discusses in some detail the success with which Bunting follows the technical ideal of Villon's poetry in this section:

Bunting employs the same verse form as Villon, octosyllabic quatrains with a basic rhythm, rhyming ABAB, with the only exception being that he arranges his lines in groups of four instead of in the groups of eight of Villon where the rhyme sound B of the first four lines is repeated as A of the second. One may note how both Bunting and Villon are masters of alliteration: for example, the labial consonants in 'pay me your pulse and breath' and the *f* and *m* sounds in '*La mort le fait fremir...*'[6]

The theme of the inhuman prison situation, reminiscent of the grave, is displaced in the second half by the theme of the inevitability of death. Threaded through the darkness of both halves is the motif of

the Emperor with the Golden Hands, the Virgin in blue.
(– A blazing parchment,
Matthew Paris his kings in blue and gold.)

Bunting wrote to me that 'Matthew Paris embellished his historical chronicle with lovely miniatures. The reference is to them' [4 July 1973]. Villon too wrote of the Emperor with the Golden Hands. Poetry, therefore, and these miniatures with their gold and blue, and later, silver, with their 'word', 'tint' and 'tone,/ insubstantial – glorious' are symbols of art and permanency. In the beginning this is associated with lies, with all that is unreal and not true to life:

My tongue is a curve in the ear. Vision is lies.
We saw it so and it was not so,
the Emperor with the Golden Hands, the Virgin in blue.

But this life is insupportable; the senses cry out for at least imagined comfort:

I stammer to my ear:
Naked speech! Naked beggar both blind and cold!
Wrap it for my sake in Paisley shawls and bright soft fabric,
wrap it in curves and cover it with sleek lank hair.

What trumpets? What bright hands? Fetters, it was the Emperor
with magic in darkness, I unforewarned.
The golden hands are not in Averrhoes,

All is silent and dark in the real situation. Besides sight and hearing, each of the other senses is restricted:

eyes lie and this swine's fare bread and water
makes my head wuzz. Have pity, have pity on me!

To the right was darkness and to the left hardness

It was

Then he saw his ghosts glitter with golden hands,

Here this motif reveals another, life-supporting aspect which finally at the end of Part I unfolds to become that aspect of art – poetry, painting, music – which outlasts individuals in its permanence:

The Emperor with the Golden Hands

is still a word, a tint, a tone,
insubstantial – glorious,
when we ourselves are dead and gone
and the green grass growing over us.

Although the contrast of verse forms emphasises the one dominant contrast in each part, the contrasts and associations within each of these halves adds a further complexity. In Part II the complex opposition is between reality supportable only by art in the first half and art too strong to be reduced to scientific reality in the second half. In the resolution of Part II, just as in Part I, art survives as something more than the reality of life and death.

Part II opens with a curse on his imprisoner which Villon only hints at in *Le Gran Testament*, but which Bunting makes explicit by quoting Psalm 109:

Let his day be few and let
his bishoprick pass to another

Although a strong contrast in form separates the first ten lines in free verse from eight rhymed couplets in iambic tetrameter, they are linked by the ballad refrain 'Whereinall we differ not'. This faintly echoes the refrains in Part I, 'Death is written over all' and 'Fellmonger Death gets every skin'.

Besides incorporating the curse Villon only suggested, Bunting throughout the poem has been alluding to lines from Villon's poetry. Here the 'mouldy bread' and 'dry crust' allude to lines in *'Ballade pour laquelle Villon crye mercy à chascun'*, and the vanished dancers and somersaulters recall lines in the *'Espistre, en forme de ballade, à ses amis'*:

But they have swept the floor,
there are no dancers, no somersaulters now,
only bricks and bleak black cement and bricks,
only the military tread and the snap of the locks.

The next line, 'Mine was a threeplank bed whereon', is a remarkably economical transition: it continues the cadenced rhythm of the preceding section and introduces the first rhyming word of the section of rhyming couplets which follows. This next passage is marked by a lilting rhythm and rhyme by which the prisoner grimly mocks the torturous reality of his situation. The shift from the free, cadenced verse to the steady beat of the rhymed couplets dramatise his desperateness; controlled rhythm parallels

the rational control the speaker must maintain to keep himself from
going insane:

> They took away the prison clothes
> and on the frosty nights I froze.
> I had a Bible where I read
> that Jesus came to raise the dead –
> I kept myself from going mad
> by singing an old bawdy ballad
> and birds sang on my windowsill
> and tortured me till I was ill,

At the same time the verse itself is an objective correlative to what
Bunting is asserting more clearly in the poem by now: human
beings must make life supportable through imagination and art in
some form:

> but Archipiada came to me
> and comforted my cold body
> and Circe excellent utterer of her mind
> lay with me in that dungeon for a year
> making a silk purse from an old sow's ear

Bunting's answer to me about Archipiada strengthens this interpretation:

> Archipiada is a mysterious person mentioned in Villon's *Ballade des
> Dames*, etc. Guesses are no use – most editors tell you that St Thomas
> made some confusion and thought Alcibiades was a woman, but I think
> that is based on a misreading of St Thomas' text, and anyway that
> Villon, who was far from profound in his theological studies, probably
> never read St Thomas with sufficient attention to remember such a
> minute detail. So for me she is any product of the imagination. [23 May
> 1972]

The last lines

> till Ronsard put a thimble on her tongue.
>   Whereinall we differ not...

contains a neatly expressive image of the restrictions the classicists
imposed on poetry, and by this line the necessary, rigid control has
been loosened.

The poetry in this section depends on a technique at the farthest
remove from Ronsard's formalism, Whitmanesque syntactical
parallelisms:

> But they have named all the stars,
> trodden down the scrub of the desert, run the white moon to a schedule,
> Joshua's serf whose beauty drove men mad.
> They have melted the snows from Erebus, weighed the clouds,
> hunted down the white bear, hunted the whale the seal the kangaroo,
> they have set private enquiry agents onto Archipiada:

The emphasis has shifted from the restricting prison conditions to the unrestrictable freedom of imagination which only the foolish think they can reduce to facts. Bertillon, the Paris police chief who invented anthropometrics, a system of identifying persons by measuring and recording their features, is one such mistaken person.

Throughout his poetry Bunting has written lines which substantiate critics' claims of his antagonism toward science. Michael Hamburger in *The Truth of Poetry* chooses this section of *Villon* to illustrate the persistence of 'an anti-scientific, anti-positivist bias' among most modern poets:

> [This section] renders a whole complex of traditional poetic antagonisms – to scientific positivism, to the interference of men in the life of nature, to the interference of technically aided administrations in the lives of individuals.[7]

It is true that in a letter to Zukofsky [1 January 1947] Bunting says outright, 'I hate Science', but this unequivocal statement must be considered in its context:

> On a different plane, I'd like to suggest that Science is only another religion, much like many old ones...I dont admire the contemporary efforts to "reconcile" a scientific outlook with an aesthetic one which is in fact based ultimately on a different religion (nor a moral one; nor least of all, a hybrid theological one)...I hate Science. It denies a man's responsibility for his own deeds, abolishes the brotherhood that springs from God's fatherhood. It is a hectoring, dictating expertise, which makes the least lovable of the Church Fathers seem liberal by contrast. It is far easier for a Hitler or a Stalin to find a mock-scientific excuse for persecution than it was for Dominic to find a mock Christian one.

Closer to the time of *Villon*, he explains his position in two articles in the *Outlook*. In the first 'Philosophic Criticism' [LX, 6 August 1927] he scorns science because it pretends that 'its universe of exact measurement and strict logic' exhausts 'all the subjects of thought and knowledge':

> There remain two realms at least that cannot be explored by scientific methods, that of Religion on the one hand, that of Art on the other; both wide regions in which the mind must wonder without a chart, in which the dominant mode of thought is not logical but intuitive.

Bunting praises the philosopher, Ramon Fernandez, for at least stating the problem of the philosopher's living 'at the cross-roads where Art, Science and Religion meet...[in order to] explore all these roads as and when required instead of treading one alone monotonously'.

This attitude which gives a background to the anti-scientific section in *Villon* is explored further in a second article, 'The Whole Man' [LXI, 19 May 1928]. Once again he points out the narrowing perspective of Science which 'deals only with measurables or with facts submissive to the forms of logic'. He continues: 'What these two instruments, mathematics and logic, cannot reach, it neglects and is inclined, in self-protection, to deny, lest the vastness of the universe should overwhelm it.' In this article he urges the philosopher to recognise the necessity of returning from his abject dependence toward science and to realise 'the need for a broader base in all human experience, the emotional, moral, aesthetic, religious, as well as the spatial and mechanical'.

Bunting's antagonism toward science is focused chiefly on its blindness toward other forms of thought and knowledge. In fact, in this article he upholds the need for scientific truths as an essential part of human knowledge, but only as one essential part within the whole spectrum. A further point which balances his position and is actually far more liberal than that of most modern poets is his comment to Zukofsky that 'there is a scientific case for poetry (it will not be heard in this age)' [21 January 1947]. In the *Outlook* article he agrees with Henry Osborne Taylor, author of *Human Values and Verities*, that 'intuition and feeling alone would be as insufficient and fallible a guide as reason alone'. It is only the pretence of science that it is the sole arbiter of truth that Bunting despises.

His satiric tone in Part II corroborates all these aspects of his attitude toward science. Homer and Dante, with Villon raised to their company, are never to be pinned down and analysed by logical, scientific investigations.

In Part III the poet attempts to harmonise all thematic oppositions of the poem by elevating reality through imagination to art. Reality or experience, the raw material of imagination, must be formed artistically for the creation of lasting beauty in life. The real and the imagined are harmonised in art and poetry in the first section of Part III, and the art process itself is elevated to art by being described in poetry in the second section. Finally the sea is seen as a symbol of the origin and the harmonisation of all opposites: life, death, permanence, impermanence, reality, imagination, time and timelessness. The brief coda is the poet's exclamation at his imperfect attempt to create in this sonata a work of art which would objectify what he is trying to express.

The culmination of the sonata, Part III, offers a contrast to the first two Parts by placing against the realistic description of the

imprisonment an imaginative description of the freedom gained by
harmonising imagination and art with life. The themes of life and
death and imagination and art are interwoven in a lyric passage of
delicately rhythmical phrases held together by parallelisms of
structure and cadence:

> Under the olive trees
> walking alone
> on the green terraces
> very seldom
> over the sea seldom
> where it ravelled and spun
> blue tapestries white and green

The unpunctuated lines suggest material from life taking shape in
the imagination:

> below me the ports
> with naked breasts
> shipless spoiled sacked
> because of the beauty of Helen

Immediately afterwards tight, economical lines attempt to
illustrate the possibilities of art. Through synthesis and metaphor
many arts are implied, but poetry is basic:

> precision clarifying vagueness;
> boundary to a wilderness
> of detail; chisel voice
> smoothing the flanks of noise;
> catalytic making whisper and whisper
> run together like two drops of quicksilver;
> factor that resolves
>   unnoted harmonies;

The image of two drops of quicksilver, which Bunting in his Notes
gives E. Nesbit credit for, carries from *The Story of the Amulet* the
connotation of the union of fact and fancy. What is more striking is
the integration of past and present which is effected once the two
pieces of the amulet are finally joined, 'as one bead of mercury is
drawn into another bead'. This effect, which Bunting is accom-
plishing here, he will do more skilfully in the integration of Then
and Now in *Briggflatts*.

The next few lines enlarge this concept. The sea contains all
diversity in unity:

> The sea has no renewal, no forgetting,
> no variety of death,
> is silent with the silence of a single note.

Appropriately enough, as a symbol in the poem it is complex, representing all that must be given form and at the same time the union and harmony of all opposites into 'the silence of a single note'. This line here in his first sonata looks forward to the end of his last one: 'For love uninterrupted night.'

When Harriet Monroe asked Bunting about the last word of the poem, he answered:

> ...you ask me 'Why salmon?' It would be easy to answer why not? But though I am shy of giving partial explanations which often seem to mislead people, which is probably worse than leaving them in the dark, I will say that by line 180 odd I have been angling a long time for a very big fish and only landed something for which the Board of Fisheries formula seems an exact and fitting description.[8]

Zukofsky in a review of *Redimiculum Matellarum* a few months later discussed Bunting's evaluation of the poem in the coda:

> [Bunting's] indictment of Bertillon in this poem is violence that an intelligent man confronted with historical fact has had to express, even if the name has joined the decorative scheme of his poem. The coda of Villon –
>
> > How can I sing with my love in my bosom?
> > Unclean, immature and unseasonable salmon. –
>
> is the logical humility consequent on Mr Bunting's bitterness. The rhetorical wrench of the last line is self-mitigated because the writer's metaphor has become the objective equivalent of his personal irony.[9]

Kenneth Cox interprets it as something less serious: '...it finishes with a mocking kick of the heels, a twirl typical of the twenties, which slights the poet's own achievement and puts the poem back to his actual situation'.[10] Since Bunting revealed in the poem those whose art he was striving toward, Homer, Dante, and more immediately, Villon, his exclamation against all he attempted and was unable to accomplish in 1925 is optimistic.

ATTIS: OR, SOMETHING MISSING

In a letter to Harriet Monroe Bunting warned against reading *Attis: Or, Something Missing*, his second sonata, as if it had the logic of a prose narrative:

> Ezra says *Attis* is obscure, from which he deduces that he is getting old. It certainly wouldnt be easy to write a synopsis, but I think it's really fairly plain for all that, if the reader doesnt spend time and energy looking for a nice logical syllogistic development which isnt there. I dont like formal logic. There are better ways of connecting things up and

anyway Wittgenstein reduced logic logically to the noble conclusion *'Woruber man nicht reden kann, daruber musz man schweigen'* some years ago and there seems nothing more to be done with that instrument after that. [13 July 1931][11]

By classifying *Attis* as a sonatina, Bunting expected readers to recognise it as a shortened, simpler form of the sonata. Since it is longer than his sonata, *Villon*, and more complicated than the sonata *Aus Dem Zweitem Reich*, the mockery of Attis and all he symbolises which began in the title continues in this classification of the poem.

The Attis myth the sonatina is based on is important in sources already mentioned in connection with Bunting's poetry, Lucretius and Catullus. In his renowned *Commentary on Catullus*, Robinson Ellis traces the cult of Cybele and its associations with the Attis cult from remote beginnings to its established religious form in the time of Catullus and Lucretius. The procession which Lucretius describes in Book II (ll. 700ff) of *De Rerum Natura* is in honour of the Earth Goddess or Great Mother to whom even Jupiter, her son, gives way, and the highest places are for those who have castrated themselves in her name, as Attis had.

In the earliest versions of the myth, Attis, the young shepherd loved and pursued by Cybele, is transformed into a pine tree after his self-mutilation, and violets spring from his blood. Catullus's version however omits this ending.[12] In Carmen LXIII, Attis, a young Phrygian leader, sails away from the mainland with his friends, and at the foot of a mountain dedicated to Cybele, they emasculate themselves in a religious frenzy. But when the religious fervour wears off, Attis alternately mourns and rages at his unalterable deed. Cybele, hearing him, sends one of her lions to the shore where Attis is looking toward his fatherland, to drive him back among the mountain pines as her subservient eunuch.

The connection between Lucretius and Bunting that Suter finds rests on the supposition that 'much of Bunting's argument depends on aspects of the Latin poet's thought; the atheism of Lucretius, his desire to banish superstitious fear from people's minds'. This the critic sees as 'effective counterpoint to the way in which Bunting mocks the Attis myth'.[13] It seems to me that the mockery is not of the myth so much as it is of Attis, a kind of archetype, and his modern counterpart, emasculated man in modern society.

The connection between Bunting's and Catullus's version is unmistakable. As his epigraph, Bunting uses the last lines of

Carmen LXVIII, the Attis poem:

> *Dea magna, dea Cybele, dea domina Dindymi,*
> *procul a mea tuus sit furor omnis, era, domo:*
> *alios age incitatos, alios age rabidos.*

The best translation I could find of this was Peter Whigham's:

> Great Cybebe, Mother Goddess, Berecynthian Queen,
> avert your fury from Catullus' house
> goad others to your actions,
> others trap in the snarl of frenzy.[14]

But Bunting wrote that 'Whigham's version tries to ornament Catullus. "Drive others frantic, drive others mad" is the real last line – no "snarl of frenzy" etc.' (4 July 1973). Bunting bases the parody in Part III on this 'most famous'[15] of Catullus's poems. Yet the parody never diminishes the scope that Bunting gains by basing his poem about modern man on the classic Attis myth. He enriches his version by adding 'a colloquialism and realism from the comic-satiric tradition' which Peter Whigham discusses in the introduction to his translations of Catullus. This, according to Whigham, is the measure of a poet's greatness, 'the extent to which he is able to effect a synthesis of preceding traditions while producing something that has not been achieved before'.[16]

   In the Catullus version of the Attis myth, the main idea, according to Ellis, is the revolt against nature, or as it might more truly be called, the passion of unnaturalness. Throughout the poem Bunting mocks this characteristic quality of modern man:

> Out of puff
> noonhot in tweeds and gray felt,
> tired of appearance and
> disappearance;
> warm obese frame limp with satiety;
> slavishly circumspect at sixty;
> he spreads over the ottoman
> scanning the pictures and table trinkets.
>
> (That hand's dismissed shadow
> moves through fastidiously selective consciousness,
> rearranges pain.)

The modern Attis is not impotent physically, but in the sense that he lacks an inner fibre of character. This renders him spiritless and enervated, a type of the Attis who is able to be kept subservient. Just as it is to the original Attis, the past to the persona is the occasion of painful, but ineffectual regrets. Until Part III the anti-theme of past wholeness and the possibility of future renewal is kept muted:

.... reluctant ebb:
          salt from all beaches:
disrupt Atlantis, days forgotten,
extinct peoples, silted harbours.
He regrets that brackish
          train of the huntress
driven into slackening fresh,
expelled when the
          estuary resumes
colourless potability;
          wreckage that drifted
in drifts out.

At the conclusion of the poem this theme is predominant in quite another tone.

With the mention of the mythical Atlantis with its allusion to Bacon's metaphor of the ideal commonwealth, the theme broadens in the same centrifugal movement as in *Villon* to include society in general. The particular social scene that the modern Attis looks back on, as if in the remote past, is the hunt, associated in great literature with bygone happiness, youthful freedom, and natural beauty.

The natural countryside Attis vaguely recalls is contrasted with the present defacing of natural landscape and depleting of rich soil:

'Longranked larches succeed larches, spokes of a
stroll; hounds trooping around hooves; and the stolid horn's
sweet breath. *Voice*: Have you seen the
fox? Which way did he go, he go?
There was soft rain.
I recollect deep mud and leafmould somewhere: and
in the distance Cheviot's
heatherbrown flanks and white cap.

Landscape salvaged from
evinced notice of
superabundance, of
since parsimonious
soil.....
          Mother of Gods.'
Mother of eunuchs.

The dualism in Cybele's nature supplies one of the chief oppositions in the poem. With the Giant Kronos, her brother-husband, Cybele had brought forth the race of the Gods. The Great Mother, the Earth Goddess, is associated in the poem with vitality, procreative energy, and abundance under the title of 'Mother of Gods'. Under the title of 'Mother of Eunuchs', she is the source of natural, but irrational and even self-destructive energy in this section. Part I concludes with the ambiguous praises of her dual aspect reflected in the world:

> Praise the green earth. Chance has appointed her
> home, workshop, larder, middenpit.
> Her lousy skin scabbed here and there by
> cities provides us with name and nation.
>
> From her brooks sweat. Hers corn and fruit.
> Earthquakes are hers too. Ravenous animals
> are sent by her. Praise her and call her
> Mother and Mother of Gods and Eunuchs.

When I suggested that these rhythms were from the Psalms, Bunting responded: 'You'll find this metre not in the psalms but in Horace' (4 July 1973).

Part II focuses on the spiritual and emotional emasculation of society. The horizontal movement which connects the past with the present operates in a different way from Part I. Here the past is not vaguely remembered, but runs parallel with the present through the parody of Milton's sonnet. Besides this variation of juxtaposing the past with the present, the scope is enlarged by the constant shift between the supernatural and the natural with dramatic transitions in between.

The persona's response in the opening lines of Part II entitled '(*Variations on a theme by Milton*)' is so opposite to Milton's in his sonnet, 'Methought I Saw My Late Espoused Saint', so low-key and so unnatural a love-response, it is humorous:

> I thought I saw my late wife (a very respectable woman) coming from Bywell churchyard with a handful of raisins. I was not pleased, it is shocking to meet a ghost, so I cut her and went and sat amongst the rank watergrasses by the Tyne.

His response suggests the distancing of modern man from a traditional source of poetry and art, love, strong enough in the classical world to recall the dead to life. Besides the dream of Milton, and Alcestis named in his sonnet, Orfeo, mentioned in the next few lines recalls the powerful love of Orpheus as well as the love of Orfeo in the medieval version of the myth and in Monteverdi's opera. The love of each of these which bridged life and death adds layers of irony to the poem.

A later variation of Milton's theme in Bunting's poem discloses another kind of unnatural love:

> Long loved and
> too long loved, stale habit, such decay of ardour,
> love never dead, love never hoping, never gay.
> Ageslow venom selfsecreted. Such shame!

Intermittently, Medusa, the gorgon, is begged in a frenzy to 'come' to 'enamel him' in the words of the Furies which Dante creates for them in Canto IX of the Inferno: *'Venga Medusa; si'l farem di smalto.'* *'The gorgon's method'* introduces a description of progressive deterioration and degradation in the diurnal round of the city. Lethargy and paralysis characterise the population which daily and unthinkingly batters down the suggestion of renewal.

In the next section the active gods intermingle with men and women who must cooperate with them in order to release their power 'to hurt or endow'. In this present society Polymnia, the muse of sacred song and poetry to the gods, is reduced to keeping a cafe in Reno, the modern symbol for the divorce of love, a source of life and art, from life. The response of emasculated men, too frightened of rebuffs to attempt any creative or positive action, is one to be ridiculed. The aside to Cino da Pistoia, one of Dante's best friends, may remind a few readers of Rossetti's criticism of Cino's 'elaborate and mechanical tone of complaint which hardly reads like the expression of true love'.[17] The aside itself, a quotation from Pound's 'Cino' is a parody of the *dolce stil nuovo* which Dante advocated and encouraged Cino to use. Most importantly, the aside recalls that in any age the source of art itself has 'something missing' without the wholeness of true love. Each line in the section with its mechanical and superficial, injured tone emphasises this:

> Polymnia
> keeps a cafe in Reno.
> Well, (eh, Cino?)

Bunting's mockery extends to his designation of Part III as *'Pastorale arioso (falsetto)'*, i.e., a pastorale which is neither wholly song nor wholly recitative, but a combination, to be rendered here in a falsetto voice. In Bunting's parody Catullus's poem is combined with the legend of Attis's transformation into a pine tree. Appropriately then, the setting of the opening, reminiscent of a Greek chorus, is a grove of pine trees. From the first line the keynote of conflicting emotions characteristic of Attis is heard:

> What mournful stave, what bellow shakes the grove?
> O, it is Attis grieving for his testicles!
> Attis stiffening amid the snows
> and the wind whining through his hair and fingers!

Just as in the Catullus poem, this Attis mournfully recalls his past experience in athletic events, and his attractiveness to other young men and women, contrasting it with his present state: 'Now I am out of a job. I would like to be lady's-maid to Dindyma.' However, his recollections are tainted, as the classic Attis's are not, by the kind of social gathering in which he was awarded prizes: 'the annual sports and flowershow'. The comparison of this with the original Attis's boasts hints satirically at the deterioration of men and all society:

> *ego gymnasi fui flos, ego eram decus olei*
> Once the flower of the athletes.
> Once the pride of the young wrestlers.[18]

Attis describes his vegetable condition in three sections each beginning with the musical first line, 'Pines, my sisters, I your sister', in which the short and long *i*'s and the *s*'s strengthen the image of his whining and sighing. In each section his lament accentuates his present condition by contrasting it with the past. His individual state is emblematic of the general modern condition.

During the festival in honour of Bacchus, 'procreative energy is honoured by carrying the phallus in procession and by singing hymns in trochaic dimeter brachycatalectic metre'.[19] Bunting parodies the persona's forgetfulness of the hymns, the syntax and the paradigms by writing lines in varied dimeter and trimeter trochaic mixed with feet of other metres:

> I have forgotten most of the details,
>   most of the names,
>   and the responses to
>   the ithyphallic hymns:
>   forgotten the syntax,
>   and the paradigms
> grate scrappily against reluctant nerves.

His final cry to Dindyma, 'Shall we be whole in Elysium?' is ambiguous, just as his weak love-hate feelings have been throughout the poem:

> Shall we be whole in Elysium?
> I am rooted in you,
>   Dindyma!
>   assure me
>   the roses and myrtles,
>   the lavish roses,
>   the naively
>   portentous myrtles,
> corroborate the peacock.

The scorn of Cybele's answer to his beseeching is rooted in her dual nature. As the dominant woman who keeps her castrated lovers in subordination, she castigates him for his futile attempt at maintaining self-respect here and now by hoping for a future renewal. As the fertile Mother of the Gods, the source of power and abundance, she scorns him as one who under the power of Polymnia has effected his own dismemberment and is now unable to respond to her creative energy. Besides, she dashes his hope of any future wholeness. His submission and dedication to Dindyma and this way of life is defrauding her of the once energetic vitality a man could channel into creativity of all kinds in society.

The final cryptic note:

> Attis his embleme:
> *Nonnulla deest.*

clinches the sarcasm directed at Attis and all he stands for. 'Something is missing' written in Latin, *Nonnulla deest*, strengthens the satire since '*nonnulla*' accumulates the pejorative suggestions of *none* and *nullify*, and '*deest*' adds the aural connotation of *deus*, god. Outside of these, the word *deest* itself is powerful enough to build the ending to a climax with its idea of something taken from (*de*) the essential being of Attis (*esse-est*) – 'Something *is* missing' from essential human nature in modern society.

As far as music is concerned, Bunting demands a great deal from his readers. Besides seeing the sonatina form in the three parts of the poem, they must follow satiric instructions about one movement being 'Pastorale arioso (falsetto)' and another a group of 'Variations on a theme...' Music and dance are an integral part of the Attis myth so that Bunting demands that a reader hear

> measured shaking of strings,
> and flutes and oboes
> enough for dancers

to enhance the pattern of the whole. This same thing happens in Part II in which the progressive movement from the stately dance to frenzy is emphasised:

> Centrifugal tutus! Sarabands!
> music clear enough to
> pluck stately dances from
> madness before the frenzy.
> Andante.... ....*Prestissimo!*
> turbulent my Orfeo!

In both cases the introduction of the music and dance motifs provides a transition that is both dramatic and functional in the manner of J. C. Bach's. In Part I the musical transition carries the movement from the external description of the arranging of thoughts and images to the internal movement of the images themselves:

> (That hand's dismissed shadow
> moves through fastidiously selective consciousness,
> rearranges pain.)

> There are no colours, words only,
> and measured shaking of strings,

In Part II the music and dance motifs bridge the contrast between the prosy rhythms of the first 'variation on a theme' and the second. The section itself matches the generally more dramatic and emotional tone of Part II in which the image of the 'tumult softly hissed' is in musical terms and the image of spoken sounds is in musical terms, an appropriate part of the *'Pastorale arioso'*:

> A tumult softly hissed
> as by muted violins,
> Tesiphone's, Alecto's
> capillary orchestra.
> Long phrases falling like
> intermittent private voices
> suddenly in the midst of talk,

The musical motif is interwoven continuously throughout the whole poem. Part III, the *Pastorale arioso*, brings together these motifs which have been working together to provide a musical background. Since Bunting does a similar thing in *Briggflatts*, that is, write lines in which the reader must imagine instruments and their sounds, the overall effect will be better discussed later when a comparison can be made.

AUS DEM ZWEITEN REICH

When Michael Hamburger singles out Bunting as a poet of place,[20] a reader may think first of his poems set in Northumberland and last of his sonatas set in Germany. Yet one of his most vividly realised places is the Berlin of the Thirties in *Aus Dem Zweiten Reich*. His lines evoke not just physical landmarks:

> past the Gedächtnis Kirche
> to the loud crowded cafés near the Bahnhof Zoo

but the pervading tone of German society and its culture by means of vivid vignettes. In keeping with the atmosphere of a post-war society subsisting on a mediocre level of culture, the diction never rises above the ordinary, nor do dramatic contrasts ever move far above or below the level of mediocrity. In Part I a jazz rhythm, suggestive of vitality and authentic life rhythms, is weak:

> shadows on sweaty glass,
> hum, drum on the table
>   to the negerband's faint jazz.
> Hundrum at the table

and dies away as the boredom of a new and sterile social milieu takes its place:

> Hour and hour
> meeting against me,
> efficiently whipped cream,
> efficiently metropolitan chatter and snap,
> transparent glistening wrapper
>   for a candy pack.
>
> Automatic, somewhat too clean,
> body and soul similarly scented,
> on time,
> rapid, dogmatic, automatic and efficient,
> ganz modern.

The lack of vitality and depth in relationships between women and men is underlined by the artificial relationships on the screen and broaden to include young and old in 'a consolingly mediocre/ neighbourhood without music'.

Excelling the British in pornography, the French in naked cabarets, and the Americans in large second-rate department stores is the source of Herr Lignitz's pride in the two four-line stanzas of Part II. In Part III, the key figure, the shallow dramatist, is Gerhart Hauptmann. Bunting wrote to me: 'As for the author of more plays than Shakespeare, he was Gerhart Hauptmann. He and his entourage are perfectly recognisable, but not of course, from acquaintance with his writings only' [23 May 1972]. Prolific in quantity, but without quality, he represents the popular artist who to Bunting is always the truest indicator of the cultural level. Straightfaced satire culminates in urbane insults which includes the whole of German society at this time.

Appropriately, there is little variety in form except in rhythm and length of lines in the three parts of the sonata. The consciousness of the one persona behind the entire poem remains the same throughout so that his indifference and distaste colour the voices he records. The voice and personality of Herr Lignitz, for example, are filtered through this consciousness. With hidden scorn it allows the German to reveal himself:

> 'You have no naked pictures in your English magazines.
> It is shocking. Berlin is very shocking to the English. Are you shocked?'

In the third Part the lines contract as if the few syllables are all that is needed to convey the 'nothing at all' the 'renowned author of more plays than Shakespeare' speaks on every subject:

> Who talked about poetry,
> and he said nothing at all;
> plays,
> and he said nothing at all;
> politics,
> and he stirred as if a flea
> bit him
> but wouldnt let on in company;
> and the frost in Berlin,
> muttered: 𝖘𝖈𝖍𝖗𝖊𝖈𝖐𝖑𝖎𝖈𝖍

The final compressed stanza is spoken as if to indicate the slighting scorn they deservedly receive:

> Viennese bow from the hips,
> notorieties
> contorted laudatory lips,
> wreaths and bouquets surround
> the mindless menopause.
> Stillborn fecundities,
> frostbound applause.

Although the contrast between Parts is not as remarkable as in the other sonatas, certain points of technique are interesting. Besides the suggestion of jazz in the first Part, the brief descriptive passage of the Berlin winter is technically beautiful:

> ('to keep warm')
> under street trees whimpering to the keen wind
> over snow whispering to many feet,

The near rhyme of 'to keep warm' and 'to the keen wind' is linked by the assonance of 'keep'/'street'/'trees'/'keen'. The parallel syntax of the last two lines is enriched by the opposition of 'under street' – 'over snow' and by the variation of rhythm between 'whimpering to the keen wind' and 'whispering to many feet'. The winter setting, fitting for a lifeless society, is capitalised on in the last section. After bringing in this motif through the 'frost in Berlin', Bunting incorporates it in the last line to epitomise the lifelessness of the society: 'frostbound applause'.

No great masterpiece, *Aus Dem Zweiten Reich* would perhaps fare better if it was considered by itself instead of being dwarfed by comparison with the other sonatas. If Christopher Isherwood's *Berlin Stories* could be renamed *I am a Camera* for a dramatic version because of its objectivity and detailed observation of scenes, the same qualities in Bunting's poem could merit for it a similar retitling. However, just as Bunting differs from Eliot in never becoming so withdrawn as to be uninvolved and indifferent, in this case too Bunting differs from both Eliot and Isherwood by more humanly revealing his distastes and mocking scorn. In comparison with the other sonatas, the theme is slight, but for the vividness and immediacy of each vignette and urbane, controlled tone of distaste, it ranks among his best.

THE WELL OF LYCOPOLIS

Bunting's constant effort is toward achieving organic unity within each poem. In a letter to me he unequivocally states: 'Always the complete architecture is implied in every line' [23 May 1972]. In *The Well of Lycopolis* this emphasis is especially important. Here the search for a 'nice logical syllogistic development'[21] is futile, yet the cumulative effect is difficult to miss. Each part is essential to this overall effect, and just a glance at the number of discarded lines should convince anyone that Bunting's goal is to eliminate all nonessentials from the sonata, to remove anything that does not contribute to the architecture of the whole. Three versions of the poem, whole or in part, are in the Louis Zukofsky Collection at the University of Texas at Austin. In Part I the meeting of Venus, the Muse Polymnia, and the poet-lover is grounded in a vivid realism:

> Slinking by the jug-and-bottle
> swingdoor I fell in with
> Mother Venus, ageing, bedraggled, a
> half-quartern of gin under her shawl,

As mythical figures, the old women have a symbolic value dramatised by Polymnia's emphatic words:

> 'What have you come for? Why have you brought the Goddess? You who
> finger the goods you cannot purchase,
> snuffle the skirt you dare not clutch.'

Polymnia's nostalgic lament:

> Leave me alone. A long time ago
> there were men in the world, dances, guitars, ah!

echoes Venus's: 'It's the times have changed. I remember during the War...'

The double level of realistic drama and metaphorical meaning continues through Part II which begins with the persona cursing both goddesses. For his inadequate response to love and poetry, he blames unfavourable happenings out of his control:

> Windy water slurred the glint of Canopus,
> am I answerable? Left, the vane
> screwing perpetually ungainlywards.
> What reply will a
> June hailstorm countenance?

In this part Polymnia is asked to open her eyes to the actions of 'sleek, slick lads', pale, smooth, and effeminate like Butler's 'smockfaced boys' [LZ, 28 October 1935], hardly a healthy condition for love and poetry. Images from Longus's Greek pastoral romance, *Daphnis and Chloe*, and of virgin and virgin who 'taste/ wine without headache' lead to the description of decadent Bloomsbury and all it stands for in love and the art:

> We have laid on Lycopolis water.
> The nights are not fresh
> between High Holborn and the Euston Road,
> nor the days bright even in summer
> nor the grass of the squares green.

The Latin phrase from Lucretius, '*aequora pontis*' (the level ocean),[22] adds a special colour to the forceful image in the last section of Part II. Taken from the invocation to Venus as the personification of the creative force of Nature, it transfigures the setting and involves Venus as an alluring natural force in the struggle being described. The strong tension in the lines themselves adds a further dimension to the conflict:

> Neither (*aequora pontis*)
> on the sea's bulge
> would the 'proud, full sail'
> avail
> us, stubborn against the trades,
> closehauled,
> stiff, flat canvas;
> our fingers bleed
> under the nail
> when we reef.

Part III revolves about the persona's complaints first to 'Infamous poetry, abject love', and then afterwards to 'Abject poetry, infamous love', with images of debasement set one after another to create a vision of degraded love and poetry. A jazz parody of a popular song, 'The Liverpool girls have got us in tow' [LZ, 28 October 1935] as 'The Gadarene swihine have got us in tow' brings this part to a climax. Besides associating men with images of dehumanisation and subjugation from the Bible, the image also faintly suggests the power of Circe.

Although it is not far from the 'swihine' of Part III to the damned and the mud of Part IV, the simultaneous juxtaposing of the parody of a popular song and the direct quotations from Dante's poetry in Italian and in English require a mental leap of some distance. Men muttering in the quagmire suggest the reality of Flanders, especially when all their mutterings concern wartime happenings, but the context of the poem suggests that many more than those involved directly with war are involved in the poem's satire. Throughout this last part the poet hints that an opposite condition exists:

> But the rivers of Paradise,
> the sweep of the mountains they rise in?
> Drunk or daft hear
> a chuckle of spring water:
> drowsy suddenly wake,
> but the bright peaks have faded.

The play on the theme of water in the last lines suggests, no matter how obscurely, an anti-theme which will be better described in the subsequent discussion of the moods and tones of this sonata:

> Look where you will you see it.
> The surface sparkles and dances with their sighs
> as though Styx were silvered by a wind from Heaven.

The Well of Lycopolis, originally much longer, was designated from the first as a sonata with a directive, later removed, for each part except the first: Part II – *'Damn slow movement'*; Part III – *'Slump'*; and Part IV – *'Dead March and Polka'*. These alone would have been enough to disclose the predominant mood of the poem. In addition, the title together with the first two epigraphs points to the reason for the despondency. The epigraph of the entire poem is from a footnote in Edward Gibbon's *Decline and Fall of the Holy Roman Empire*:

> *cujus potu signa*
> *virginitatis eripiuntur*
> [by whose potion the seal of virginity is broken]

Immediately following this is the epigraph of Part I from Villon's *'Les Regrets de la Belle Heaulmière'*:

> *Advis m'est que j'oy regretter*

Bunting translated these lines for me as 'Oh dear! where do these mournful sighs come from? I am reminded (or I notice) that I heard

(the beauty) regretting...' (4 July 1973). The way the directives
build up a cumulative effect is, on a small scale, the way in which
the parts of the poem create the final, larger one. The original
designation of each part reveals gradations of mood and tone
which, by omitting, Bunting let the reader discover from the poetry
itself. Coloured by the epigraph, the drama of Part I provides the
introduction to the sonata in the mood of *'Les Regrets'*. The first
lines of Part II, which shift the focus from the lamenting goddesses
to the chief persona of the first part, slow down the tempo
considerably and add a further heaviness:

> May my libation of flat beer stood overnight
> sour on your stomach, my devoutly worshipped ladies,
> may you retch cold bile.

There is no way in which these lines, especially the last, can be
hurried. In this part and in Part II, even parodies of light, popular
songs are laced with such sarcasm that in these also the heavy mood
continues. In Part III, previously the 'Slump' movement, the
despondency becomes deeper, but an underlying anger and
ridicule often rises to the surface, quickening the tempo and
providing a strong tension:

> – with their snouts in the trough,
> kecking at gummy guts,
> slobbering offal, gobbling potato parings,
> yellow cabbage leaves, choking on onion skin,
> herring bones, slops of porridge.
> Way-O! Bully boys blow!
> The Gadarene swihine have got us in tow.

In Part IV Bunting intersperses his translation of lines 117-26 of
Canto VII of the *Inferno* with no parody of Dante's poetry, but only
a redirection of its meaning so that it satirises human nature and
the social condition:

> Stuck in the mud they are saying: 'We were sad
> in the air, the sweet air the sun makes merry,
> we were glum of ourselves, without a reason;
> now we are stuck in the mud and therefore sad.'
> That's what they mean, but the words die in their throat;
> they cannot speak out because they are stuck in the mud.
> [*Inferno*, VII, 121-26]

Although Part IV expresses the heaviest and angriest tone of the
sonata, it is relieved by the possibility of a condition opposite to the
one described in most of the poem. From the first line of the
epigraph of Part IV, the persona speaks as one who is separated
from those 'under the water'. Near the end of the poem this

epigraph, translated, is incorporated as part of the climax:

> and besides I want you to know for certain
> there are people under the water. They are sighing.
>
> [*Inferno*, VII, 117-18]

The possibility of a contrasting condition is woven continuously throughout this part except in the central section. This section together with approximately thirty discarded lines may have composed most of the 'Polka' that Bunting had designated as a contrast to the original 'Dead March' of the beginning and end. From this polka-like interval introduced originally by the line, 'Manly Mars for Coda!' he eliminated lines which introduced but weakened the concretely imaged section though they stated his satirical attitude more explicitly:

> War
> Natural, necessary, glorious war,
> ennobles and elevates man.

After this muttering of the dead voices, the first slow rhythm and serious tone of Part IV are resumed and the missing lines, 119-20, of Canto VII become part of the poem's climax. Here, the overall mood of pessimism is played against the loveliest lines of the poem:

> The surface bubbles and boils with their sighs.
> Look where will you see it. [*Inferno*, VII, 119-20]
> The surface sparkles and dances with their sighs
> as though Styx were silvered by a wind from Heaven.

Bunting told me:

> It might be worth noting that in Dante the boiling sighs of the Styx *are* presently submitted to a wind from Heaven, when the angel arrives to open the gate of Dis. The whole passage of the Inferno is indelibly in my mind. The gorgon in Attis is from the same page. (Whereas EP, who could remember the angel, had forgotten all the rest, which I think is bound up with the angel indissolubly.) [4 July 1973]

In his recent 'debate', Geoffrey Hill defends Simone Weil's idea that 'simultaneous composition on several planes at once is the law of artistic creation, and wherein, in fact, lies its difficulty'.[22] He sees this as a foundation for the conception of lyric poetry as 'necessarily dramatic': 'Indeed the "different planes" actually available to a director on his theatre-stage could even be regarded as an indication of what takes place "simultaneously" in the arena of the poem.' It is on one of these planes that *The Well of Lycopolis* does not come up to the standard set by Bunting's best sonatas. In a different way from his other poems, voices and tones are interlayered and echo against each other; but in the other sonatas the reader is never distracted from enjoying the poem in an effort to discern the predominant tone and voice. In Part I the overlaid tones create a rich texture. For example, in the drama of this part the lines spoken by the two old women are recorded by a persona whose own attitude is created by the anonymous poet. On another level, the two old women are the goddesses of Love and Poetry, Venus and Polymnia, lamenting the good old days in the presence of a poet-lover persona who is recording their words in tones expressed actually by another voice further removed. Beneath all this is Bunting's parody of Villon who himself in '*Les Regrets de la Belle Heaulmière*' is speaking in the persona of a woman whose words he is pretending to dictate to his imaginary clerk, Fremin. Through this accumulation of voices and tones with their texture of relationships, Bunting's thoughts and feelings about the condition of love and poetry in this era is expressed.

During Part I these multiple voices mesh together well. But when the dramatic scene is removed in Part II, ambiguity develops. The tones of voice, rather than compose a rich texture, tend to blur. It is not always clear if the speaker is including himself in the castigation of society ('We have laid on Lycopolis water'), or if he is standing aloof, pointing at the weaknesses. In this second case, he sometimes speaks with scathing ridicule in the first person:

> Open your eyes, Polymnia,
> at the sleek, slick lads treading gingerly between the bedpots,
> stripped buff-naked all but their hats to raise,
> and nothing rises but the hats;
> smooth, with soft steps, *ambiguoque voltu.*

Most often he speaks in the voice of the type being mocked:

> I shall never have anything to myself
>
> but stare in the tank, see
> Hell's constellations,
> a dogstar for the Dogstar:
> women's faces
> blank or trivial,
> still or rippled water,
> a fool's image.

The ambiguity lessens the bite of the satire because the predominant tone is not clear enough to colour and unify the others. Commenting on all this, Bunting wrote to me: 'I am inescapably part of a detested generation. To see, and to have a mirror amongst what you see, is less than usual in satire. Hence the difficulty' [4

July 1973]. In his next sonata, especially in Part I, Bunting is able to work with many voices so that each contributes a particular note which blends into an unmistakable unified tone.

CHAPTER 7

The Spoils

By February 1951, Bunting had completed half of the first draft of
what he referred to for a long time as the 'Fifth Sonata'.[1] Although
originally planned in four movements, he explained to me it was
finalised in only three, and entitled *The Spoils* [23 May 1972]. He
gives some background for his selection of the title in a letter to
Zukofsky:

> Poem's title at last: *The Spoils*. Motto from the Qor'an: Al-anfal li-llah,
> the spoils are for God (to God, God's. God gets the booty.) (Fifth
> Sonata wasn't intended for a permanent name, mere means of
> identification. But I do claim copyright, and bugger TSE. He was
> before me with Preludes, but I'd a bunch of Sonatas before he thought
> up his Quartets.) [22 March 1951]

Later Bunting conceded to Zukofsky's objections about the title up
to a certain point:

> If the title as set down sounds religiose, I'll not translate the Arabic
> motto at all. But I don't see why the word, "God" which has a million
> meanings need be abandoned to the pious. *The Spoils*, all alone, is a little
> more enigmatic than I'd intended, but a title is nearly always an enigma
> anyway. [19 April 1951]

This title does cover adequately the general intention of the
poem which Bunting 'in great haste and without much thought,
merely for [Zukofsky]' [19 April 1951] attempted to indicate while
the poem was in progress. In the simplest terms, *The Spoils* is an
expression of human attitudes toward life and toward death. When
the poem is considered in its entirety, the emphasis on the
interdependency of these attitudes is clear. Throughout the poem
the choice of one, life or death, as the more important, necessarily
subordinates the other, and subsequently colours attitudes toward
all related values. Finally though, whichever one is placed first, life
or death, the spoils are God's no matter in what terms 'God' is
defined.

In this sonata Bunting contrasts differing attitudes toward life

and death in Eastern and Western societies by presenting a
fundamentally Eastern point of view which by implication underlines the general Western attitude. The stress throughout is on the
Eastern point of view because this is the attitude that Bunting
believes must inform the point of view of his own culture to give it a
wholeness it now lacks. Within the overall Eastern point of view
Bunting contrasts the two chief variations in the first two
movements. In each of these movements he compares and
contrasts variations within that point of view.

The first movement describes the attitudes of those Easterners
who measure life against the unalterable fact of death which they
accept as the ultimate end-all of existence. The second movement
describes the attitudes of Easterners who believe in life itself as a
higher value, yet who finally accept the fact of death as inevitable.
The contrasts in these first two movements are somewhat explained
by Bunting in answer to Zukofsky's question about the 'general
intention' of the poem:

> General intention? If I could put it in prose I wouldn't take the trouble
> to write a poem. First movement, the *anschauung* or better the
> *vorstellung*, general no doubt, but more or less particularly characteristic
> of the Semitic peoples, which takes life as a journey (to Zion, to Jinnat)
> best performed with few impedimenta, and is indifferent to the
> furniture at the inn. (The second movement contrasts that with the
> people who go in for architecture and furnish as though they intended to
> live here forever.) The advantage of the journey idea is that death
> becomes a familiar, almost a friend. No Lucretian cold-comfort
> required. Limits, their arts are those of the camp-fire (They write poetry
> and play the fiddle.) They cannot share the illusion of tree-like semi-
> permanence needed by a good cultivator, and so when they cease to be
> shepherds they become merchants (fundamentally, therefore, parasites,
> on beasts or on farmers, which may have something to do with the
> irritation they so commonly arouse: but I've not attempted to display
> that aspect.) This is alien to my bent, but I believe I see the good, and I
> think it idiotic to denounce (à la Voltaire-Ezra, as you observe) what has
> nobility and discipline. [13 March 1951]

Later in the letter he discusses the general intention of Part II.

> And part two, eastern also so as not to provoke irrelevant contrasts, as
> well as because the matter is fresh in my mind; life well-padded, itself a
> source of enjoyment, to which the thought of death comes close to the
> end, and which must then invent specious (though often beautiful)
> comforts. This familiar enough and also a regular source of sentimen-
> talities. To avoid them is not entirely easy, at least without sardonic
> remarks which would be out of tone and might seem to deny the general
> desirability of a good life.

Besides the contrasts of these two movements, Bunting planned

to include war as another aspect of life which necessarily includes
an attitude toward death:

> But I want also war: not as a horror, not as an opportunity for self-
> congratulating glory (dear Hem[ingway] again, I'm afraid), but simply as
> an activity which has pleasures of its own, an exercise of certain faculties
> which need exercise: in which death is neither a bugbear nor a
> consummation, but just happens...part of the fun.

This material eventually becomes the content of the third and final
movement of the sonata.

Although the mosaic pattern of Eastern poetry discussed in
Chapter 3 is discoverable in each of Bunting's sonatas, because of
the subject matter perhaps, it is especially evident in *The Spoils*.
Part I in particular sets up a definite mosaic pattern. In this first
part Bunting uses four speakers to express the various attitudes of
Eastern peoples who see life as a journey and death as a
companion. According to the poet (LZ, 13 March 1951), these four
speakers represent an 'arbitrary choice among the duly registered
legitimate sons of Shem', the son of Noah, whose names appear in
Genesis 10. 31. Bunting makes this explicit in the epigraph which
follows the Arabic motto:

> *These are the sons of Shem, after*
> *their families, after their tongues,*
> *in their lands, after their nations.*

However arbitrary the choice of names may have been, the group
that each represents is not: 'Asshur suggests the merchant-soldier.
Aram the later prophets, and hence my stand for later Judaism,
down to the Zionists. Lud...suggests to me Lot, Sodom, the city
Arab' [LZ, 13 March 1951]. Somewhat later Bunting describes
Arpachshad: '(By the way, luck or instinct or what not, Arpachshad
turns out to be claimed as an ancestor by the Harb, the Aniza, and
the Shammar (the three largest desert tribes) and also by the
Koraish. Muse taking care of me?)' [LZ, 19 April 1951]. At another
time he stated their types in single words: 'the Bedoin, the
Baghdadi and the adventurer'; the fourth speaker, Aram, represented 'the better modern Jewish mind (or emotions)' [13 March
1951]. Although all four view life as a journey and death as a
familiar, the interest lies in the variety of outlooks within this
similar point of view and in the way in which Bunting builds each
part of his design on the viewpoint preceding it until the mosaic of
the Eastern viewpoint is complete.

The four opening lines of Part I establish the main themes and
are the heart of the mosaic pattern on which each speaker builds

until the total pattern of this basic point of view is perfected. In
musical terms these first four lines of the sonata state the theme of
the first movement just as the motto states the theme of the entire
sonata. The four-line opening includes an Eastern attitude toward
life, but more importantly, an attitude toward death:

> Man's life so little worth,
> do we fear to take or lose it?
> No ill companion on a journey, Death
> lays his purse on the table and opens the wine

Here death is as real as a human companion on a journey. His
continuous presence does not prevent enjoyment of possessions
and sensual pleasure, but provides a perspective that is a constant
reminder of the impermanence of all things.

Emphasis on 'Death' rather than 'life' in these lines is stressed by
the revision Bunting made in an earlier version. As is the case with
all revisions throughout the poem, this too is in favour of greater
economy of expression. Instead of

> Death is no ill companion on a journey.
> He lays his purse on the table and opens the wine,

the revised lines lay a heavier dramatic emphasis on 'Death' by
making it the climactic last word and by forcing the reader to linger
on the concept in order to complete the next line:

> No ill companion on a journey, Death
> lays his purse on the table and opens the wine.

Moreover, this revision further subordinates 'life', already sharing
the emphasis of a pair of spondees in 'Man's life', besides better
coordinating the rhythm of the two verb phrases, 'lays his purse on
the table and opens the wine'.

Once the basic Eastern viewpoint has been established, the first
speaker, Asshur, the merchant-soldier representative, begins his
variation of the theme. His section is divided into two major parts:
the description of his own present situation as an assessor and the
contrasting situation of the soldier. Each of these parts contains
further contrasts. In the first half the speaker is set against each of
those he is assessing and in the second half, the two-part camp
sequence, he is opposed to the 'then' – 'now' section of the last
lines. This kind of mosaic design can be traced in finer and finer
detail to show its beauty and intricacy. Formally, it is as if the
techniques acquired from translating Persian poetry have been
meshed with the basic techniques refined under Pound's influence
to become in *The Spoils* Bunting's own unique method. The

content combines his own background as a soldier, consul, journalist, and poet in the Middle East with his opinions about modern civilisation reinforced by living with Pound and his friends.

After the four-line introduction Asshur, the first speaker, begins to describe an Eastern scene in which he places himself immediately:

As I sat at my counting frame to assess the people,

For ten lines he creates a design suggestive of Persian poetry by balancing half-line against half-line and line against line:

marking the register, listening to their lies,
a bushel of dried apricots, marking the register,
three rolls of Egyptian cloth, astute in their avarice;

The incremental repetition of 'marking the register' added to the sound effects of alliteration and assonance enhances the music of this section. Ten participles within ten lines unify them through sound and structural parallelisms; for example:

counting and calling the sum,
ringing and weighing coin,

Within this series only two phrases could not have been completely visualised by a camera, 'listening to their lies' and 'astute in their avarice'. These two subjective comments reveal an attitude of a speaker who is consistently set against his partner 'Abdoel squatting before piled pence' and those he is dealing with, men whose lives revolve around gain. This entire group is contrasted with the person introduced in the eleventh line:

one stood in the door
scorning our occupation,
silent:

In most respects this new figure is different from the speaker. Identified as a soldier by his 'greaves' of 'polished bronze', the newcomer subtly gains superiority over the speaker-assessor by reflecting 'a man like [him] reckoning pence' in his lower leg-armour. The reflection contrasts the soldier with a man who has never experienced the adventure of living precariously:

never having tasted bread
where there is ice in his flask,

To explain this last line to Zukofsky Bunting wrote: 'Mine froze at Wadi Mohammerah as late as March, and it's not uncommon in the Syrian desert or that of Northern Arabia, let alone the high desert of Persia' [3 March 1951].

This transitional passage from the Eastern market to the high desert pivots on quite an original cinematic device: 'so in his greaves I saw...' Once the scene has shifted, the movement continues with an even greater emphasis on colour: dazzling white of snow, yellow and blue, besides copper which complements the bronze of the greaves.

The dawn sequence is alive with imitative rhythms ('Camels raise their necks from the ground') and transitive verbs with imitative sounds ('cooks scour kettles, soldiers oil their arms'). Dawn itself is described in military terms:

> snow lights high over the north,
> yellow spreads in the desert, driving blue westward
> among banks, surrounding patches of blue,
> advancing in enemy land.

The breaking-camp sequence parallels the dawn sequence, but a strong contrast is achieved by no mention of people and the use of the passive voice:

> Kettles flash, bread is eaten,
> scarabs are scurrying rolling dung.[2]

The appearance of 'thirty gorged vultures' seems only a vivid detail until the focus shifts in the middle of a line to the speaker; then the relation between their life pattern and that of the desert people is clear:

> Thirty gorged vultures on an ass's carcass
> jostle, stumble, flop aside, drunk with flesh,
> too heavy to fly, wings deep with inner gloss.
> Lean watches, then debauch:
> after long alert, stupidity:
> waking, soar. If here you find me
> intrusive and dangerous, seven years was I bonded
> for Leah, seven toiled for Rachel:
> now in a brothel outside under the wall
> have paused to bait on my journey.

In these last lines of Asshur's speech, Bunting's use of 'bait' introduces a series of long a's which musically rounds off the section:

> have paused to bait on my journey.
> Another shall pay the bill if I can evade it.

The second son of Shem, Lud, the city Arab, begins his first speech with a striking description of the yearly flooding of the Tigris:

> When Tigris floods snakes swarm in the city.

According to Bunting, this scene has been common for centuries:
'The description of Baghdad in the spring floods would stand for
Ctesiphon or Nineveh – dead Kurds have floated down every year
since before Xenophon at least' [LZ, 3 March 1951].

As vivid as the vignettes were that Asshur depicted, the city and
village scenes that Lud describes are even stronger in their appeal
to each of the senses; for example:

> Dead camels, dead Kurds,
> unmanageable rafts of logs
> hinder the ferryman, a pull and a grunt,
> a stiff tow upshore against the current.
> Naked boys among water-buffaloes,
> daughters without smile
> treading clothes by the verge,
> harsh smouldering dung:
> a woman taking bread from her oven
> spreads dates, an onion, cheese.
> Silence under the high sun. When the ewes go out
> along the towpath striped with palm-trunk shadows
> a herdsman pipes, a girl shrills
> under her load of greens.

On another level, the aural reinforcement of the sensory beauty is
equally outstanding. In the first line the *s* sound in five words
simulates the sound of snakes:

> When Tigris floods snakes swarm in the city,

and in the second line not only the colours, but the sounds and
number of syllables in a word create a miniature design:

> coral, jade, jet, between jet and jade, yellow,

This long *o* of 'yellow' is repeated in the last word of the next two
lines, 'Toads', and 'Jerboas', and is echoed several lines later in
another last word: 'water-buffaloes'. Such alliterative patterns as

> weary, unwary, may be taught to feed
> from a fingertip. Dead camels, dead Kurds,

are enriched by cross patterns of whole syllables:

> unmanageable rafts of logs
> hinder the ferryman,

The final sentence is Lud's comment on his particular Eastern
viewpoint on life, and, by implication, death:

> There is no clamour
> in our market, no eagerness for gain;
> even whores surly, God frugal,
> keeping tale of prayers.

Arpachshad, the third son, begins in a matter-of-fact tone to
describe the day-to-day situation of his tribesmen:

> Bound to beasts' udders, rags no dishonour,
> not by much intercourse ennobled,
> multitude of books, bought deference:

Physical, emotional, and intellectual pleasures which are simple
but satisfying are underlined by the directness and simplicity of the
poetry:

> meagre flesh tingling to a mouthful of water,
> apt to no servitude, commerce or special dexterity,
> at night after prayers recite the sacred
> enscrolled poems, beating with a leaping measure
> like blood in a new wound:
> *These were the embers...Halt, both, lament...:*
> moon-silver on sand-pale gold,
> plash against parched Arabia.

Answering some queries from Zukofsky, Bunting supplies interesting background for these lines:

> *The mo'allaqat* (singular cat, plural cart) were written in highly
> ornamented character on gilded scrolls to be hung at Mecca. 'Halt,
> both, lament...' tries to give the Arabic dual while preserving the
> abruptness of that most celebrated opening, which is currently rendered
> (O ye Muses!) 'Pause, O ye two, and let us bewail...' Incidentally the
> moon-silver pool on the sand-pale gold of the desert, below, is an
> imitation of Manuchehri's imitation of another line from this famous
> and lovely poem. [13 March 1951]

Judged from the compression of the final version, this earlier one,
although so lyrical, must have seemed too rich to Bunting:

> *Halt, both, lament,*
> a fountain sprung, spurts of clear sound,
> rhyme-plash in a still pool
> moon-silver on sand-pale gold
> against the parched bakehouse taste of Arabia.

The shrug of Arpachshad's final comment sums up his
tribesmen's attitude: 'What's to dismay us?'

Since Bunting has stated that the matter of the poem is 'more or
less permanent' [LZ, 13 March 1951], fittingly, parodies of Old
and New Testament lines compose the speech of Aram, the type of
the latter day prophets. Echoes of Psalm 137 interweave with those
of Matthew's parable of the hired labourers in the vineyard (20. 1-
6) to become a lament for all eras:

> By the dategroves of Babylon
> there we sat down and sulked
> while they were seeking to hire us

to a repugnant trade.
Are there no plows in Judah, seed or a sickle,
no ewe to the pail, press to the vineyard?
Sickly our Hebrew voices far from the Hebrew hills!

In this section repetition of motifs becomes more noticeable. For example, the 'ewes' so integral to the life Lud described, which 'go out along the towpath striped with palm-trunk shadows', are mourned by Aram as a part of a life pattern that is missing. Although the synonym 'hogg' will replace the word in one instance, the 'ewe' motif will continue as a connecting note in each of Lud's next speeches, and the 'vineyard' motif will be repeated in Aram's. Aram first mentions Babylon by name in the derogatory biblical sense, and Asshur and Lud, the next two speakers, repeat this motif to create a counterpoint of complaints, each type focusing on his peculiar grievance. Asshur, the merchant figure, in a biblical parody mocks the merchants who place all their trust in possessions:

We bear witness against the merchants of Babylon
that they have planted ink and reaped figures.

Lud speaks out

Against the princes of Babylon, that they have tithed of the best
leaving sterile ram, weakly hogg to the flock.

and Arpachshad simply adds a rhythmical listing of businessmen to those Asshur and Lud have already indicated: 'Fullers, tailors, hairdressers, jewellers, perfumers'. Aram, returning to his more pronounced biblical themes, repeats the art motif of Arpachshad's first speech and climaxes this second series of brief speeches by a telling comment on the artist's situation, as familiar in the time of David as in a more modern era:

David dancing before the Ark, they toss him pennies.
A farthing a note for songs as of the thrush.

The third and final round of speeches focuses on the simple, physical pleasures already prepared for in several earlier ones; e.g., Lud's and Arpachshad's. The Eastern attitude toward life as a journey with death as an inevitable ending colours each group's attitudes toward sensual pleasure as a normal part of life. When Bunting explained his rejection of "amendments" Zukofsky suggested, he shared some important insights about this last series of speeches:

Within the [first] movement, the relief is the sensual counterpart (or counterpoint) of that way of life: which seems to me more needed in the modern west. You Ashkenazim have put it partly aside because it shocks the people you live among: and since it is nevertheless a part of your inheritance, the effort to suppress it in an individual is apt to make a Jewish prude the most ticklish of all. We need sensuality because without it we stumble into the ways of hollering he-man Hemingway sentimentality, or else the medical text-book school which forces itself unwillingly to admit, item by item, what is really half our life. (The last I expressed a dislike for in 'Lycopolis') [...] Fucking on principle and fucking to keep one's courage up are both repulsive to me, and, I believe, damaging to mankind. Since I'm not after notoriety and suppression, I confine myself to thighs since I can just get away with them...What I mean can be presented, not said. [13 March 1951]

In each of these speeches the speaker presents the variation of his group's attitude toward sensual enjoyment, a reflection of his attitude toward life and death. Besides this emphasis, dominant motifs are interwoven to unify the movement in this last series of speeches. Although Asshur is addressed this time as 'Soldier', echoes of his merchant role connect his first speech with this one. As a merchant he has already mentioned 'copper', 'bronze', and the metallic sound of 'coin'. Here he is concerned with another kind of 'gold', 'golden skin scoured in sandblast', a repetition of the motif Arpachshad introduced with 'sand-pale gold', and another kind of 'bronze', 'Very much like going to bed with a bronze.'

One of the first versions of Asshur's speech more specifically connected the 'golden skin' with the 'vulture's wing' of the next line:

Golden skin scoured in a sandblast
glowed like a vulture's wing.

The 'vulture's wing' itself is an echo of the 'wings deep with inner gloss' of Asshur's first speech.

'The child cradled beside her sister' and the girl's gesture of tossing the pence aside are incidental aspects which spell out the attitude of the East towards men's sensual pleasure as an integral part of a life of poverty for some women from childhood, and for which payment is scorned, but accepted for survival.

Lud's description of his bride faintly suggests the ancient lines of the Song of Songs, but the intricate weaving of motifs from within *The Spoils* itself is more immediate. Repetition of 'kettle', 'bed', 'bread from the oven', and 'meagre' lightly keynote Eastern life, while the bride, 'alert without smile', recalls the 'daughters without smile' Lud described earlier. 'Jet, jade', and 'coral' appear on his bride's forehead in this speech, and her married life pattern is appropriately summarised in simple phrases. The expression of her eyes mocking 'the beribboned dancing boys' not only reveals her full knowledge of the situation but the almost passive acceptance of the life style which this child-bride is powerless to change:

> My bride is borne behind the pipers,
> kettles and featherbed,
> on her forehead jet, jade, coral under the veil;
> to bring ewes to the pail, bread from the oven.
> Breasts scarcely hump her smock,
> thighs meagre, eyes
> alert without smile
> mock the beribboned dancing boys.

Like Lud, Arpachshad repeats motifs chiefly from his own earlier speeches, 'gold', 'silver', 'moon', 'sand', and 'embers', to continue to unify the movement. 'Breasts' and 'thighs', key words of the 'counterpoint' of Part I, appear here, as in every speech in this last series.

The scope of Aram's last speech is even broader than his previous ones. Describing conditions as suitable to Old Testament times when Abishag 'lent her warmth to dying David' (I Kings 1. 1-4) as to the present, he looks forward to a distant future:

> Chattering in the vineyard,
> breasts swelled, halt and beweep
> captives, sickly, closing repugnant thighs.
> Who lent her warmth to dying David, let her seed
> sleep on the Hebrew hills, wake under Zion.

Echoes of former speeches would have been even more pronounced if Aram's last line had remained: 'sleep on Hebrew hills, and waking soar', but the revision strengthens the overall Jewish emphasis, as well as the pattern of sound. By this time, the simple repetition of 'vineyard', 'halt and beweep', 'warmth', 'seed', and 'Hebrew hills' is easily recognised as a point of added enjoyment.

Each of these groups treats sensual pleasure as something natural and transitory, but the focus of each is on a particular aspect: casual intercourse, marriage, vital passion; Aram's speech suggests the modern Jewish dilemma that Bunting pointed out in his letter and to which American Jewish writers are giving expression in modern literature.

Finally, the last four lines of Part I which parallel the opening complete the symmetrical frame of the movement. The theme of life as a journey is universalised to include the ideas of all four speakers:

> What's begotten on a journey but souvenirs?

The attitude introduced in the first four lines becomes a stronger conclusion with actions described in this section symbols of a philosophy of life:

> Life we give and take, pence in a market,
> without noting beggar, dealer, changer;

Death in the first lines 'lays his purse on the table and opens the wine'; here the unrebellious Eastern response to this life's 'companion' is as simple and direct as the poetic line:

> pence we drop in the sawdust with spilt wine.

Part II provides a rich contrast with Part I in accordance with the freedom of the preclassical sonata form Bunting uses as a model. Movement contrasts with movement, not according to any rigidly formal rules, but freely in a variety of ways. Instead of four speakers as in Part I, an anonymous persona addresses the reader directly, yet at times almost as if he is allowing his musings to be overheard. The variety of tones which each speaker employs in Part I is opposed in Part II to the closely related tones of only one speaker. The length of lines, in general, is shorter in Part II which consequently effects a contrast in rhythm and in cadences. Although both parts have 121 lines, in Part I sixty-two lines have ten or more syllables whereas in Part II only seventeen lines contain ten or more, and all these lines occur after line 72, more than half way through the movement. This not only affords a contrast with Part I but points up one within the movement itself, another reflection of the loose early sonata form.

These technical contrasts serve to underline the deeper one between Parts I and II, that of the differing attitudes toward life and death in these Eastern groups which Bunting had summarised in his letter to Zukofsky. His description of Part II as 'life well-padded; itself a source of enjoyment, to which the thought of death comes close to the end, and which must then invent specious (though often beautiful) comforts' focuses chiefly on the arts, central to their culture. Rather than the impermanent arts 'of the campfire' [LZ, 3 March 1951] this Eastern group creates lasting masterpieces which make clear their predominant interest in this life. Their energies were, however, expended in creating works of beauty, not in gaining easily dissipated wealth for its own sake. This is the contrasting fact Bunting uses throughout Part II to counterpoint the description of their creativity with ironic comments about foreigners' tasks:

> They despise police work,
> are not masters of filing:

always a task for foreigners
to make them unhappy,
unproductive and rich.

Eastern arts described in this movement range from kinds of architecture to miniature-painting, music and varieties of literature. Furthermore, graceful life styles suggesting gracious, unhurried living point up further their predominant interest in deeply savouring this life:

> On a terrace over a pool
> vafur, vodka, tea,
> resonant verse spilled
> from Onsori, Sa'di,
> till the girls' mutter is lost
> in whisper of stream and leaf,

Although Bunting claimed that this poem depends 'less on erudition than on the language and imagery employed',[3] some knowledge of Eastern culture would certainly enhance the reader's appreciation of all that is included in Bunting's lines; this is more true of Part II than of I or III. The number of proper names mentioned here is a proof of this: Avicenna, Nezam-ol-Molk, Taj-ol-Molk, Veramin, Malekshah, Khayyam, Qor'an, La Giralda, Abu Ali, Seljuks, Hajji Mosavvor, Naystani, Taj, Hafez, Moluk-e-Zarrabi, Shir-e Khoda, Sobhi, Onsori, and Sa'di. Generally, they are in contexts which explain their essential significance; for example:

> Flute,
> shade dimples under chenars
> breath of Naystani chases and traces
> as a pair of gods might dodge and tag between stars.
> Taj is to sing, Taj,
> when tar and drum
> come to their silence, slow,
> clear, rich, as though
> he had cadence and phrase from Hafez.

For the enjoyment of the way the sound reinforces the meaning in these lines no further background is necessary. However, Bunting's elaboration of this scene in a letter to Zukofsky two years later strengthens the imaginative reinforcement of this poetry. To his Note in the *Collected Poems*, 'Naystani: a celebrated virtuoso of the nose-flute', he adds:

> A *Tar* is a stringed instrument played with bow and pizzicato, the basis of Persian classical music as the fiddle is of ours. Borrowed by the Arabs, it was modified into the lute. Reduced to three strings (se tar) it re-evolved into zither and guitar by different roads. The word tar

originally meant merely a gut string, but the present instrument must be at least as old as Hafez and probably a few centuries more. A *nay* is a flute (nose-flute) cut from a cane (nay) and is at least as old as the tar. Both are in use, apart and together, in unison and in a kind of counterpoint, as solo instruments, as accompaniment to dancing and as the preface and coda and intermezzo of classical singing. The voice itself is usually, but not always, accompanied by the drum alone, and almost always begins, after a rather long rest, without even drums. But when the singer pauses the instruments get going again. I have, however, sometimes heard the instruments accompanying the voice, quietly, the nay making a kind of subdued descant, very florid.

I remember escaping, vexed, from an overcrowded illtempered hotel in Shiraz into its lovely garden, and there, under the huge chenars (oriental plane trees) whose shadows were making a dance of sundapples on the ground, I found Naystani, the virtuoso, just taking his flute from his pocket, and he played most beautifully for a couple of hours, the flute music as kaleidoscopic as the shadow pattern, getting in a single line that feeling of extreme multiplicity that Byrd gets in many parts, and that is nearer reflecting life than any simpler art. Nobody joined us, Naystani said nothing beyond 'Salaam', it was unlike the same thing over the radio: not addressed to an audience, but almost as though addressed to the trees and the sun. The great player celebrating the first of spring in his own natural talent. [6 August 1953]

Even in such a passage as

From Hajji Mosavvor's trembling wrist
grace of tree and beast
shines on ivory
in eloquent line.

Bunting's note that this 'greatest of modern miniature painters' 'suffered from paralysis agitans' is barely necessary. But a reader who knows that the title Hajji (pilgrim)[4] is generally given to a Moslem who has completed the pilgrimage to Mecca has added a new dimension to the lines, and, better yet, the one who has seen Persian miniatures will be best equipped to appreciate Bunting's ability to parallel in words the beauty of Mosavvor's art. This is true also of the arts of Moluk-e-Zarrabi, Shir-e Khoda, and Sobhi whose beauty Bunting has experienced and is attempting to share in poetry with his readers. In the same way, in the first half of Part II which introduces the Seljuk culture, Bunting is drawing on his wide knowledge of Persian history and culture to outline the attitude of the Seljuks and their cultural descendants toward life and death. Although broad erudition is not necessary for the enjoyment of the poetry, more knowledge than the poem and its notes provide can only enrich the reader's appreciation.

Bunting's note to Zukofsky, 'Second movement. Begins with the

Masjid-e Jom'a of Isfahan, a Seljuk building' [2 February 1951], would not be necessary to anyone who knew of the Friday Mosque, 'the oldest dated monument in Isfahan', 'the most important surviving mosque of this [classic architectural] type', and 'probably the major monument of Seljuk architecture in Iran'. In less qualified terms, it has been called 'the epitome of Persian architecture from Seljuk to early Safavid times' and 'among the finest products not only of Persia but also of all architecture'.[5] It is an appropriate choice for this poem because it represents a product of beauty and a creative system of building. A group which expends its energies on the creation of lasting monuments reveals its attitude about the importance of life on this earth.

To describe in the first twenty lines of Part II a building 'notable for its sheer formal beauty of structural perfection'[6] Bunting uses simple, direct language in which long vowels and unstopped consonants contribute to the smoothness of the description:

They filled the eyes of the vaulting
with alabaster panes,
each pencil of arches spouting
from a short pier,
and whitewashed the whole, using
a thread of blue to restore
lines nowhere broken,
for they considered capital
and base irrelevant.
The light is sufficient
to perceive the motions of prayer
and the place cool.
Tiles for domes and aivans
they baked in a corner,
older, where Avicenna may have worshipped.
The south dome, Nezam-ol-Molk's,
grows without violence from the walls
of a square chamber. Taj-ol-Molk
set a less perfect dome
over a forest of pillars.

His use of architectural terms in the first sentence, 'vaulting', 'pencil', 'arches', 'pier', culminates in a pun on 'capital' and 'base' which somewhat interrupts the description. However, the counter-pointing thread of ironic comments throughout the movement is not merely a Poundian throwback but an important means of contrast which incorporates the Western viewpoint of a group which also concentrates its energies on this life but does not obtain any like return in satisfaction and enjoyment. The pun also serves

G

to bring out the contrast in cultures by emphasising the primary meaning of the words in each one, in the East, a term of art, in the West, economics. Further, it is possible that this is a subtle link with an architectural contrast in the next section:

> For all that, the Seljuks avoided
> Roman exaggeration

This will become clearer in the discussion of those lines.

The Seljuk dome Bunting describes first has been called 'a miracle of construction'[7] in which 'the problem of setting a circular dome on a square base...that challenged generations of architects' was solved by the Seljuks. Bunting presupposes our appreciation of this feat when he writes simply:

> The south dome, Nezam-ol-Molk's,
> grows without violence from the walls
> of a square chamber.

Further, the vaults of the aivans anticipated developments in the Gothic world by centuries in the way that 'ribs were used as frames in which the masonry of the domes and vaults was supported'.[8] Bunting's awareness of the relation of the aivan to the Gothic arch is evident in a description he sent Zukofsky:

> *Aivan.* Gigantic arch, pointed, apparently remotest ancestor of gothic: formerly framing the crowned King for audience, as the ruined specimen at Ctesiphon, early AD: later giving access to the covered parts of a mosque and the mihrab. Seljuk mosques have several, later mosques two or only one. Tile decorated, the tiles matched and renewed as they crack or fall. Sometimes there is decoration in raised brick; Safavi mosques have the upper part of the aivan often filled with honeycomb-work, and some have the honeycomb set with mirrors, very lovely when there is enough cash to keep the mirrors silvered, as at the shrine of Imam Reza at Meshhed. [3 February 1951]

In the final version Bunting omitted these superfluous lines about the accomplishment of the aivan:

> Without this
> knowledge you cannot explain the Gothic
> and stand in some danger
> of sentimentalising the Middle Ages.

He also abbreviated the lines:

> At Veramin
> and Gulpaygan
> they built smaller mosques and Malekshah
> cut his prides in plaster
> which hardens by age, the same
> who found Khayyam a better reckoner
> than the Author of the Qor'an

to

> At Veramin
> Malekshah cut his pride in plaster
> which hardens by age, the same
> who found Khayyam a better reckoner
> than the Author of the Qor'an.

Beneath this simplicity and economy of description lies an historical level which Bunting draws on sparingly but whose filled-in outline fleshes out the movement. Under the Seljuk conquerors who imperfectly unified the Persian territories the Persians enjoyed greater cultural and economic development than previously. Bunting humanises this aspect by musing in the first person:

> I wonder what Khayyan thought
> of all the construction and organisation afoot,
> foreigners, resolute Seljuks, not so bloodthirsty
> as some benefactors of mankind; recalling
> perhaps Abu Ali's horror of munificent patrons;
> books unheard of or lost elsewhere
> in the library at Bokhara,
> and four hours writing a day
> before the duties of prime minister.

Wisely, the Seljuks appointed powerful viziers or prime ministers who were frequently Persian. Bunting mentions Malekshah (465-485/1072-1092) under whom the Seljuk Empire reached its zenith and Nezam-ol-Molk, his wise prime minister, whose prose work on government, *Siasat Namah*, is a classic. His sworn rival, Taj-ol-Molk, favourite of the Shah's most powerful wife, replaced him and attempted to surpass Nezam-ol-Molk's sanctuary by his Gumbad-i-Khaki or Brown Dome, the second one Bunting describes in the poem. Bunting only hints at the rivalry in order to emphasise instead the architectural accomplishments which reflect the Seljuks' priority of values.

Omar Khayyam, according to the story 'still current in Fitz-gerald's day', was a friend of Nezam-ol-Molk, but Bunting wrote to me that actually, though Khayyam's life overlaps his, the old minister must have been an old man, Khayyam a young one if they ever met. But Khayyam, under Malekshah's patronage was more renowned as a mathematician-astronomer than poet-philosopher in Iran. That Malekshah found him a 'better reckoner' than God, the Author of the Qor'an (LZ, 7 February 1951), alludes either to his reform of the calendar which preceded the Gregorian reform by five centuries or to his sceptical outlook which stressed the importance of this life. Khayyam as author of one of the best

medieval treatises on algebra is linked to the line following
Malekshah's judgment which summarises the attitude of the entire
group Bunting is including here: 'Their passion's body was bricks
and its soul algebra.' Bunting left the next line more cryptic by
revising

> Poetry
> they remembered but made it out of itself

to

> Poetry
> they remembered
> too much, too well.

Piling up details to add to the description of the Seljuks'
downfall, easily universalised, Bunting draws on a famous anecdote
based on Khayyam's belief in metempsychosis. The sage convinced
'a recalcitrant ass' used to bring bricks to repair the college that he
recognised it as a former lecturer there so that the animal would
enter the building. According to Browne, the Sage went up to the
donkey and extemporised the following quatrain:

> O lost and now returned 'yet more astray',
> Thy name from man's remembrance passed away,
> Thy nails have now combined to form thy hoofs,
> Thy tail's a beard turned round the other way!

In Bunting's lines the satire is more direct:

> 'Lately a professor in this university'
> said Khayyam of a recalcitrant ass,
> 'therefore would not enter, dare not face me.'
> But their determination to banish fools foundered
> ultimately in the installation of absolute idiots.
> Fear of being imputed
> naive impeded thought.

The lines contain a biting warning.

Pictures of 'the belfry at Seville' [LZ, 7 February 1951], La
Giralda, support the poetic evidence Bunting gives of its inferior
design worked out 'heavily, languidly':

> Eddies both ways in time:
> the builders of La Giralda
> repeated
> heavily, languidly,
> some of their patterns in brick.

Immediately after the first-person musings of the poet, the
transitional passages between the Seljuk past and the reflection of
its attitudes in the present is a series of four three-line stanzas

introduced by one slightly longer. The ironic tone heard only sporadically in the first fifty lines now predominates as the poet compares and contrasts the eastern culture with the great civilisations of those whose attention was centred on self-aggrandisement:

> For all that, the Seljuks avoided
> Roman exaggeration and the leaden mind of Egypt
> and withered precariously on the bough
> with patience and public spirit.
> O public spirit!
>
> Prayers to band cities and brigade men
> lest there be more wills than one:
> but God is the dividing sword.
>
> A hard pyramid or lasting law
> against fear of death and
> murder more durable than mortar.
>
> Domination and engineers
> to fudge a motive you can lay your hands on
> lest a girl choose or refuse waywardly.

These few lines contain a disciplined restraint that only Bunting's replies to Zukofsky's objection to the adjective in the phrase 'leaden mind of Egypt' reveal:

> *Leaden mind of Egypt.* I suppose no civilisation ever failed to produce some delightful things. The Egyptians did in their off-moments when they werent attending to what they were doing. But pyramids, gigantic statues, (horrible huge statues of Zaghlul today too), buildings – Qasr-an-Nil for example – more hideous than any Europeans except Germans can produce: Egyptian gestures are heavy, jowls heave, they speak Arabic heavily, G for J, D for TH, B for W, their syntax, with the demonstrative after the noun, thickened in pronunciation and holding up the sense...Heavy wits, abuse and the cudgel; heavy, lifeless spite. No Egyptian has managed to rule or even much influence the rulers of his country since Cambyses conquered it – Persian, Greek, Roman, Arab, Turk – even Zaghlul was part Turk. And their rulers have failed to influence them. The mosques, so famous, are all foreign, and everything light and pleasant in Egypt except what birds and foliage provide is foreign. Or sometimes Nubian. [13 March 1951]

How seriously he meant the transitional stanzas is evident from his second reply to Zukofsky:

> No doubt Egypt had merits, has some of them still: so has Prussia: so had Rome (more than either of them). It is also true that colossal statues are capable of having very simple and grand lines, and that pyramids serve more purpose than merely oppressing the face of the earth. With *all* allowances made, the disease of mind that conceives pyramids and colossi is continually evident in Egypt today and throughout Egyptian

history. People group bads and goods too easily, dont admit that heavy
brutality may coexist with aesthetic merits. [19 April 1951]

Although in Part I attention has been called to the refined
techniques Bunting is using in this sonata, the intricate pattern of
half-rhymes and alliteration in 'pyramid'/'fear of death', 'lasting
law', 'hard'/'murder'/'more'/'durable/'mortar' in the stanza above,
for example, should not be overlooked.

The next section, the long, sonorous description of contemporary arts and timeless, yet modern living styles: whose roots are in
the past, has only one philosophical note, 'Nothing that was is.'
Otherwise, the focus is on the musical short lines filled with vivid,
sensuous images rather than on the shadowed speaker who spoke
in the first person previously. In his Notes Bunting explains further:

> Proper names explain themselves and can be found in books of
> reference. A few are not yet filed. *Hajji Mosavvor*, greatest of modern
> miniature painters, suffered from paralysis agitans. *Naystani*, a cele-
> brated virtuoso of the nose-flute. *Taj* sings classical odes with
> authenticity; *Moluk-e Zarrabi* moulds them to her liking. *Shir-e Khoda*
> begins Teheran's radio day with a canto of the epic. *Sobhi* is the most
> perfect teller of tales, his own.

To Zukofsky he not only added that he tried to reinforce the
meaning with the sounds but he also shared the background for the
musical lines:

> Flute,
> shade dimples under chenars
> breath of Naystani chases and traces
> as a pair of gods might dodge and tag between stars.

'*Chenar*. The oriental palm tree, a splendid tree. A great double
avenue of them runs through the centre of Isfahan. We were sitting
under chenars at Shiraz when Naystani, in a hotel room, began to
practise his flute, and the play of notes and the play of light through
the leaves seemed to work together.'

The progression from early morning to the silence of night is
accomplished effortlessly:

> A fowler spreading his net
> over the barley, calls,
> calls on a rubber reed.
> Grain nods in reply.
> Poppies blue upon white
> wake to the sun's frown.
> Scut of gazelle dances and bounces
> out of the afternoon.
> Owl and wolf to the night.
> On a terrace over a pool

vafur, vodka, tea,
resonant verse spilled
from Onsori, Sa'di,
till the girls' mutter is lost
in whisper of stream and leaf,
a final nightingale
under a fading sky
azan on their quiet.

Bunting's note on 'azan' enriches yet further the uniquely Eastern atmosphere:

> The *azan* is the mo'ezzin's call to prayer. You hardly hear its delicate, wavering airs at other times, but an hour before sunrise it has such magic as no other music, unless perhaps the nightingale in lands where nightingales are rare.

After the counterpointing lines contrasting the culture of this people with 'foreigners', 'unhappy,/ unproductive and rich', the final section begins with an allusion which Bunting expected few to notice: 'The falcon has an echo probably unperceived by readers, since the name of Toghril, first Seljuk conqueror, means falcon' [LZ, 7 March 1951].[10] Apart from this neatness in rounding out the movement, the final section metaphorically epitomises a cyclical progression recognisable in individual lives as well as in history, especially the Eastern history encompassed in this movement:

> Have you seen a falcon stoop
> accurate, unforseen
> and absolute, between
> wind-ripples over harvest? Dread
> of what's to be, is and has been –
> were we not better dead?
>
> His wings churn air
> to flight.
> Feathers alight
> with sun, he rises where
> dazzle rebuts our stare,
> wonder our fright.

Part III opens with thirteen lines which had been compressed from twenty-one in an earlier version. This is indicative of the extensive cutting and revising Bunting did throughout this movement, which may account for some of the very abrupt transitions. The atmosphere in these first lines is still faintly Eastern, but the omission of the names of those with whom the persona would barter, 'Tubai', 'Hiram', and 'Ben Hada', helps universalise both time and place. This is appropriate in the final movement which combines both Eastern and Western attitudes in a war setting which involves both cultures. When the theatre of war shifts from the Middle East to the North finally, nothing of the East remains but what is essential to this poem, the attitude toward life and death which has been blended with all that the persona believes and fully accepts.

The introductory lines which begin with the barest statement of Xenophanes' belief [LZ, 19 April 1951], 'All things only of earth and water', succinctly depicts the strong simplicity of practical life in a timeless, uncomplicated society. The fundamental simplicity is reinforced by the form of the poetry which is basically a three-stress line made up of predominantly monosyllabic words. Bunting is able to vary even this simple pattern:

All things only of earth and water,
to sit in the sun's warmth
breathing clear air.
A fancy took me to dig,
plant, prune, graft;
milk, skim, churn;
flay and tan.
A side of salt beef
for a knife chased and inscribed.
A cask of pressed grapes
for a seine-net.
For peace until harvest
a jig and a hymn.

But the simple bartering carries seeds of conflict, so that in the next stanza this essential simplicity of societal living is interrupted by the more complicated business of rulers who can exact far greater tribute for peace than 'a jig and a hymn'. The change from simple living to greater complications is subtly underlined by the shift away from the predominance of monosyllabic to di- and trisyllabic words and by the move away from spondaic feet ('sun's warmth', 'clear air', 'salt beef', 'pressed grapes') toward the substitution of dactylic feet ('Lydian', 'Solomon', 'hampering') which complicates the rhythm in the second part. The greatest reinforcement of the sense is the twisted syntax in the second half of this section:

tribute of Lydian pebbles
levy and lay aside,
that twist underfoot
and blunt the plowshare,
countless, useless, hampering
pebbles that spawn.

The 'obsessiveness' of the Lydian pebbles [LZ, 25 June 1951], symbols of the tribute exacted by the greedy and powerful, permeates every line here in which paired activities ('Quarry and build', 'levy and lay aside') are opposed to the earlier series of peacetime activities listed in strong monosyllables (dig, plant, prune, graft, milk, skim, churn, flay, tan). The interruption of normal activities characterised by the blunting of the plowshare suggests an ironic reversal of Micah's prophecy of peace (4.3-4):

> He will wield authority over many peoples
> and arbitrate for mighty nations;
> they will hammer their swords into plowshares,
> their spears into sickles.
> Nation will not lift sword against nation,
> there will be no more training for war.
> Each man will sit under his vine and his fig tree.

Through a series of verbs and adjectives, the transformation from peaceful existence to one which encourages war is highlighted, so that finally the poet's scorn of the cause of disruption is expressed strongly in his description,

> countless, useless, hampering
> pebbles that spawn.

To understand the background from which Bunting writes the next abrupt transitional passage, it is necessary to recall the place of tradition in human understanding of self and culture which Pound and Eliot dwelt on. All that is included in Pound's dictum 'Make it new'[11] presupposes that the artist drink deeply from the 'artesian well of our past'. T. S. Eliot insisted that 'the poet must develop or procure the consciousness of the past and that he should continue to develop this consciousness throughout his career'. Tradition, according to Eliot, involves 'the historical sense', which itself involves a 'perception, not only of the pastness of the past, but of its presence'.[12] Bunting compresses his own thoughts and feelings on this subject in lines of poetry charged with an emotional impact. The position of this section in the whole movement seems to emphasise particular insights that the patterns of the past bring into sharper focus: contrast of life styles and the development of the causes of war:

> Shot silk and damask white
> spray spread from
> artesian gush of our past.
> Let no one drink unchlorinated
> living water but taxed tap, sterile,
> or seek his contraband mouthful

> in bog, under thicket, by crag, a trickle,
> or from embroidered pools
> with newts and dytiscus beetles.

The emphasis in the metaphor is on the 'living water' whose biblical echoes form a connection with all other biblical allusions to add another layer of density to the meanings. 'Taxed tap, sterile' is the only mention of its opposite in these nine lines, as though it were a waste to write poetry about its effects.

The fates of those who dare to drink and share with others are listed:

> One cribbed in a madhouse
> set about with diagnoses;
> one unvisited; one uninvited;
> one visited and invited too much;
> one impotent, suffocated by adulation;
> one unfed:

Although Pound is easily recognised, the point is greater than that involved in the six individual cases. Bunting explained to me:

> The poets whose fates are listed in the 'One cribbed in a madhouse' paragraph are not individuals in particular, but there are plenty of instances of poets who have been destroyed or hampered by all the means suggested. The reader can supply what names he pleases. [23 October 1972]

The importance of the lines is that the reality of such situations exists.

This section culminates in metaphors whose two lines vary interestingly the Anglo-Saxon alliterative line which is further complicated by a sound pattern of "vowel-r" combinations. The sea imagery is a foreshadowing of the finale of the sonata:

> one unfed: flares on a foundering barque,
> stars spattering still sea under iceblink.

In response to Zukofsky, Bunting answered: 'I think everyone but you, my dear New York cockney, would know the iceblink by reputation without having to try the dictionary. I'm familiar with the thing itself, on the Banks in the Gulf of St Lawrence, and "between Lofoten and Spitzbergen".' [25 June 1951]

Although the movement to this point has had a timeless quality, with the mention of Roosevelt and Churchill the setting is placed solidly in the Second World War. In Parts I and II Bunting has deliberately prepared for the introduction of war into the poem, the style of life which presupposes the constant companionship of death. Hardy soldiers appear in Asshur's first speech and their rigorous way of life seems admirable. Bunting himself pointed out to Zukofsky [13 March 1951] that the 'public spirit triplets' are part of the preparation for the subject matter of the last movement. Although the falcon section at the end of II is more universal in scope, the fact of war in the process of decay and renewal is at least implicit.

By line 41 in Part III Bunting has established his abhorrence of the causes of war so firmly that he can in a balanced way emphasise his primary theme of 'war not as a horror, not as an opportunity for self-congratulatory glory...but simply as an activity which has pleasures of its own,...in which death is neither a bugbear nor a consummation, but just happens...part of the fun' [LZ, 13 March 1951]. Although Bunting had gone to prison as a conscientious objector in World War I, after his involvement in World War II he defended the merits of war convincingly:

> People group goods and bads too easily, dont admit that heavy brutality may coexist with aesthetic merits, just as they dont admit there may be merits in war, which is associated in their minds with the stupid slaughters of 1914-18 or the last battles of your Civil War to the exclusion of all virtue except endurance. But resolution and effort can be gay instead of grim, and the death and ruin have had their importance exaggerated. That is not to deny their existence nor to advocate multiplying wars. But freedom from war, like freedom from poverty, can be pursued at the expense of things better worth preserving than peace and plenty, of which, I should say, the most important, and the most threatened, is personal autonomy. Free will entails sin! I dont want my acts determined by any authority whatever. [LZ, 19 April 1951]

Peacetime occupations of men converted to wartime create strange scenes, but the focus is rather on the attitude of those who live close to death and do it jauntily and wholeheartedly:

> Tinker tapping perched on a slagheap
> and the man who can mend a magneto.
> Flight-lieutenant Idema, half course run
> that started from Grand Rapids, Michigan,
> wouldnt fight for Roosevelt
> 'that bastard Roosevelt,' pale
> at Malta's ruins, enduring
> a jeep guarded like a tyrant.
> In British uniform and pay
> for fun of fighting and pride,
> for Churchill on foot alone,
> clowning with a cigar, was lost
> in best blues and his third plane that day.

Bunting's Note ensures the reader won't miss the essential tone: 'Gaiety and daring need no naming to those who remember others like Flight-Lieutenant Idema.' Bunting explained to me further: 'Idema was the son of a smallish mid-western manufacturer who, like all his kind, hated Roosevelt. He found an excuse for it when Churchill and Roosevelt successively visited Malta in the circumstances described' [4 July 1973].

From Bunting's comment to Zukofsky, it is clear he was trying to write his poetry without any other voice intruding: 'You provide the key, though not the exact formula, for rearranging the Idema paragraph and losing a part at least of the unwanted echo of EP I couldn't get rid of.' Just a glance at the many lines omitted in the final version proves how rigorously he removed 'unwanted' echoes [25 June 1951].

The timeless Middle East depicted in Parts I and II is transformed into an almost surrealistic landscape by modern wartime scenes which Bunting describes in the next section. In order to create the illusion of a long desert journey similar to the one he himself experienced [LZ, 4 May 1943; 23 July 1944], Bunting composes a sentence of seventeen lines by adding phrase after phrase to create a powerful montage:

> Broken booty but usable
> along the littoral, frittering into the south.
> We marvelled, careful of craters and minefields,
> noting a new-painted recognisance
> on a fragment of fuselage, sand drifting into dumps,
> a tank's turret twisted skyward,
> here and there a lorry unharmed
> out of fuel or the crew scattered;
> leaguered in lines numbered for enemy units,
> gulped beer of their brewing,
> mocked them marching unguarded to our rear;
> discerned nothing indigenous, never a dwelling,
> but on the shore sponges stranded and beyond the reef
> unstayed masts staggering in the swell,
> till we reached readymade villages clamped on cornland,
> empty, Arabs feeding vines to goats;
> at last orchards aligned, girls hawked by their mothers
> from tent to tent, Tripoli dark
> under a cone of tracers.
> Old in that war after raising many crosses
> rapped on a tomb at Leptis; no one opened.

Traces of the timeless Eastern life style central to Part I are unobtrusive links between this section and other parts of the poem.

The ever present theme of death concludes this section with the mention of the Punic cemetery at Leptis which dates as far back as the fifth century. This is a strong device to universalise the concept of war and death and also to move the reader back in time as a preparation for the next part which reintroduces the Age of the Caliphs.

Bunting filled in the background of the next few lines:

Blind Bashshar bin Burd saw,
doubted, glanced back
guessed whence, speculated whither.

by explaining to me:

Bashshar bin Burd was an Arabic poet of Persian race who was put to death for heresy in the eighth or ninth century. It's not clear exactly what his heresy was, but it seems that he 'glanced back' at the achievements of the Sassanian kings and the Zoroastrian religion, and in particular at the ideas of the communist rebellion of Mazdak which was put down after a temporary triumph in about 570 a.d. He was probably some kind of pantheist, though he didnt get as far as Hallaj, who said, 'Ana' l-hagg' ['I am the True One', or 'the Fact', i.e. God] or some kind of Manichaean, but most likely a bit of both. He 'speculated whither' by foreseeing only evil from the caliphate and rousing a rather vague spirit of rebellion. The first great Persian poets who wrote in Persian, a century or more later, thought well of Bashshar, at least as a poet. You'll find an adequate account of him in the first and second volumes of Browne's *Literary History of Persia* [11,361]. I forget now where my supplementary information came from, apart from mentions of him by the poets. [23 October 1972]

The considerations of a counsellor and poet who weighed the values and results of power is opposed here by the attitudes of

Panegyrists, blinder and deaf,
prophets, exegesists, counsellors of patience

who in a paraphrase of Micah's words, 'All are lurking for blood,/every man hunting down his brother' (7. 2),

lie in wait for blood,
every man with a net.

The smooth undulations of Swift's satiric line [LZ, 16 May 1951]:

Condole me with abundance of secret pleasure.

pinpoint the underlying dishonesty of this group. The poet's straightforward prophecy against them paraphrases the words of Christ in Matthew 10. 26 and in Luke 12. 1-3 where he speaks against the hypocrisy of the Pharisees:

What we think of him in private
will be said in public
before the last gallon's teemed
into an unintelligible sea –

Besides being a term of the metaphor, the sea shifts the scene back to the actual world in levels of society far from the powerful:

old men who toil in the bilge to open a link,
bruised by the fling of the ship and sodden
sleep at the handpump. Staithes, filthy harbour water,
a drowned Finn, a drowned Chinee;
hard-lying money wrung from protesting paymasters.

The poetry underscores their hardships by lines made heavy by
words which must be spoken slowly: 'old men', 'toil', 'bilge',
'sodden', 'handpump', 'drowned', 'hard-lying', 'wrung...protesting
paymasters'. 'Finn' and 'Chinee' [LZ, 25 July 1951] help to shift
the scene from the Middle East so that the next section which
begins with a sharp transition to the North is somewhat prepared
for.

More important than the scene shift is the sudden change of
atmosphere, a return to the lightheartedness of the Idema passage,
accentuated even more in this one. This spirit surges through lines
in which the word 'sang' is a vibrant refrain. Twice the words of the
tide, 'rippling round the anchor chains of the ships assembling in
the Firth of Forth for the Archangel convoy', punctuate the lines:

Rosyth guns sang. Sang tide through cable
for Glasgow burning:
  'Bright west,
  pale east,
  catfish on the sprool.'

. . .

Tide sang. Guns sang:
  'Vigilant,
  pull off fluffed woollens, strip
  to buff and beyond.'

Bunting pointed out to me in these words of the tide 'the contrast of
leisurely fishing with the need to prepare to face very ultimate
things' [23 October 1972]. Using nautical terms, he creates a
metaphor for the sun and a strongly musical comment which
underlines the prevailing response of the men to this kind of life
with its mortal dangers:

Sun leaped up and passed,
bolted towards green creek
of quiet Chesapeake,
bight of a warp no strong tide strains. Yet
as tea's drawing, breeze backing and freshening,
who'd rather
make fast Fortune with a slippery hitch?

With the word 'meditative' Bunting begins to slow the tempo of
the movement which still contains irrepressible vitality in the final
lines of this section:

In watch below
meditative heard elsewhere
surf shout, pound shores seldom silent
from which heart naked swam
out to the dear unintelligible ocean.

The 'unintelligible sea' has now taken on a more mysterious
character which elicits a wholehearted response from anyone who
wills to live life fully and face squarely 'very ultimate things'.

Lyric apostrophe fits in smoothly with wartime subject matter in
the next lines:

From Largo Law look down,
moon and dry weather, look down
on convoy marshalled, filing between mines.

The time, the place, and the occupation are not as important as the
individual's free response to the richness of living which is a share
of 'the spoils'. This richness can be savoured fully only with a life-
view which accepts death as the natural end of all things. From the
hot desert sands of the Middle East, central to the first two
movements of the sonata, the scene has moved to the cold waters of
northern Europe:

Cold northern clear sea-gardens
between Lofoten and Spitzbergen,
as good a grave as any, earth or water.

Xenophanes' belief, used in the first lines of Part III in the context
of living is echoed here at the end in the context of dying. The
Eastern attitude toward life and death is integrated with all that the
persona accepts when he asks the final rhetorical question:

What else do we live for and take part,
we who would share the spoils?

Bunting has revealed that although he thinks highly of *The Spoils*,
he is dissatisfied with its symmetry which seems to him 'lopsided':
'I don't mean it is a bad poem, it is lopsided, it's not, it's not got the
symmetry it should have had and was planned to have.'[13] He has
qualified this by saying it was 'musical' lopsidedness he meant.
When I asked him about this, he replied:

The Spoils was planned in four movements and was first written so, in an
interval between pretty strenuous doings in Italy which obliged me to
hurry the last two movements far too much. Louis Zukofsky pointed out
to me that the substance had run very thin in the last two movements,
and as soon as I had time to consider them again I saw that he was right,
but I had no leisure to rewrite them. So I cut away, probably more than
Zukofsky wanted me to, and shrank the two movements into one, thus

keeping a dense tissue, but losing the symmetry I had planned. That makes it lopsided. And too obscure. [23 October 1972]

If there is any criticism about his accomplishment in this poem, Bunting has stated it here. After reading each of the first two movements which have no slackness about them, but which, line by line and section by section, build an intricate but relatively clear design about a central theme, the reader is not prepared for the much denser tissue of Part III. This Part contains sections abruptly juxtaposing disparate eras, cultures, environments, situations, and fictional and nonfictional characters with their varied responses to values. This is not to judge that this part is not unified in itself or disconnected from the other movements; all of that has been discussed. If the first two movements had not been written in a style less dense, the whole would not have lost its symmetry. But this sonata is a step in Bunting's development which led to *Briggflatts*. It is in his last sonata that Bunting combines the best qualities of Parts I and II with the best of III, definite and vivid sensual images, the sense of place, and 'clean' writing with 'no fluff',[14] that interweaves contrasting details into an intricate design. He harmonises this with abruptly juxtaposed motifs, tones, and rhythms in the swift and musical development of a complicated theme.

CHAPTER 8

Briggflatts

Before Bunting began writing *Briggflatts*, he mentioned two unrelated factors which seemed to have influenced him to write a sixth sonata. One was his dissatisfaction with *The Spoils*, not because of its lopsidedness but rather because it did not embody ideals he found in the *Art of the Fugue*, in Beethoven's last quartets, and in the music of Byrd and Monteverdi:

> No...concessions to eclairegobblers...nothing recondite, but only a complete purge out of irrelevancies; compression; but there was a good deal to say, nothing precious. So I re-read Lycopolis and the Spoils and saw they aren't good enough (questions of technique omitted); Rhone wine when I wanted Mouton. And still, let me boast, I dont think any of our contemporaries has got nearer. (LZ, June the New Moonth, 1953]

The second was the debt he felt he owed to

> Peggy Greenbank and her whole ambience, the Rawthey valley, the fells of Lunedale, the Viking inheritance all spent save the faint smell of it, the ancient Quaker life accepted without thought and without suspicion that it might seem eccentric: and what happens when one deliberately thrusts love aside, as I then did – it has its revenge. That must be a longish poem. (LZ, 16 September 1964)

As an autobiography, *Briggflatts* is, according to Bunting's emphatic statement, not 'a record of fact'; 'the truth of the poem is of another kind'. The truth *Briggflatts* does express is an essential one; this is clear from Bunting's comment to Jonathan Williams after he had written for publication the factual details of the poet's life: 'Jonathan, I'm surprised at you. What the hell has any of this to do with the public? My autobiography is *Briggflatts* – there's nothing else worth speaking aloud.' [D].

Herbert Read sees the truth of the autobiography as one of first impressions recovered and evaluated.[1] However, they are all filtered through the poet's memory which gives the lightest, gayest lines a poignancy, although never a sentimental nostalgia.[2] From the first line the posture of the definitely masculine persona is

energetic and strong. This is no speaker slumped in a chair by the
fireside. If he is recovering first impressions, he is not luxuriating in
soft, disordered memories. His recollections are expressed in what
Read aptly terms 'resonant and durable verses'.[3]

This autobiography concerns the man as an individual human
being, as poet, as native of Northumberland, as world traveller, and
in all the other aspects of his life. Themes that describe his human
actions, feelings, and aspirations, are so often inseparably interwoven with themes that describe those of contemporary or
historical figures that single lines can reveal several aspects of this
man and many others also. Yet this happens chiefly through
remembered echoes of other themes in the lines rather than
through many voices speaking simultaneously. This is a result of a
deliberate technique closely connected with Bunting's ideas about
the relationship between poetry and music:

> Poetry can carry only one line of sound at a time, music many. Pound, I
> think, and certainly Zukofsky, tries to get some of the effect of many
> voices by letting them work, not simultaneously, but in quick succession,
> much as Bach managed to give an illusion of fugal writing on an
> unaccompanied violin, each voice implying what went on while it was
> overlaid (or suspended) by a different one. I have never been happy with
> that. I prefer to let the poem be shaped by the fact that only one voice is
> ever really audible at a time. [23 May 1972]

The overall tone of *Briggflatts* is quieter than *The Spoils* and
remarkably more subdued than the other sonatas generally. It is
Wordsworthian in the sense that it is recollected in tranquillity,
though not in the manner in which it was written. When questioned
about this Bunting answered:

> 'Tintern Abbey' is all of a piece. 'Tintern Abbey' was not finished, of
> course, but it was all got down on paper in the thirty-six hours it took to
> get from Tintern back to home. The finishing of it of course would be a
> much longer job, but it was on the whole got down in a go. No,
> *Briggflatts* took a year to write down.[4]

Whatever the comparison with Wordsworth, the tone of reminis-
cence carries a more modern and contrasting Hardyesque tone of
acceptance of uncertainty, of the impossibility of certain metaphysical knowledge in a universe in which all seems obscure and
even chaotic. As Bunting wrote in *A Note on 'Briggflatts'*: 'Hierarchy
and order, the virtues of the neo-Platonic religion . . . are not virtues
to me, only expedients that chafe almost as vilely as the crimes they
try to restrain.' This statement, however, does not repudiate the
relational aspect of all things which underlines his poetry:

> Amongst philosophers I have most sympathy with Lucretius and his

masters, content to explain the world an atom at a time; with Spinoza who saw all things as God, though not with his wish to demonstrate that logically; and with David Hume, the doubter. The men I learned poetry from did not value these. Perhaps that is why it took me so long to make a poem that reflects, fragmentarily, my whole mind.[5]

The theme of the mortality of the individual and eventually of all men and women moves in and out of the foreground as an everpresent human limitation. Finally, 'uninterrupted night' 'for love' is accepted, though not without the simultaneous painful uncertainty of the future. Even the fact of the cosmos with its own larger continuum, as well as the varied beauty and cyclical order of nature does not entirely mitigate the pain heard in the final stoic expression of the sonata. This pain Bunting described to me as 'the pain...of wrong unrighted or unrightable' [4 July 1973].

Another modern attitude is the emphasis through the form of the poem itself on the individual as a centre of consciousness in the modern universe. This central 'experiencing consciousness'[6] is individualised in every one of Bunting's sonatas by the personae's attitudes which are anonymous but not as impersonal and detached as T. S. Eliot demanded for the goal of modern poetry. In this sonata, above all, the attitudes are individual and personal, yet anonymous enough to be generally representative, one of the most difficult accomplishments of modern poetry.

Bunting has taken pains to explain that the sonata form he is using is the free, pre-classical form that allows him the formal freedom which is necessary for the creation of his poetry. Yet freedom from the classical sonata form in no way presupposes freedom from form itself. The discipline that shaped approximately seven hundred lines of the final poem from over 20,000 proves that this freedom is not undisciplined energy but energy directed toward some kind of formal order. A quest for form is proved even more conclusively by the fact that Bunting's first move toward writing *Briggflatts* was to draw a symmetrical diagram:[7]

Even though Bunting admits that in actuality the sonata does not
'follow exactly the diagram', although it does 'come near to it', the
diagram was important in the planning of the poem:

> You have a poem. You're going to have five parts because it's got to be
> an uneven number. So that the central one should be the one apex,
> there. But what is new, the only new thing that I knew of, in doing it, was
> that instead of having one climax in the other parts you have two. In the
> first two the first climax is the less and another immediately comes out
> of it when you're not expecting it. So you have it for those two. In the
> others the first climax is the greater and it trails off...

Furthermore, Scarlatti's B minor fugato sonata (L. 33) was in his
mind from the outset.[8]

Bunting makes it clear that in no stage of the poem's
development was the sonata form in control from the outside. The
constraint of trying to fit a form to content is farthest from his
considerations:

> I never have, on the one hand, something I want to say, and on the
> other, a form I want to say it in. My matter is born of the form – or the
> form of the matter, if you care to think that I just conceive things
> musically. There's no fitting, at least consciously. Whatever you think I
> am saying is something I could not have said in any other way. [23 May
> 1972]

Once Bunting had planned the entire structure with its
emotional peaks, he provided for both variety and unity by
assigning a motto to each part: I. – '*Son los pasariellos del mal pelo
exidos*' ('The spuggies are fledged'); II. – 'Bloodaxe'; III. – '*Longe
processit e flammantia moenia mundi*' ('He went far beyond the
flaming walls of the world'); IV. – 'Aneurin'; and V. – '*Nox est una
perpetua dormienda.*' In the final version all the mottos are omitted
but the first which becomes the epigraph for the entire sonata, and
the last which is translated and rephrased to become the final line
of Part V.

Although the five mottos already begin to bring content to the
poem, the next step in the planning, according to Bunting's
account, was to 'look at the diagram' and to 'say obviously what any
poet thinking of shape would say which is Spring, Summer,
Autumn, and Winter'. This leaves the central section, already
settled on as Alexander's interview with the Angel on the mountain,
as 'something different'. The chronological movement through the
parts eventually became symbolic of the stages of a lifetime,
involving spatial as well as chronological progression. In the Hall
interview Bunting explained: 'Spring is around Briggflatts,

Summer is all over the place – London, the Arctic, the Mediterranean, Autumn is mostly in the Dales, and the last part is mostly on the Northumberland coast.' Later he expanded this explanation in a simple yet profound summary:

> Commonplaces provide the poem's structure: spring, summer, autumn, winter of the year and of man's life, interrupted in the middle and balanced around Alexander's trip to the limits of the world and its futility, and sealed and signed at the end by a confession of our ignorance. Love and betrayal are spring's adventures, the wisdom of elders and the remoteness of death, hardly more than a gravestone. In summer there is no rest from ambition and lust of experience, never final. Those fail who try to force their destiny, like Eric; but those who are resolute to submit, like my version of Pasiphae, may bring something new to birth, be it only a monster. What Alexander learns when he has thrust his way through the degraded world is that man is contemptibly nothing and yet may live content in humility. Autumn is for reflexion to set Aneurin's grim elegy against the legend of Cuthbert who saw God in everything, to love without expectation, wander without an inn, persist without hope. Old age can see at last the loveliness of things overlooked or despised, frost, the dancing maggots, sheepdogs, and particularly the stars which make time a paradox and a joke till we can give up our own time, even though we wasted it. And still we know neither where we are nor why.[9]

But none of this can be separated from music, the formally integrating factor of the sonata. As Charles Tomlinson expresses it so accurately:

> The achievement of the poem – and here one is reducing to abstraction all that is art and art's particulars – derives from the attempt to bring Then into as close a relation with Now as possible. The aligning of the two comes about by the central device of imitating 'the condition of music'. Then and Now are brought to bear upon each other as are the different voices in a madrigal. In the poem this cannot be done simultaneously; but, by juxtaposition, Now can be played over against Then as Then – summoned up by motif and left echoing in the mind – stands forth, counterpoised rather than counterpointed, against the ensuing motif of Now.[10]

Playing a Scarlatti sonata before and after each part helps impress the similarities between the music and poetry on the listener. By having the audience listen to an entire sonata between each movement Bunting is bringing to its attention such parallels between the Scarlatti music and the poetry as structure and variations of tempo, tone, and cadence.

Bunting's use of musical interludes is possibly a further blending of his classical Persian cultural background with his poetry which underlines subtly one aspect of his theme, 'Then is Now'. He

Peggy Mullett at Briggflatts farmhouse.

described the Persian blending of music and poetry to Zukofsky much earlier:

> Anyway, the instrumental half of any classical ghazal is a serious thing, often as long as a movement from a symphony at the beginning and of quite respectable dimensions every now and then when the singer gets out of breath or whatever the criterion is for setting the tar and drums and nay to work again. [9 July 1953]

Although the poetry of *Briggflatts* is able to stand alone as it does so well in Bunting's recording, once it has been heard with the music, it never again sounds quite complete without it. Unlike the seemingly random use of music by the Persians, Bunting's use of Scarlatti is deliberate and integral to the full rendition of the poem. Besides telling interviewers that the B minor fugato sonata was in his mind from the outset in the planning of this sonata, in a letter to me he designates it as 'the key' to *Briggflatts* [6 June 1971]. To help ensure its position, he has it played twice during the poem. The Bloodaxe Books record *Basil Bunting reads 'Briggflatts'*[11] shows how closely Scarlatti's sonata is echoed in the poem in the second part of Part IV, where it first accompanies Bunting's reading, and then is allowed to finish before Bunting starts his reading of Part V; it is played again at the end of the Coda to conclude the entire sonata. Bunting's plan for a full reading of *Briggflatts* included other sonatas between the movements: L.204 (1 – 2), L.25 (2 – 3), L.275 (3 – 4) and L.58 (4 – 5).

The title *Briggflatts* 'comes from the "name of a small hamlet in the Pennine mountains in a very beautiful situation in what [Americans] call a valley but which [Northerners] call a dale'.[12] Michael Hamburger calls attention to Bunting's 'highly developed sense of place and of particular ways of life rooted in particular localities'.[13] This characteristic is strongly evident in this latest sonata which begins and ends in the North. Though many other ways of life in various localities are described, none are so naturally and empathetically represented as the localities around Briggflatts. The sonata is entitled appropriately since, in the words of Herbert Read, it is a 'poem of return...after long sojourns in exotic lands', and since it is a 'celebration of origins, or remote blood and ancestry, of a natal landscape'.[14]

Bunting begins simply by stating that *Briggflatts* is 'An Autobiography for Peggy'. It is not important who Peggy is, he tells enough about her part in his life in the sonata itself. Through a letter he wrote to Edward Lucie-Smith we know he had to find her to ask her permission for the dedication:

> Yes. *Briggflatts* is now mentionable by name. My hand was forced by Tyne Tees Television, who smuggled it in, in a question in an interview to be shown sometime in August. So I took my courage in both hands and wrote to the person most concerned and she must put up with it, though she can still have her name removed from the dedication if she likes.[15]

Immediately after the simple dedication, the epigraph is presented in two languages: '*Son los pasariellos del mal pelo exidos*' from *Libro de Alexandre*[16] with the translation into Northumbrian speech as 'The spuggies are fledged'. Both the form and the content of the epigraph highlight many of the key ideas of the sonata so it is appropriate that Bunting made this serve as the epigraph of the entire poem instead of the motto of the first part as it had originally. The lines in two languages, one in thirteenth-century Spanish and the other in a contemporary local idiom, immediately juxtapose 'Then' and 'Now', the central juxtaposition of the poem, and the meaning itself reinforces the parallel theme of a continuous cycle of change which nothing can reverse. The juxtaposition also includes the past in the way that Pound and Eliot would have it included to enrich the culture of the present. Through the use of a medieval language the poet is expressing more poignantly than he can in his own idiom the deep feeling evoked by this whole irreversible process of change. The Spanish line is from the medieval book which recounts the life of Alexander the Great in more than ten thousand lines of poetry; this is another detail which is neatly tied in with the highest point of the entire sonata in Part III, Alexander's interview with Israfel on the mountaintop. The choice of this one line is especially appropriate as an introduction to Part I with its reminiscences of May and childhood. One of the most remarkable sections in *Libro de Alexandre* is the description of spring, a 'truly inspired' passage, according to one critic.[17] It is from this description which begins 'The month was May, a glorious time' that the epigraph is taken.

This same lighthearted spirit of spring is felt in the sonata which is played immediately after the epigraph as an introduction to Part I. The Scarlatti sonata (L204/K105) Bunting chose is one which contains the 'most obviously Spanish phrases in all Scarlatti',[18] an extension of the mood of the Spanish epigraph and again a weaving of cultures that is more deftly accomplished in *Briggflatts* than in any of the other sonatas. But more important to the poem are the qualities of the music which Bunting parallels in his poetry. The sonata's compactness and its single melodic line are characteristics which are important to Bunting. He patiently explained this second concern to me:

> The most fundamental limitation [in the analogy of poetry and music] is that poetry can carry only one line of sound at a time, music many...I prefer to let the poem be shaped by the fact that only one voice is ever really audible at a time. [23 May 1972].

Besides the compactness and single melodic line, Scarlatti's readiness to change back and forth between the light and shade of major and minor[19] has a correspondence in Part I also. Although the spirit of spring and the beginning of life predominates in the first stanza and is a dominant note in most of Part I, the more sombre note of betrayal and death is introduced within the first few stanzas. Here in the beginning of the sonata the accent is on life, with death a contrasting element in a subordinate sense. As the sonata proceeds, the thought of death becomes more dominant and life is weighed from that ultimate perspective.

At first all elements in the first stanza speak of the fullness of new life. The note of the 'sweet tenor bull' is heard in the first word, 'Brag', a sound which had intrigued Bunting much earlier. As he described it to interviewers:

> The bull had been in my mind for ages, but hadn't been put down as having anything to do with this poem until quite late in the process...the bull I noticed one day in a farm near Throckley where I was living at the moment; and, you know, it struck me, at once, nobody had noticed the bull has a tenor voice. You hear of the bull bellowing and this, that, and the other. But in fact he bellows in the most melodious tenor, a beautiful tenor voice, quite different from the rather raucous contralto of the cow. And, in the spring, the bull does in fact, if he's with the cows, dance on the tips of his toes, as part of the business of showing off, showing that he is protecting them, you see. He's not really doing anything, but he sees somebody walking by the hedge and he begins to dance at once, just to demonstrate what an indispensable creature he is. It is delightful, and it bears such a, a strong resemblance to the behaviour of young men in general and...well...all creatures.[20]

From the outset the setting is clear, the countryside about the Rawthey, with nature and music inseparably woven:

> Brag, sweet tenor bull,
> descant on Rawthey's madrigal,
> each pebble its part
> for the fells' late spring.
> Dance tiptoe, bull,
> black against may.
> Ridiculous and lovely
> chase hurdling shadows
> morning into noon.
> May on the bull's hide
> and through the dale
> furrows fill with may,
> paving the slowworm's way.

This first thirteen lines also introduces the stanza form for Part I, the only one so formally composed: twelve stanzas of thirteen lines, the last two of which rhyme. The rhythm is always harmonised with the themes and moods so that the rhyming lines are never merely rhymed couplets in a regular metre which finish off the stanza neatly, but rather two ending lines which capture the mood of the entire stanza. Thus they range from

> furrows fill with may,
> paving the slowworm's way

to

> becks, flocks,
> and axe knocks

and to such a variation as

> Delight dwindles. Blame
> stays the same.

The second stanza introduces the mason who is important not so much because he is Peggy's father, but because he becomes the image of the kind of poet the persona wishes to be, a craftsman who carves words in stone. This figure speaks in the 'Then' of the poem as the man for whom, Bunting told me, he 'with his sons did a bit of rough work from time to time to help out' [4 July 1973]. This is the man whom he so attentively watched and listened to that years later the larger meaning of his words and actions are effective in writing this poetry. In the 'Now' of this sonata his craftsman's actions have a significance which reach out to include art and mortality:

> A mason times his mallet
> to a lark's twitter,
> listening while the marble rests,
> lays his rule
> at a letter's edge,
> fingertips checking,
> till the stone spells a name
> naming none,
> a man abolished.
> Painful lark, labouring to rise!
> The solemn mallet says:
> In the grave's slot
> he lies. We rot.
>
> . . .
>
> Brief words are hard to find,
> shapes to carve and discard:

The theme of mortality is enriched by being paralleled with the Hardyesque image of the lark, a symbol of all nature, especially man, 'labouring to rise' painfully. But the solemn couplet places a death sentence over all, which the mason's mallet, like a judge's, ratifies. But from the death and decay life springs renewed:

> Decay thrusts the blade,
> wheat stands in excrement
> trembling. Rawthey trembles.

With an acknowledgement of fear of spring and pain, the poet introduces the innocent adolescent love theme which is con-tinuously shadowed with images of temporality and death:

> Stone smooth as skin,
> cold as the dead they load
> on a low lorry by night.
> The moon sits on the fell
> but it will rain.
> Under sacks on the stone
> two children lie,

Spare descriptions trace the progress of the children and the mason:

> In Garsdale, dawn;
> at Hawes, tea from the can.
> Rain stops, sacks
> steam in the sun, they sit up.

Herbert Read's conception of *Briggflatts* as a series of first impressions is most true in this section. Sound, sight, taste, touch, all senses are called on by the poet to gently attain the emotional climax describing the two children together 'till bird dawn'. When the 'mason stirs' and speaks, his words may be attributed chiefly to the poet-craftsman in the 'Now' of the poem, yet they echo the words the mason 'Then' might have uttered:

> Words!
> Pens are too light.
> Take a chisel to write.

The progress to this point has been steady and uncomplicated, but contrasting motifs have enriched the texture of the sonata. The place of the murder of Bloodaxe, the key figure of the next part, is pointed out by the mason whose physical appearance is mentioned in the same stanza. Consciously or not, he resembles the poet himself:

> Copper-wire moustache,
> sea-reflecting eyes
> and Baltic plainsong speech

so that three eras are represented in the lines, an underlining of the theme 'Then is diffused in Now'. The words

> By such rocks
> men killed Bloodaxe

foreshadow a 'murder' the persona himself feels guilty of and describes later in this Part.

'Knotty wood, hard to rive' and 'smell of October apples' look forward to similar lines in Part IV which describes autumn in the dales. Images of nature on all levels, human, animal, and plant, are blended together to communicate the remarkable richness and unity of experience the persona enjoys.

Bunting diagrammed each part with two emotional high points. The second one in Part I seems to be naturally in the stanza following the delicate love scene, in which the reader is told that this innocent love was murdered and the persona takes the blame with 'No hope of going back'. The connotations are larger though. The mason as draftsman pronounces his judgment of the birth and life of every person back to Adam and Eve:

> Every birth a crime,
> every sentence life.
> Wiped of mould and mites
> would the ball run true?

Statement after statement which is particularised in the persona's case holds true for everyone who has ever wished that a part of life could be lived over again in a different way. The theme of murder which returns now 'jogging the draftsman's elbow' leads into a kind of exorcism of this guilt by confession:

> Love murdered neither bleeds nor stifles
> but jogs the draftsman's elbow.
> What can he, changed, tell
> her, changed, perhaps dead?
> Delight dwindles. Blame
> stays the same.

The motif of Bloodaxe reappears with a deeper significance in the next stanza. His destiny drives him from one place to another, and his life pattern includes betrayal and flight. In the single-mindedness which enables a person to shunt aside even 'insufferable happiness', Bloodaxe and the persona become inextricably mixed in the stanza:

> Bloodaxe, king of York,
> king of Dublin, king of Orkney.
> Take no notice of tears;
> letter the stone to stand
> over love laid aside lest
> insufferable happiness impede
> flight to Stainmore.

Sadly contrasting 'Now' and 'Then', image after image suffers some degradation as Part I ends on a note quite different from its light-hearted beginning. Images of dung, 'sodden trash', of the Rawthey, 'truculent, dingy', and of fog replace each of the Edenic images of the past to underline the self-condemnation of the youthful response:

> Guilty of spring
> and spring's ending
> amputated years ache after
> the bull is beef, love a convenience.
> It is easier to die than to remember.
> Name and date
> split in soft slate
> a few months obliterate.

Instead of only the last two lines rhyming as in all the rest of the stanzas, in the last stanza the last three rhyme to draw Part I to a more definitely final close.

The formality of twelve stanzas each ending with rhyming lines echoes the order and simplicity the youth finds in his world. The 'brief' and 'lean' words at times flow like music:

> Ridiculous and lovely
> chase hurdling shadows
> morning into noon.

and at other times are 'axe knocks':

> In the grave's slot
> he lies. We rot.
>
> . . .
>
> By such rocks
> men killed Bloodaxe.

In the midst of portents of mortality, the children go innocently on their way:

> In such soft air
> they trudge and sing,
> laying the tune frankly on the air.

Only the 'poet-mason' remembering 'Then' sees finally those patterns of life that were foreshadowed, repeated in contemporary human history.

The direct, uninvolved syntax underlines the simplicity and orderliness of the time of youth. If connections are at all obscure or if sombre notes seem to have nothing to do with their youthful lives, this is only in keeping with a time of life in which experience has not given the perspective and insight to clarify them.

Often directness and brevity are achieved by not repeating the verb in a long series:

> hear the horse stale,
> the mason whistle,
> harness mutter to shaft,
> felloe to axle squeak,
> rut thud the rim,
> crushed grit

or by omitting it entirely; for example, "Her pulse their pace," or:

    The road again,
    at a trot

so that the overall effect is one of 'lean words' carved in stone. Kenneth Cox singles out lines in this part to show Bunting's achievements in the use of colloquial language, which 'usually crown a lifelong exercise in revision, imitation and translation'. He judges its use in *The Well of Lycopolis* as 'imitative and self-conscious', in *The Spoils* as 'accomplished but still mannered', but in *Briggflatts* as 'an easy and unassuming mastery'.[21] Any of the lines already quoted from Part I corroborate Cox's judgment about Bunting's achievement in this poem.

The decisive and 'flamboyant' opening of Scarlatti's sonata (L25/K46) provides a fitting transition from youth, looking from 'discarded love' toward new horizons which will bring his vocation as poet to fruition. But more interesting is its division into smaller contrasting sections which parallels the general form of the next movement of *Briggflatts*. Kirkpatrick explains that in this Scarlatti sonata it is necessary to think in blocks of rhythm. What unifies the sonata and, according to Kirkpatrick, is most important to Scarlatti is the coherence of all thematic material around a basic tonal center.[22] This seems easily translatable into literary terms with the substitution of 'thematic' for 'tonal' in order to see a similar unity in this movement and finally in the whole poem.

Part II in which the persona spends time on land and sea in various parts of the world is shaped block by block, like the Scarlatti sonata, into a whole by the underlying theme of 'Summer', the second of the four seasons used in the poem, and by 'Bloodaxe', one of the mottoes Bunting used to unify each movement. The movement is further unified in itself by the central consciousness which permeates all the blocks as well as the entire poem.

Another parallel between the Scarlatti sonata and Part II is the use of comparatively startling effects, the sudden long pause in which the whole course of the rhythmic movement hangs in suspense:

                    sing, sing,
        laying the tune on the air,
        nimble and easy as a lizard,
        still and şudden as a gecko,
        to humiliate love, remember
        nothing.

The long pause here in Bunting's reading of the poem dramatises this sudden stop even more than it does for a silent reader. Both Bunting and Scarlatti ignore 'bar lines' so that the parts are able to establish their own 'irregular rhythmic pattern'.[23]

Although the spacing, the punctuation, and the general layout on the page provide the diagram for the reader, every one of these effects is more remarkable in Bunting's reading of the sonata. This after all is the proper rendition of his poetry as he insists. Further, this Scarlatti sonata, one of 'the richest in thematic content, rhetorical pauses, and opposing phrases', has these qualities heightened by 'conspicuous contrasts of forte and piano'.[24] These qualities Bunting parallels in reading his poem also.

In the first large block of Part II, three sentences contained in twenty-three lines describe the time spent in London during the 'summer' of this 'autobiography'. The poetry moves restlessly from one phrase to another just as the poverty-ridden poet moves about the city struggling to express exactly and precisely the sights and sounds of his experience:

> Secret, solitary, a spy, he gauges
> lines of a Flemish horse
> hauling beer, the angle, obtuse,
> a slut's blouse draws on her chest,
> counts beat against beat, bus conductor
> against engine against wheels against
> the pedal, Tottenham Court Road, decodes
> thunder, scans
> porridge bubbling, pipes clanking, feels
> Buddha's basalt cheek
> but cannot name the ratio of its curves
> to the half-pint
> left breast of a girl who bared it in Kleinfeldt's.

His failure in creating poetry is connected with his failure in love and his self-judgment is harsh:

> he lies with one to long for another,
> sick, self-maimed, self-hating,
> obstinate, mating
> beauty with squalor to beget lines still-born.

The disciplined emotion of the first block carries into the second which is an apostrophe spoken from the double perspective of 'Then' and 'Now'. The two self-contained stanzas had been sent to Zukofsky on the same day, 10 November 1964, that Bunting had finished the first draft of Part I. The accompanying note added:

> ...tonight it seems to be words for music. If you dont play bowls
> (not ten-pins, but on the grass with biased bowls) in America you may
> not quite get it...

You who can calculate the course
of a biased bowl,
shall I come near the jack?
What twist can counter the force
that holds back
woods I roll?

You who elucidate the disk
hubbed by the sun,
shall I see autumn out
or the fifty years at risk
be lost, doubt
end what's begun?

'Spheres' in an earlier version sent to Zukofsky was changed to
'woods' and a comma was removed after 'out' to add more fluency.
The intricate rhyme scheme abcacb and defdfe, and the parallel
number of syllables, 8, 5/4, 6, 7, 3, 3, in the six lines of each stanza
strengthens the underlying framework, but the differences in
rhythm, in the number of stressed syllables, and primarily in the
cadences provide the interesting variations which Bunting's oral
phrasing makes even clearer. Although each stanza is read slowly
and deliberately, the first six lines are read in three breaths. The
only pause is at a punctuation mark, the comma and the two
question marks. In the last line 'I' is emphatically stressed. The
next stanza begins like the first with the first pause at the first
comma, the second again at the end of the third line, but with only a
short pause instead of the full stop of the first stanza. The third
breaks the fifth line at the comma in order to slow down the ending
to the final full stop after three spondaic beats. Spondees
strengthened by internal rhyme have already introduced each
stanza; a strongly stressed 'You' is echoed in each second word
'who'. Phrasing which moves naturally across several lines makes
the rhyme scheme become a subordinate element with such sound
effects as internal rhyme ('You who elucidate', and 'hubbed', 'sun',
'autumn', 'begun') to tighten the lines musically.

With all the questions unanswered, the poem continues in the
third block with the same kind of a sweeping turn that the poet
himself makes and which he describes in these comparatively long
lines:

Under his right oxter the loom of his sweep
the pilot turns from the wake.

Vivid sailing images predominate in this block in which the
differences between north and south provide the chief contrast.
The increased clarity of the clear-cut images is worth any amount

of time spent locating definition of nautical terms. Bunting had already answered Zukofsky's objections to a specialised vocabulary during the writing of *The Spoils* when he said: 'I dont think my sea is overspecialised (compared, lets say, with TSE and his garboard-strakes)...But the reader doesn't need to know...Most people know something about the sea from reading or imaginary adventures' [25 June 1951]. The frequent contrast of such images as 'tilled acre', 'steading smell', and 'hearth's crackle' sharpens the physical and psychological situation in which 'Summer is bergs and fogs, lichen on rocks'.

Besides the thematic contrast of sea and land, a syntactical contrast is the minimum use of a verb or adjective to strengthen the impression of paucity or scarcity ('gold scarce,/ walrus tusk, whalebone, white bear's liver' or 'Scurvy gnaws, steading smell, hearth's crackle') and the maximum use of verbs to build an impression of deliberateness or length of time ('he blends, balances, drawing leagues under the keel' or 'Days jerk, dawdle, fidget'). Characteristically, short lines are balanced with a long 'flexible, unrepetitive line':

> Crew grunt and gasp. Nothing he sees
> they see, but hate and serve. Unscarred ocean,
> day's swerve, swell's poise, pursuit,
> he blends, balances, drawing leagues under the keel
> to raise cold cliffs where tides
> knot fringes of weed.

The image of the poet-mason is recalled in

> Who cares to remember a name cut in ice
> or be remembered?

The words the 'Wind writes in foam on the sea' speak appropriately of impermanence and temporality. Bunting sent one longer version of this self-contained fragment to Zukofsky [6 December 1964] with the note that the 'way [it] subsides to next to nothing is intentional':

> Who sang, sea takes,
> flesh brine, bone grit.
> Keener the kittiwake.
> Fells forget him.
>
> Fathoms dull the dale,
> slime voices.
> Watchdog the whale,
> gulfweed curtain.

The power Bunting achieves by condensing these lines with their

resonances of Old English poetry and by leaving the last line
incompletely articulated is a good example of his method:

Who sang, sea takes,
brawn brine, bone grit.
Keener the kittiwake.
Fells forget him.
Fathoms dull the dale,
gulfweed voices...

The punctuation strengthens the effect he wanted, of subsiding to
next to nothing, but this is sharply cut off by the first words of the
next stanza: 'About ship!' With this cry the persona moves abruptly
to the south, just as Bunting, dissatisfied, moved from place to
place when he was younger. The persona's efforts are divided
between dissipating his early experience of love which he tries to
denigrate and realising his vocation as a unique poet. But the
division itself and the attitude which causes it dooms his attempts,
though at times there is something as slight and tenuous as 'the
water's surface between/ appetite and attainment'.

The next four quatrains are closely connected by the opening
phrases 'It tastes good', 'It sounds right', 'It feels soft', and 'It looks
well'. Since each of the first three stanzas consist of one sentence,
the 'flexible, unrepetitive line' takes the reader through the entire
stanza. Each one focuses on a different sensual consideration with
telling details that unobtrusively fill in the Italian setting: 'the half-
sweet white wine of Orvieto', 'where the ramparts cuddle Lucca',
'Apennine sage', and 'Amalfitan kisses'. It is only in the fourth
stanza that the reader is brought up short with

It looks well on the page, but never
well enough. Something is lost
when wind, sun, sea upbraid
justly an unconvinced deserter.

Italy is still the setting in the next large block, another long
section of twenty-three lines, but the thematic emphasis here is on
the poet-mason and his connection with tombstones and death.
Although the region of the Garfagnana, Parma, La Cisa, and the
Apuan Alps is far from the Pennines of Part I, the same
transporting of tombstones down roads recalls the theme of the life
and death cycle introduced in the first part:

clouds echo marble middens, sugar-white,
that cumber the road stones travel
to list the names of the dead.

Instead of the lark's twitter and slowworm's mosaic of Part I, here

> Frogs, grasshoppers
> drape the rice in sound.
> Tortoise deep in dust or
> muzzled bear capering
> punctuate a text whose initial,
> lost in Lindisfarne plaited lines,
> stands for discarded love.

Lyrics which Herbert Read describes as 'adamantine'[25] seem carved out of the rock he has been speaking of in the next block of four four-line stanzas. This 'self-contained fragment' which appears in the sonata with no changes was sent to Zukofsky with the brief remark that the 'debt (if any) [is] to Kipling' [6 December 1964]:

> Win from rock
> flame and ore.
> Crucibles pour
> sanded ingots.
> Heat and hammer
> draw out a bar.
> Wheel and water
> grind an edge.
>
> No worn tool
> whittles stone;
> but a reproached
> uneasy mason
>
> shaping evasive
> ornament
> litters his yard
> with flawed fragments.

By 'heat and hammer' and 'wheel and water' men transform unformed, natural material into 'flame and ore' or are able to 'grind an edge', but the 'reproached uneasy mason' whose situation is underlined by broken lines of two or three words, or even one, only 'litters his yard with flawed fragments'. The short lines in the first stanzas seem almost incantatory, while perfect and imperfect end rhymes ('ore'/'pour', 'rock'/'ingots'), the repetition of vowels heard against the alliteration of consonants, and a sentence broken between stanzas create the impression of the difficult struggle of the uneasy mason whose lack of success is connected, characteristically, with reproaches.

This motif becomes a transition to the next block. For the third time in Part II, a long section, twenty-four lines this time, is contrasted with a contingent section of short, formal stanzas. This time the murder of Eric Bloodaxe, the dominant figure in the diagram of Part II, leads to an emotional peak in this part. In this autobiography in which Bloodaxe is a central image, it seems obvious that the historical figure is closely connected with the persona. This connection has been mentioned in the discussion of Part I, but there the brief references to Bloodaxe only fore-shadowed his larger role in II. The 'lies', 'king of Orkney, king of Dublin, twice/ king of York', are repeated in this part with greater significance. Somehow his moral failure is connected with his physical downfall:

> Loaded with mail of linked lies,
> what weapon can the king lift to fight

Moral failure as the cause of lack of success in his destiny suggests the situation of the persona whose lack of success too seems always connected with his partially dishonest response to love. The parallel seems even more evident when the poet includes in his description:

> long flight
> from who knows what smile,
> scowl, disgust or delight

The death and dissolution of the king is graphic, and the action is suspended abruptly while a question of the murderer's identity interrupts the death blow:

> trampled and hewn till a knife
> – in whose hand? – severs tight
> neck cords?

The significance of this ambiguous rhetorical question is not felt until it is followed much later by another one of even deeper significance at the end of the entire sonata:

> Who,
> swinging his axe
> to fell kings, guesses
> where we go?

In a complete change of tone and tempo, the next block of four six-line stanzas presents images in nature which 'figure' music for dance and song, such as galliards and madrigals by such composers as Byrd, Monteverdi, and Schoenberg. Bunting once admitted to me modestly: 'It is perhaps fortunate that though I knew Scarlatti well I did not then know much of Corelli, or I would have tried to emulate his aetherial largos and the way he makes the angels dance jigs, and I would have failed utterly instead of only relatively' [23 May 1972]. If ever Bunting may have wanted to emulate Corelli, it

seems that this section along with the slowworm's song at the end
of Part III may have been the place for it. As it is, the influence of
Scarlatti and other musicians is evident in these lines filled with
vitality and beauty; in the words of Bunting, these lines are 'lithe
and alert'.

The synaesthesia is effective and creative and in keeping with the
architecture of the whole. In a poem which is a sonata, it is
appropriate that music is made tangible and visual, and elements of
experience transformed into art forms. But these stanzas are not
merely a technical accomplishment. The motif of the persona's
dissatisfaction with his artistic achievement and his conception of
the possibilities reappears in the design of these stanzas without
disturbing the synthetic effects:

> But who will entune a bogged orchard,
> its blossom gone,
> fruit unformed, where hunger and
> damp hush the hive?
> A disappointed July full of codling
> moth and ragged lettuces?

Yet in a more optimistic tone the description returns to the
beautiful synaesthetic images of the first of these stanzas, and
almost as if in a seesawing argument, the forces of renewal working
through the transformation of experience into art gain the
upperhand:

> Yet roe are there, rise to the fence, insolent;
> a scared vixen cringes
> red against privet stems as a mazurka;
> and rat, grey, rummaging
> behind the compost heap has daring
> to thread, lithe and alert, Schoenberg's maze.

Against 'unformed fruit' and 'ragged lettuces', images of vitality are
balanced until the final judgment is made:

> So is summer held to its contract
> and the year solvent

However, this use of image and design from nature to figure
music is only a step toward the goal the artist is striving for. In the
conclusion Cyril Connolly describes as a 'precisely Yeatsian
evocation of Pasiphae',[26] the persona's recent judgment is recognised as only temporary when he imagines the combination of
human and divine, divine and bestial, flesh and spirit, to describe
the kind of union of which his art ideally must be an expression.

In these lines Bunting makes use of his wide knowledge of

classical mythology, one of the few instances since the earlier poems, for example, *The Well of Lycopolis*. It seems unnecessary to classify it as Connolly does, as 'precisely Yeatsian', when one considers the emphasis on the classics in Bunting's formal education and his modern use of myths from the earliest odes such as 'Chorus of Furies', 'Narciss', and 'Farewell, ye sequent graces'.

Each Scarlatti sonata is by no means to be analysed carefully for parallels with the part preceding or following it; it is enough to see the appropriateness generally to be convinced of their contribution to the whole. However, the opening chords of the Scarlatti sonata (L10/K84) underline the emphatic statement which closes Part II. This one serves particularly well as a transition between II and III since its ordered, yet 'diffuse thematic organisation' echoes the organisation of Part II which was more accurately paralleled in the 'blocks' of the sonata (L25/K46) preceding it. The sonata is representative of the transition from Scarlatti's full realisation of harmony to the 'lean and muscular delineation of the later slow movements'.[27] The delineation in Part III which moves upward to the highest emotional peak of the poem could easily be described as 'lean and muscular', especially as it moves closer to the climax:

> but he
> reached to a crack in the rock
> with some scorn, resolute though in doubt,
> traversed limestone to gabbro,
> file sharp, skinning his fingers,
> and granite numb with ice, in air
> too thin to bear up a gnat,
> scrutinising holds while day lasted,
> groping for holds in the dark

When Bunting outlined the diagram of his poem, he made it clear that the central part is a 'different thing'. As he described it, 'the middle one is a nightmare or dream or whatever you fancy'. In discussing 'free form' in the baroque sonata, William Brandt offers an explanation that should give an insight into this part of *Briggflatts*. Within music the free form, entitled "fantasie", is 'intended to sound as though it were being made up on the spur of the moment', although it is 'clearly organised in some loose way'. It only appears to be free because of the 'seemingly capricious use of thematic material, sudden changes of tempo', etc. 'The improvisatory forms are almost always linked to some more strictly defined form or procedure for contrast and formal balance.'[28] By placing this part in the centre of the sonata, the "fantasie" is formally balanced by the two parts before and after it, and its contrast with the other movements is sharpened since it is the only one of five parts which is a 'nightmare or dream'. One of the strongest contrasts of the entire sonata occurs within Part III when the persona awakens from his nightmare world to the natural one. This is probably what Bunting was indicating by drawing a vertical line dividing the middle peak of the diagram.

In an interview Bunting summarised the central part of the poem, 'Alexander's interview with the Angel on the top of the mountain', a Persian version of the legend from Firdosi's *Shahnameh*:

> Alexander wanders through country after country where the most horrible things are going on, and ultimately comes to the mountains of Gog and Magog on the edge of the world. And his troops refuse to follow him, but all alone he climbs up to the top of the mountain, and there he sees the Angel sitting exactly as in my poem, with the trumpet ready to his lips to blow, and looking anxiously to the east for the signal to blow the trumpet and put an end to the world. And that of course does Alexander's business for him: he falls off the mountain, comes to, and leads everybody home in peace to Macedonia.[29]

In the beginning Bunting's motto for this Part was '*Longe processit e flammantia moenia mundi*': which he translates as 'He went out far beyond the flaming walls of the world.' This would be a fitting description of the situation of the interview on the mountaintop. Before the legendary Alexander reached this peak, he barely endured a variety of hardships and sufferings in the adventures Bunting mentioned in his summary. The nightmare is in the form of a gradual Dantean journey which begins ominously and mysteriously and reaches a climax only after the horror becomes progressively more intense. The scene shifts from places where excrement is the key image, a commodity of the market-place, where turd-bakers would be slaughtered if leave were given, to places where pieces of brined and long-rotten corpses are stolen and where beggars advertise 'rash, chancre, fistula'.

Bunting relieves this nightmare landscape by a delicately beautiful description of dawn and by finally switching from disgusting human imagery of disease and death to unnatural nature imagery:

> we heard the teeming falls of the dead,
> saw kelts fall back long-jawed, without flesh,
> cruel by appetite beyond its term,
> straining to bright gravel spawning pools.

At this point another amazing obstacle is encountered which Bunting explained to me: ' "Banners purple and green" etc. are the

Northern Lights, Aurora Borealis, a formidable magnetic barrier
which was until lately thought to "pen in mankind" and make moon
voyages impossible' [4 July 1973]. These 'Banners purple and
green...pennants of red, orange blotched pale on blue' introduce
Alexander and his companions who refuse to follow him to a peak
they 'deemed...unscaleable'.

> But we desired Macedonia,
> the rocky meadows, horses, barley pancakes,
> incest and familiar games,
> to end in our place by our own wars,

The harsh difficulty of Alexander's scaling the peak alone is made
vivid from the series of phrases piled on top of each other for the
eight lines already quoted until at the utmost point 'far beyond the
flaming walls of the world'

> ...the morning star reflected
> in the glazed crag
> and other light not of the sun
> dawning from above
> lit feathers sweeping snow
> and the limbs of Israfel,
> trumpet in hand, intent on the east,
> cheeks swollen to blow,

According to legend Alexander (Sikander) overcame super-
human obstacles to attain the peak in order to see 'visions of his
futurity'. At the summit he learned indelibly the lesson of human
mortality, and especially of the short span of his own life. In
Atkinson's translation Sikander (Alexander) sees the vision of one

> Wrapt in his grave-clothes, and in gems embedded.
> In gold and precious jewels glittering round,
> Seemingly to show what man is, mortal man!
> Wealth, worldly pomp, the baubles of ambition,
> All left behind, himself a heap of dust!
>
> None ever went upon that mountain top,
> But sought for knowledge; and Sikander hoped
> When he had reached its cloudy eminence,
> To see visions of futurity
> Arise from that departed, holy man!
> And soon he heard a voice: 'Thy time is nigh!
> Yet may I thy career on earth unfold!
> . . . .
> Renowned and glorious shalt thou be; thy name
> Immortal; but, alas! thy time is nigh!'
> At these prophetic words Sikander wept,
> And from that ominous mountain hastened down.

In Bunting's version the climax of the journey through the

nightmare vision of society is Israfel's sigh:

> Yet delay!
> When will the signal come
> to summon man to his clay?

In a scene reminiscent of medieval dream literature, the sleeper awakens from his dream journey to see the world with a new vision articulated in the slowworm's song. Nothing could afford a greater contrast to the preceding nightmare than the natural scene which ends Part III. Even the difference in form underlines the contrast. The first part of the movement leading to the climax on the mountain-top is written in a long section of ninety-five continuous lines. This is contrasted with the last part of the movement written in seven short sections.

The slowworm, an essential element of spring and a phallic image of life in the first part of *Briggflatts*, from the beginning has also been a symbol of death and dissolution of the body in the grave. Instead of the 'cold squirm snaking [the sleeper's] flank' affirming death and mortality in these lines, it presages an affirmation of life and the vitality and renewing qualities of nature which will be celebrated in the slowworm's song. In his uncomplicated philosophy his concern is with being himself, 'neither snake nor lizard', living simply by using whatever is naturally available, uninterested in the more complicated concerns of others, and, above all, delighted by the beauty and variety of nature which cleanses and renews. Aside from the lively way in which Bunting reads the lines, the format and content of the lines indicate the allegro tempo:

> Vaults stored wiť slugs to relish,
> my quilt a litter of husks, I prosper
> lying low, little concerned.
> My eyes sharpen
> when I blink.
>
> Good luck to reaper and miller!
> Grubs adhere even to stubble.
> Come plowtime
> the ditch is near.
>
> Sycamore seed twirling,
> O, writhe to its measure!
> Dust swirling trims pleasure.
> Thorns prance in a gale.
> In air snow flickers,
> twigs tap,
> elms drip.

Finally, the section ends in a kind of crescendo:

> Swaggering, shimmering fall,
> drench and towel us all!

The finality of the last lines:

> So he rose and led home silently through clean woodland
> where every bough repeated the slowworm's song

brings to a climax the twofold vision of Part III in which the nightmare living men and women have made of community life is contrasted and complemented by the possibility of a simple life lived in harmony with nature. In both cases though, mortality and death colour the situation. The end of the world is symbolised by the vision of Israfel, the Angel of Judgment in Persian culture, and the death of the individual is in the background of the second section by the very presence of the slowworm. But the final mood of Part III is one of quiet thoughtfulness and acceptance of life.

Besides the more general parallels between the Scarlatti sonata and *Briggflatts* already discussed, the sonata played at the conclusion of Part III presents two specific points of comparison which strengthen the movement of this Part. First, the sonata (L275/K394) is divided into two parts that seem so independent that it has been disputed whether or not they form one or two sonatas. This echoes the strong division in thematic material, mood, tone, tempo, and form in the part of *Briggflatts* just heard. Further, the sonata opens with a descending melody which seems a continuation of the descending movement of the poetry. This began at the highest emotional peak with Alexander's interview on the mountain top and followed his descent in the "fantasie" to the last line in which the ambiguous 'he', Alexander and the poet, 'led home silently'. This sonata looks forward to the next part in its 'free unfolding of melodic material in which one theme spontaneously suggests another'. The 'easy flow from one theme to another'[30] can also be considered a unifying characteristic of the entire poem.

Part IV begins with a montage of precise images from nature which convey the impression that the 'height' of all that has been described to this point 'has subsided':

> Grass caught in willow tells the flood's height that has subsided;
> overfalls sketch a ledge to be bared tomorrow.

It is finally a picture of a subdued homecoming to the familiar Dales where 'Rats have left no potatoes fit to roast' and where 'gamey tang' and 'tomcat stink' recall distant exotic scenes where ibex and leopard were the game.

Killing game leads naturally to visions of more serious killing which are somehow connected with the very fact of being 'adult male of a merciless species'. Aneurin, the key figure of this autumnal section, is described by Bunting as someone who 'ought to be known to all, but probably isn't, the great Welsh poet of the early Dark Ages who left a splendid poem called *Gododdin*, mourning the men killed at the battle of Catterick by the newly arrived English'.[31] Lines reminiscent of Whitman's syntactical parallelisms are connected by a sentence which is central to Bunting's concern with the past and present:

> I hear Aneurin number the dead, his nipped voice.
>
> . . .
>
> I hear Aneurin number the dead and rejoice,
> being adult male of a merciless species.
> Today's posts are piles to drive into the quaggy past
> on which impermanent palaces balance.
> I see Aneurin's pectoral muscle swell under his shirt,
> pacing between the game Ida left to rat and raven,
> young men, tall yesterday, with cabled thighs.

Bunting who in a letter to Zukofsky [6 August 1953] coupled Aneurin with Taliesin as two poets who 'belong with the best and straightest' mentions them as a pair again years later in these lines:

> Clear Cymric voices carry well this autumn night,
> Aneurin and Taliesin, cruel owls
> for whom it is never altogether dark, crying
> before the rules made poetry a pedant's game.

If Aneurin and Taliesin belong to the Dark Ages, Columba, Aidan, and Cuthbert 'put on daylight'. Here Cuthbert at least marks a deliberate symmetry with Bloodaxe of the early parts of the poem, but aside from admitting that, Bunting refuses to pedantically set other symmetries for questioners:

> There are symmetries – matching one another here and there. They are not followed out pedantically in full detail and so forth, but they are there. There's the contrast between Bloodaxe and Saint Cuthbert here, the extreme opposites of each other in things...There's the way in which these two parts are connected which I can't put a name to which quite closely resembles the way these two are...You're asking for things which are too far down, hid in the subconscious, to be brought out without falsifying in a way.[32]

A more immediate contrast follows in the comparison of the perspectives and outcomes of these men with those figured by the fox, leech, and weevil, or by cattle whose perspective is too narrow for them to consider anything beyond their own 'hedge horizon', or by runts who

> murder the sacred calves of the sea by rule
> heedless of herring gull, surf and the text carved by waves
> on the skerry.

that is, by a narrow perspective that disregards larger designs of natural balance and of beauty. Positive images of men such as Columba, Aidan, and Cuthbert concerned with larger perspectives and higher values,

> not for bodily welfare nor pauper theorems
> but splendour to splendour, excepting nothing that is

are contrasted with negative images of those who are centred in a small world, existing by 'rule', heedless of larger designs and useless patterns of beauty. There is nothing in these contrasting images to be calculated logically in order to come to a neat conclusion. Just as no one can

> trace shuttles thrown
> like drops from a fountain, spray, mist of spiderlines
> bearing the rainbow, quoits round the draped moon;
> shuttles like random dust desert whirlwinds hoy at their
> tormenting sun?

so also in this case; the persona concludes:

> Follow the clue patiently and you will understand nothing.

After this long first section of Part IV, the tone and mood shift as abruptly as in a Scarlatti sonata. Nature itself echoes the skills of Domenico Scarlatti which the poet would like to emulate in his poetry:

> It is time to consider how Domenico Scarlatti
> condensed so much music into so few bars
> with never a crabbed turn or congested cadence,
> never a boast or a see-here; and stars and lakes
> echo him and the copse drums out his measure,
> snow peaks are lifted up in moonlight and twilight
> and the sun rises on an acknowledged land.

This 'acknowledged land' acts as a transition which introduces the song of praise of the persona's love. Here the key sonata (L.33/K.87), the B minor fugato sonata which was in Bunting's mind from the beginning of the plan of *Briggflatts*, begins softly in the background to continue by itself finally as the interlude between Part IV and V. This unobtrusive background cannot soften, in the pejorative sense, strong, unsentimental lines which translate into distinctly English terms, themes and expressions from the *Song of Songs* and the description of the ideal wife from Proverbs, 31. 10-31:

My love is young but wise. Oak, applewood,
her fire is banked with ashes till day.
The fells reek of her hearth's scent,
her girdle is greased with lard;
hunger is stayed on her settle, lust in her bed.
Light as spider floss her hair on my cheek which a puff scatters,
light as a moth her fingers on my thigh.

It is possible to think of the symmetry of this theme of mature love and faithfulness and the earlier one of young love and unfaithfulness as a further strengthening of the firm architecture of the whole.

In contrast with sections which are compressed as far as possible, the syntax of this section is without any kind of ellipsis. In fact, in order to echo the biblical cadences better, *and*s are added in a line that is repeated as a refrain:

We have eaten and loved and the sun is up.

Most of the beauty of the design of this love song derives from its being composed of parallelisms which also recall Bunting's assimilation of Persian poetry. The pattern of one line is repeated in the next or the pattern of the first half of a line is repeated in the second half:

The fells reek of her hearth's scent,
her girdle is greased with lard;
hunger is stayed on her settle, lust in her bed.

The 'Goodbye' that ends each section of the praise of his love is more immediately final than it appears at first. The next section moves from the repetition of images of impermanence, smouldering applewood knots and 'cobweb hair' which 'a puff would blow...away', to images of oncoming winter and death. This section then becomes a sober contrast to the picture of love, comfort, and satisfaction preceding it:

Rime is crisp on the bent,
ruts stone-hard, frost spangles fleece.

Eighteen strong, short lines beat out defiance and scorn in a section which begins:

Where rats go go I,
accustomed to penury,
filth, disgust and fury;

This bitterly angry tone shifts to a more poignant expression of increasing separation and loneliness, a second contrast with the theme of the comfort of love:

> Stars disperse. We too,
> further from neighbours
> now the year ages.

As a transitional device, this looks forward to Part V in which the star motif, heard so far only faintly and intermittently, becomes dominant in an important final theme.

The Scarlatti sonata which has been in the background for the last forty-six lines is heard clearly once Part IV is finished, and its minor key and andante movement make it seem a continuation of the autumnal movement.

The first section of Part V introduces the final descending movement of the entire sonata. Two emotional high points remain within this Part, but even these are muted in harmony with the winter setting and the mood of

> Solstice past,
> years end crescendo.

The precise descriptions of the end of a cycle with its own unique beauty is elevated by the poet's imagination into the casual, yet formally arranged order of art which recalls this kind of vision in Part II especially. The artistic vision is integrally combined with music:

> Drip – icicle's gone.
> Slur, ratio, tone,
> chime dilute what's done
> as a flute clarifies song,
> trembling phrase fading to pause
> then glow. Solstice past,
> years end crescendo.

The "music" of the sounds within the poetry itself bears out what Bunting insists is important; that ideally his work must be read aloud and ideally by someone from Northumberland. His pronunciation of 'dilute' with a long *i* links the word with 'chimes' and 'clarifies' to effect what he is describing. Further, the pronunciation forces the word to be said more deliberately and thus draws more attention to the unobtrusive internal rhyme of 'chime dilute' – 'as a flute' which plays against the imperfect end rhymes, 'gone', 'tone', 'done', and 'song'. The music of such intricate internal rhyming as

> pause
> then glow. Solstice past,
> years end crescendo

and

> sinews ripple the weave,
> threads flex, slew, hues meeting,
> parting in whey-blue haze

is not easily lost if the poetry is read aloud.

Repeated motifs of the sea and shore are primary, but here the mason and stone motif are recalled as secondary terms in a simile whose onomatopoetic sounds create a definite visual and aural image:

> Silver blades of surf
> fall crisp on rustling grit,
> shaping the shore as a mason
> fondles and shapes his stone.

The precise description of shepherds and dogs in Northumberland, timeless except for the names of trainers Wilson and Telfer, corroborate Peter Quartermain's remark about Bunting's 'observant eye':[33]

> fell-born men of precise instep
> leading demure dogs
> from Tweed and Till and Teviotdale
> with hair combed back from the muzzle,
>
> . . .
>
> Their teeth are white as birch,
> slow under black fringe
> of silent, accurate lips.

This section with its timeless description culminates in one of the key phrases of the entire poem: 'and Then is diffused in Now'. In the next large section of Part V, this key idea is repeated even more strongly.

The smooth transition to this next section about the stars is by way of the light which 'lifts from the water' and directs attention unhurryingly, through a link with all the preceding description of land, to 'Bleached sky. Cirrus...':

> Light lifts from the water.
> Frost has put rowan down,
> a russet blotch of bracken
> tousled about the trunk.
> Bleached sky. Cirrus
> reflects sun that has left
> nothing to badger eyes.
>
> Young flutes, harps touched by a breeze,
> drums and horns escort
> Aldebaran, low in the clear east,
> beckoning boats to the fishing.

Here the imagination of the poet again supplies music to augment the grand entrance of these 'Furthest, fairest things, stars'. Charles Tomlinson complains that Bunting 'goes wrong' when he brings in an orchestra which can not be heard. This 'cannot work as an analogy for comparable emotions in the poem,' he believes, 'because the sounds he asks us to imagine in such a passage are extra-verbal and hence unachievable within the poem's acoustics.' He concludes that 'music must inhere for the poet in his verbal meshings and not in "sounds off" '.[34]

It is true that it is 'precisely in those verbal meshings, rhyme disposed in its time sequence counterpoising a Then and Now, that Bunting's "musical" successes come'. However, the reinforcement of that "music" by the imagined sounds of musical instruments seems a creative combination that an imaginative reader can be expected to 'hear' with delight. These horns, drums, and flutes are leading to the finale of the sonata which the majestic opening chords of the Scarlatti sonata will translate into the kind of instrumental music that Bunting is helping the reader imagine. Further, the images of music taper off to a synaesthetic image, the kind that has been woven through the texture of the entire sonata, so that the image of music from instruments blends into one which is not unexpected or incongruous:

> flutes flicker in the draft and flare.
> Orion strides over Farne.

All the images of stars are closely linked with the sea motifs of the earlier section of this part and are spoken of familiarly as by one who knows each of them well, as Bunting does:

> Capella floats from the north
> with shields hung on his gunwale.
>
> . . .
>
>   – Betelgeuse,
> calling behind him to Rigel.
> Starlight is almost flesh.
>
> . . .
>
> watching Capella steer for the zenith,
> and Procyon starts his climb.

As mythological figures, the constellations share a kind of immortality and a kind of presence in Then and Now. As natural objects, the stars have a stability and constancy so reliable that each 'places a surveyor's stone or steadies a tiller'. Through the simultaneous permanence and transience of the light of a star, an essential assertion of the sonata is imaged: 'Then is Now.'

Charles Tomlinson discusses this aspect as the key point of the sonata. He praises the 'achievement of the poem' as one which

'derives from the attempt to bring Then into as close a relation with
Now as possible...by the central device of imitating the "condition
of music".' Later he summarises the achievement in another way:

> Then and Now: that incident of fifty years since and other incidents in
> Northumbrian history of a greater starkness...all now the spoils of time,
> are held over against the present moment and landscape, the quality of
> that wet spring night informing this present moment and demanding all
> the intricacy of musical form that Bunting brings to the confrontation.[35]

The perspective of the entire poem to this point has been the
double one. Only after the key idea, 'Then is Now', becomes
explicit is the time past spoken of in the past tense, and only then
does the double perspective become one:

> light from the zenith
> spun when the slowworm lay in her lap
> fifty years ago.
> The sheets are gathered and bound,
> the volume indexed and shelved,

Up to this point the present tense has been used to describe these
happenings, even though as an 'autobiography', all that has been
described must have taken place in the past. The use of the present
tense is not merely an arbitrary use of the "historical present"
tense, but an artistic use. The double perspective working
throughout the poem demands that the past, 'Then', be described
and felt visually and immediately, yet always played against and
coloured by the second perspective of the autobiographer's present
judgment 'Now'.

The debt which has dogged the autobiographer since the first
part of the sonata is paid for as far as possible by the very act of
writing the poem, an act which has exorcised the guilt he has felt
for 'fifty years':

> Fifty years a letter unanswered;
> a visit postponed for fifty years.
>
> She has been with me fifty years.

The time past finally does become actually the Past, yet all is
connected integrally in this one life. Even more distant pasts in
which Eric Bloodaxe, Cuthbert, Aneurin and Taliesin move are
bound up in this one human history.

The importance of the last line of Part V, 'For love uninterrupted
night', is not to be underestimated. Bunting tried to convey some of
its importance in an interview:

> But you see the Catullus line here [the motto for Part V of the diagram],
> *'nox est una perpetua dormienda'*. It's a much more complex line than any

of the translators have ever got across. The *una* is never given its full value...*Nox est perpetua*: there is an everlasting night. *Una dormienda* doesn't mean one night, it means a night that is all one, that never varies. That is the important point in the Catullus line, you see. And that sets you thinking, and that sets you going, and things come into your mind. It is from that, I should think, though I'm not sure at this stage, time has passed, that it's probably from that line that the whole train of thought started, that brought back the various things that become matter in the poem. But the poem starts merely as a shape.[36]

In Part V any sharp or bitter note of self-hatred and self-recrimination has disappeared. Here the tone is one of an alert and clear-eyed acceptance of himself, of his natural situation which is mirrored in the winter beauty of his surroundings, and finally an acceptance of the ultimate situation:

> Starlight quivers. I had day enough.
> For love uninterrupted night.

Charles Tomlinson was considering the analogous quality of 'Lindisfarne's plaited lines' in *Briggflatts* when he quoted the words Ruskin used to describe the 'verbal music' of Jean de Meung;

> There is to be rich rhyming and chiming, no matter how simply got, so only that the words jingle and tingle together with due art of interlacing and answering in different parts of the stanza, correspondent to the involutions of tracery and illumination.[37]

Although the 'rich rhyming and chiming' is a quality of the entire sonata, the Coda demonstrates this rich tissue of sounds in a brief section of three five-line stanzas. In the first five lines, for example, the most obvious 'verbal music' is the rhyming of 'strong', 'song', and 'long' interwoven with 'tows', 'follow', 'not know' and with 'earsick', 'spray flick':

> A strong song tows
> us, long earsick.
> Blind, we follow
> rain slant, spray flick
> to fields we do not know.

Every word but two in each stanza is monosyllabic; the disyllabic words lend interest by blending masculine and feminine rhymes. The long *o* rhyme sound of this first stanza is echoed in the second stanza by the strong imperative, 'float', and again in the third stanza by the end-rhyme of the first and last lines, 'knows' and 'go'. The repetition of this sound which is heard at the end of three lines in the first stanza helps give a terseness and shape to the entire Coda.

Besides the one inherent in the words, another aspect of sound is added in the recording of *Briggflatts* when Bunting strongly

emphasises 'shout' and does actually shout out the indirect
questions the 'offshore wind' must 'ask the sea':

> what's lost, what's left,
> what horn sunk
> what crown adrift.

The emphatic enunciation of all these stanzas underlines the
spondaic character of much of the rhythm by stressing words that
are set apart, such as 'Blind' and 'Night' and 'who knows'. A legato
effect is created often by the combination of stressed words and
words somewhat equivalent to quantitative long syllables, words in
which a vowel is followed by two consonants which force the
careful reader to articulate them slowly:[38] 'lost', 'left', and 'adrift'.
All these elements, especially the repeated questions ('who', 'what',
'where'), the emphatic spondees of the irregular, legato rhythm,
work together to communicate the feeling of human doubt and
uncertainty about what is ultimately unknowable, the future:

> Where we are who knows
> of kings who sup
> while day fails? Who,
> swinging his axe
> to fell kings, guesses
> where we go?

The B minor fugato sonata, heard once before, concludes the
poem, under-lining the mood by its minor key. More importantly,
the clear melodic lines which cross and echo each other and are
heard in many variations abstract, in a sense, the design of the
music from the poem. One is not an equivalent of the other, but in
their own modes each is 'an endlessly varied record of experience'
which ridicules translation into prose.[39]

Besides those quoted here – Herbert Read, Kenneth Cox,
Charles Tomlinson, Michael Hamburger, and Cyril Connolly who
made *Briggflatts* his 'Critic's Choice of the Year',[40] many other
authorities, for example, Hugh MacDiarmid,[41] Robert Creeley[42]
and Donald Davie,[43] have praised this sonata enthusiastically.

Although the words of any of these could be used to summarise
Bunting's accomplishment, Kenneth Cox integrates many aspects
of it. However, to his opening comment that '*Briggflatts*, somewhat
unfairly, makes Mr Bunting's earlier poetry look like preparatory
work', the poet has a response:

> Amongst philosophers I have most sympathy with Lucretius and his
> masters, content to explain the world an atom at a time; with Spinoza
> who saw all things as God, though not with his wish to demonstrate that

logically; and with David Hume, the doubter. The men I learned poetry from did not value these. Perhaps that is why it took me so long to make a poem that reflects, fragmentarily, my whole mind.

Kenneth Cox continues with his strong integrative summary:

[*Briggflatts*] returns to the north country with English both purified and enriched, the past and its studies absorbed. Here and there is a southern warmth, an eastern courtesy, the skill of a Latin poet in placing a long word, the audacious finality of Dante...Yet it is the long practice of the translator, the persistent testing of every word, which has made possible the unfailing discretion with which the life and appearance of the country is represented without a trace of provincialism or lapse into the banal. In addition to romantic theory and symbolism technique it infuses into the native tradition the sensuality of oriental poetry and attains, not by imitation but by a revival of its primitive elements, the standard of the King James version of the Old Testament.[44]

To this and all criticism of *Briggflatts*, Bunting repeats his simple credo: 'Let the incidents and images take care of themselves.' However, just before writing this, he composed a fuller explanation which he complained had been 'teased out of me by people who cannot be content to listen without reasoning'. In it is his firm statement that the heart of the sonata is the music: '*Briggflatts* needs no explanation. The sound of the words spoken aloud is itself meaning, just as the sound of the notes played on the proper instruments is the meaning of any piece of music.'

Here too, in *A Note on 'Briggflatts'*, he did allow a deeper glimpse into his soul than he usually permitted:

Call it God, call it the universe, all we know of it, extended far beyond our telescopes or even inferences, detailed more minutely than our physicists can grope, is less than the histology of a single cell might be to a man's body, or to his conduct. The day's incidents hide our ignorance from us, yet we know it, beneath our routine. In silence, having swept dust and litter from our minds, we can detect the pulse of God's blood in our veins, more persuasive than words, more demonstrative than a diagram. That is what a Quaker meeting tries to be, and that is why my poem is called *Briggflatts*.[45]

The achievement of the poem is the seamless combining of all these elements.

UNFINISHED SONATA

Bunting did not intend this sonata to be his last. When he arrived home after the long voyage from British Columbia through the Panama Canal, he wrote to me on 23 May 1972:

It may illuminate what I've said about sonata form or any other form if I tell you what happened on the voyage home. I'd a number of themes in my head for at least three years, some longer, but could do nothing with them because they didnt seem to join together or oppose each other in any way that suggested their proper shape. Then one night I saw the new moon, the very first new moon, emerging from the old moon as Helen, Selanna, the new moon, must have emerged from Leda's egg; and the next night I watched Jupiter as a drop of molten silver sliding down the flank of the new moon. And as I turned away from this marvellous sight I caught a glimpse of a very young girl who seemed obviously the new moon in flesh, slim, graceful, blonde; and instantly many old themes began to assemble themselves as though this were the keystone enabling them to form an arch, themes of renewal, mainly, closely bound, though I had never perceived it. And this was wonderfully reinforced when I spoke to the girl and found her name was Linnaea and she a descendant of Linnaeus who named all the flowers, as though she were Persephone as well as Selanna. There was even the germ of an anti-theme ready to fit in, though that needs more perception before I can use it. I cannot say more yet; but it seems to me that I shall soon be able to begin work on a sonata, or what is more likely to prove a sonata than not, with the transformations of the first theme all worked out though those of the second may delay me.

When I asked him if I could quote the New Moon letter, he replied: 'If you really want the extract from my letter to you about the new moon, I wont grumble too audibly. It's irrelevant to whatever finally gets onto paper...Perhaps you'd prefer 30 lines which will almost certainly be the first of the poem (provided I ever do it). I'll copy them for you.'

Such syllables flicker out of grass:
'What beckons goes'; and no glide lasts
nor wings are ever in even beat long.
A male season with paeonies, birds bright under thorn.
Light pelts hard now my sun's low,
it carves my stone as hail mud
till day's net drapes the haugh,
glaze crackled by flung drops.
What use? Elegant hope, fever of tune,
new now, next, in the fall, to be dust.

Wind shakes a blotch of sun,
flatter and tattle willow and oak alike
sly as a trout's shadow on gravel.
Light stots from stone, sets ridge and kerf quick
as shot skims rust from steel. Men of the north
subject to being beheaded and cannot avoid it
of a race that is naturally given that way.
'Uber sophiae sugens' in hourless dark,
their midnight shimmers like noon.
They clasp that axle fast.

Those who lie with Loki's daughter,
jawbones laid to her stiff cheek,
hear rocks stir above the goaf;
but a land swaddled in light? Listen, make out
lightfall singing on a wall mottled grey
and the wall growls, tossing light,
prow in tide, boulder in a foss.
A man shrivels in many days, eyes thirst for night
to scour and shammy the sky
thick with dust and breath.

His note on the bottom of the thirty lines, three ten-line stanzas, read: '*First* draft – many errors and clumsinesses to be cut out or changed' (26 February 1973).

After this buoyant letter, time and again he deplored the concerns that did not leave him the peace of mind he needed to complete a long sonata in these last years. In May 1975 he wrote:

> I've written nothing for a long time. You will easily imagine that inflation on the scale we are enduring leaves no peace to a man whose income is fixed and very small. More and more has to be done without. I never know two months in advance how we shall live. That is not a circumstance favourable to reflection, let alone steady craftsmanship. But I'll put a little bit into the envelope that I concocted for the tercentenary of Briggflatts meeting house, which is being celebrated this spring.

Six years later, in June 1981 after his move to Greystead, he seemed a little more hopeful:

> I dont expect to write any more. What a man of my age writes can seldom be any good. Nevertheless in such a splendid place, if there are no nagging worries, something might happen to get down on paper at last, even perhaps 'The New Moon'. There are sure to be visitors in the summer (this is a beautyspot, thronged on public holidays) but I dont expect any at all in the winter [he was mistaken], so that I may write out of boredom!

Lack of time and peace of mind conflict with renewed vitality and insights of beauty in this long letter just as it does in the thirty lines of the first draft he had written earlier. Both the energy and difficulty of writing as well as the deeper understanding of the transience of life are foreshadowed in the first stanza:

Such syllables flicker out of grass:
'What beckons goes'; and no glide lasts
nor wings are ever in even beat long.

Rhythm underscores meaning. The quick music of 'syllables flicker' lengthens to 'goes; and no glide lasts' to end in the broken rhythm of 'nor wings are ever in even beat long'.

But counterpointed against this tone is the keen awareness of natural beauty used refreshingly in clear images. 'A male season with pœonies' suggests that in the plants, bright and blossoming, the male part is mature and ready in late spring or early summer to produce seed before the female part is ready, oftentimes because of light conditions. Both flowers and birds, 'bright under thorn', in fresh plumage, are bursting with vitality. However, the late spring possibilities conflict with the persona's time of life in lines of imitative sounds:

> Light pelts hard now my sun's low,
> it carves my stone as hail mud
> till day's net drapes the haugh,
> glaze crackled by flung drops.

This side of the conflict is underlined by the strong music of spondees in words that must be carefully enunciated, from 'light pelts hard' to 'glaze crackled by flung drops'. Bunting had expressed something of this conflict earlier when he wrote to me that 'it looks as though I will have to try to find a job again...thus making poetry not far from impossible for a long time to come; and I haven't got a long time to come (though I'm healthy for my age).'

Ironically, the vibrancy of the next lines contradicts the despondent poet:

> What use? Elegant hope, fever of tune,
> new now, next, in the fall, to be dust.

In the second stanza the counterpoint continues, but this time, after images of energetic nature – sun, wind, plant and fish life, the shift in the simile is to man-made 'shot' and 'rust' and 'steel' as the fate of the individual is subsumed into the group's:

> Men of the north
> subject to being beheaded and cannot avoid it
> of a race that is naturally given that way.

Light in the next lines looks back to the light and sun already mentioned in stanza 1 and 2 and toward light in the next stanza. But in these lines in a variety of ways light contrasts with darkness. 'Men of the north' search 'in hourless dark' of day and of mind for wisdom, another kind of light, and 'their midnight shimmers like noon./ They clasp that axle fast.'

In the third stanza the darkness is the deeper darkness of Hel, Loki's daughter, the goddess of death who rules over nine worlds in the depths of Niflheim. All who die except men slain in battle enter her realm under the earth 'after a painful journey over the roughest road in the cold, dark regions of the extreme North...Within the gate amid the intense cold and impenetrable darkness [are] heard the rolling of the glaciers and other streams of Hel.'[46] 'Those who lie with Loki's daughter/ jawbones laid to her stiff cheek' who 'hear rocks stir above the goaf' are dumbfounded by the possibility of 'a land swaddled in light?' Music returns as the dead 'Listen, make out/ lightfall singing on a wall mottled grey'. Then more energy is heard and seen as 'the wall growls tossing light,/ prow in tide, boulder in a foss'.

In a transformation of theme that Bunting wrote to me about, the tone changes when light becomes inimical, shrivelling a living man and blinding him. Dust and breath so obscure the sky during the day that he thirsts for night in which he can see clearly:

> A man shrivels in many days, eyes thirst for night
> to scour and shammy the sky
> thick with dust and breath.

In a letter about the new moon and these thirty lines, Bunting had closed with 'As for God's graces, what can we see except in the dark? Daylight is opaque, like water we've washed our hands in' [26 February 1973]. Contrasted with daylight and life, this same complex theme of night and darkness as a symbol of death yet also a time of clarity had figured strongly in *Briggflatts*. The Dantean conclusion of 'day enough./ For love uninterrupted night' is haunting. Not placidly but with energy here, the last lines return to his theme of daylight as opaque, night as the time for seeing clearly.

In these last few lines the intricate music of rhythms and sounds – 'shrivels' 'shammy', 'eyes' 'night' 'sky', and 'thirst' 'thick' 'breath' – is just a hint of the beauty that may have been shared if the 'New Moon' sonata had been completed.

Bunting closed the letter about the plans for this sonata and its music with renewed life:

> Perhaps I expect more of myself than an old man can carry out; but I feel more confident and gayer than I've felt for years, and at least there [in the experience on board ship] is an example for you of how the matter fits itself together, with no intervention from the conscious me:...My difficulty may be to hide the myths in something more ready to the contemporary mind. Corelli would have seen in them types of the resurrected God, but he wouldn't have underlined that. It would have been hidden in jigs and long, long notes that you can take merely for delights.

In 1982 when I asked him if he was working on his poetry, he said in a confidential tone that he was. But he would never allow a sonata to be published unless he was satisfied with it. On television he spoke about cutting a poem down with care: 'The fewer words it takes to say something useful the better, the more likely it is to be remembered. What is the sense of burdening the public with things you can avoid saying.'[47]

Unfortunately, he never finished 'The New Moon', and with all the qualifications Bunting sent with this first draft, it does not seem fair to discuss these thirty lines as something final. But even in this rough stage these lines with the intricacy of their music and the transformation of their themes look toward the quality of *Briggflatts*. Judging from the progression of his sonatas and from the promise of these lines, it is not rash to believe that this could have been his greatest sonata, a great loss. However, the legacy Bunting has left in the sonatas he did complete, especially *Briggflatts*, and in all the rest of his poetry seem great enough to assure him a place among the greatest writers of modern times.

CHAPTER 9

Conclusion

'Poetry, like music...' – for Basil Bunting this combination of terms is inseparable. When he acknowledges poets who have influenced him, he refers to those whose techniques help him realise in his work qualities he finds in such composers as Scarlatti, Johann Christian Bach, and Corelli – informally balanced structure, clear outlines, a variety of contrasts and associations. He mentioned a part of this after he had helped me get a tape of his reading: 'I'm glad you enjoyed the tape of *Briggflatts*. It is much more convincing with Scarlatti's music, and may give you some notion of what I've learned from Scarlatti, Corelli, and other musicians about terseness and shape.' As a postscript he added:

> Corelli should be the one for you, the Concerti Grossi, with jigs to play in the middle of Mass. I wonder whether the congregation was stirred to dance to the glory of God, like David before the Ark? I have seen a girl in Italy charlestoning up to the altar to get her Communion, and nobody seemed to think it odd. So, perhaps, should all worship be. [23 October 1972]

More than once, Bunting spoke of dance as the antecedent of poetry and music:

> To me it seems that history points to an origin that poetry and music share, in the dance that seems to be a part of the make up of *homo sapiens*, and needs no more justification or conscious control than breathing. The further poetry and music get from the dance and from each other, the less satisfactory they seem. Within that scope, various languages set various limits on what a poet can do.[1]

Another time he connected all three with his unshakable conviction that it is "absolutely necessary to read the poem aloud, not necessarily to an audience":

> But poetry is very close akin to music. They both come directly from the dance which seems to me to be built into us, a part of the process of being a human being. And the further they get away from each other and from the dance, the slacker and more useless they become. Like music, what you put down on the page is not what matters. You don't,

unless you're a great expert, spend much time turning over Beethoven's scores. You get a piano and play or you get somebody else to play them or a record or something. And it's the same way with poetry. You won't know what it is doing until you have listened to it.[2]

For Bunting, to share experiences in a fully human way – sensually, emotionally, and intellectually – requires poetry as close to music as possible for its fullest expression. His insistence that his poetry be read aloud is underpinned by Pound's theory of melopoeia. To achieve this melopoetic quality, Bunting creates a basic surface simplicity by means of ordinary but precise diction and economically compressed syntax. His concentration on 'the immediate, the particular, the concrete' [LZ, 2 October 1932] expressed with no unnecessary word is a source of strength and beauty in his poetry but also at times the basis for just charges of obscurity. At its best the surface simplicity combines with complexities of rhythms, varied stanzaic patterns, subtle vowel modulations and alliterations to create poetry that helps the audience share more than the connotative meanings of the words, but rather emotions 'too deep to name'. In Bunting's words

[Poetry's "meaning"] is of another kind, and lies in the relation to one another of lines and patterns of sound, perhaps harmonious, perhaps contrasting and clashing, which the hearer feels rather than understands; lines of sound drawn in the air which stir deep emotions which have not even a name in prose. [D]

This poetry whose music must be heard is what he worked to perfect all his life. Unfailingly, in writing and in speech, he gives credit to the poets of the past and present who helped him learn the 'sleights' he needed to know to write this kind of poetry. It is not too difficult to see what he taught himself from some of the most important. From Horace, Dante, Wordsworth, Villon, Whitman, Zukofsky and Pound he learned ways of creating poetry 'without fluff',[3] using ordinary diction and speech patterns. Dante taught him to say a thing once, sharply and with precision; Spenser, to use music suited to his theme. From Wyatt and Malherbe, he learned metrical inventiveness. Together with Zukofsky, Bunting firmly believed in Pound's pronouncement that poetry fails when it gets too far from music and that the best music is composed in the sequence of the musical phrase.

Besides subscribing wholeheartedly to almost all of Pound's famous 'Don'ts', Bunting strongly supported his concept of direct treatment [LZ, 1 May 1953]. The only published letter of Pound to Bunting deals chiefly with technique which is best suited to content:

> The poet's job is to *define* and yet again define till the detail of surface is in accord with the root in justice. [Rot] to submit to the transient. But poetry does not consist of the cowardice which refuses to analyse the transient, which refuses to see it.
> The specialised thinking has to be done or literature dies and stinks. Choice of the *field* where that specialised analysis is made has a percentage of relevance. In no case can constipation of thought, even in the detail, make for good writing. LUCIDITY.[4]

But, as evidence proves and as Bunting insists, Pound's place in Bunting's technical development, although assuredly an important one, must be kept in perspective by anyone evaluating Bunting's work. Bunting's own summary of the influences in his development maintains a balanced view:

> I've been thinking...about how and where I got whatever I know and feel about poetry, and the more I think the bigger Malherbe's part in it seems. Wordsworth, when I was a small kid showed me what it was; Rossetti's translations from the Dolce Stil people, in my teens, and Whitman at the same time, enlarged the scope. Horace gave me the first inkling of how it was done (odes). Malherbe produced all I afterwards found in Ez's writing except what I'd already got from Horace. Ez and Spenser, great galleries of technical accomplishment. Lucretius. Dante. And after that, Hafez for what I got from Horace (and Ez from Chinese,) only more, taken further; Manuchehri, greater and more splendid gallery than Ez and Spenser; Wyat; the Mo'allaqat; and for sheer pleasure, when I am not out to learn or have my mind fixed, for diversion, for mere living, Homer and Ferdosi. Could one make a kind of 'Education of X?' out of these reflections, I wonder. [LZ, 6 August 1953]

Translations and adaptations helped Bunting learn techniques from great poets of other languages, Latin, Persian, Italian, and Japanese, but the results are mixed. One from Lucretius Bunting himself gave up on, others are among his best poems, *Chomei at Toyama*, for example, which has a section of its own in the *Collected Poems*. About the 'Overdrafts' Bunting warns in his Notes that 'it would be gratuitous to assume that a mistranslation is unintentional', evidence that he was working to go beyond the literal to create something more, in Pound's words, to 'make it new'.

The quality of the odes he wrote throughout his life is uneven. The obvious progression in tone, from the earliest odes of an immature youth ('Weeping oaks grieve', I-1; 'Farewell ye sequent graces', I-2) to the final odes of the life-experienced man ('Stones trip Coquet burn', II-10; 'At Briggflatts meetinghouse', II-11; 'Perche no spero', II-12), is as marked as the development of his craftsmanship. But the progression is not so chronological that such odes as 'To Peggy Mullett', I-3, and 'Dear, be still!' I-9, written in his twenties, or 'Vestiges', I-20 written at thirty-one, can be passed over.

As he searched for the right music in his poetry during era after era of the twentieth century, he was experiencing a cosmopolitan life that he would distill to create his best poems. But always it is much more. When an interviewer asked him near the end of his life about his statement that his poems are based on experience collected over a long time, he replied: 'That's true in a certain sense, in a certain degree. But I think that anything of the sort must begin with a pattern. It's filling up the pattern that's easier if you have a great deal of experience to pick out things you have observed which will fit into it.'[5]

Finally, the shape and pattern he found most congenial to his gift was the early sonata form. At seventy-six he seemed proud of his accomplishment: 'I think I was the first one who got the idea of imitating the form of the sonata and I have carried it to further lengths than any of the others.'[6] The first sonatas depend to some extent on the material of other older poets, but their expression is modern and the themes are always personal concerns. By 1952 both the material and the musical techniques are uniquely his own and used with originality to develop themes which are personal but more broadly universal.

In the sonatas, above all, and in *Briggflatts* especially, the balanced architecture of the whole provides the necessary framework for the full development of Bunting's art. This form through which he gained the freedom and "spirit" of Scarlatti's sonatas allows scope for the overall development of themes throughout several large movements. The means are best described in musical terms: incremental repetition of themes and recurrent motifs, contrasting rhythms, tempos, and texture of sounds, and tone colour. Within each movement subordinate thematic and technical developments through contrasts and associations parallel the larger ones. For Bunting all this is necessary for the fullest expression of the human experiences he is communicating.

The thematic and technical relationships among all his sonatas, in fact, among all his collected poems, create a unity like the *Art of the Fugue*. This is a goal he spoke of in a poignant letter to Zukofsky:

> Don't be dust yet a bit, please...No one who would even guess what I mean when I want to do an 'Art of the Fugue' or 'Grosse Fugue' (not fugal, I mean, but as plain, unadornable, solid, all the beauty in the form entire) in words; since I can't hope to do a 'Great Service' or an

equivalent of the best melodies of Monteverdi or Handel. Yours is a somewhat different art, but we've enough aims in common to keep some sort of touch, some sort of mutual pleasure. [18 June 1953]

Just as the musical development of the poems has an obvious essential unity, so do their thematic concerns. Grouped around the tensions of life and death, art and experience, permanence and impermanence, the predominant themes always express the individual's responses, and always there is the primacy of human values.

Fundamentally, Bunting insists that his poetry is 'seeking to make not meaning but beauty' [D]. In a letter to his daughter Roudaba, he wrote: 'What else can I say to my dear daughter now? Only...that I love you: that writing poetry is a skill like weaving carpets or shaping bowls on the potter's wheel and is not an intellectual exercise to make people afraid of the poet' [7 September 1966]. The beauty his skill created, his particular contribution to modern poetry, he describes in modest terms:

> My excellence, if I have one, isn't new or striking. I suppose that's what TSE misses. I'd say I remember the musical origin of poetry, the singing side of it, better than anybody except Ezra or Carlos Williams; and that the process of association or contrast or what you will that I think I derive from Horace, Hafez, and the symphonic composers, differs from Ez's 'ideogram' or the Waste Land manner, being at once less arbitrary and more under control...but if so, that won't be perceived in this generation. I've added nothing much. But I think I've done the job quite well, skilfully, unrepetitively. I hope so, anyway. [LZ, 6 July 1951]

Hugh MacDiarmid's opinion, one Bunting valued highly, is not so understated as Bunting's and more precisely describes the public judgment of an increasing number:

> History may not repeat itself exactly but poetry readers who remember how long Gerard Hopkins was kept out of print by his uncomprehending contemporaries and the great vogue and vitalising influence his work has had since are today faced in Basil Bunting with a great poet who has had to wait far longer for recognition. In my opinion his poems are the most important which have appeared in any form of the English language since T. S. Eliot's *Waste Land*...[7]

More recently, Hugh Kenner dedicated *The Sinking Island: The Modern English Writers* (1988) to the memory of 'Basil Bunting 1900-1985 "With never a crabbed turn or congested cadence, Never a boast or see-here." ' On his first page he begins his discussion of idioms 'from Venerable Bede to Basil Bunting'. This places Bunting in a sphere Kenner proves he deserves, especially in his last chapter when he singles out Basil Bunting in a lengthy discussion as one of the quartet of modern poets who are the best, 'his music firm, the semantics kept open by sparseness'.[8]

With only a little adjustment the words of the young Bunting as a music critic describe his own lifelong achievement as a poet who 'remembered the musical origin of poetry, the singing side of it...quite well':

> [This artist] is not for lazy hearers. It is impossible to lean back and dream your way through some of his recitals. He makes no compromise...and he refuses blankly to take upon himself the burden of expressing anybody's and everybody's callow emotions for them. There are plenty of performers ready to flatter their audience by debasing fine thought to the platitudes of emotional debauchery...
>
> For me it is impossible not to listen, and, listening, impossible not to follow the thought closely; and that requires considerable expenditure of energy...The effort needed to follow it is similar to that required by the exposition of a physical problem by say Dr Whitehead or Professor Eddington. Nothing can be skipped. Nothing is redundant. Yet everything is there, and the problem is so obviously fascinating that no one with the slightest curiosity could shirk it. [He] has thought the piece out from the beginning without preconceptions, and presents it so firmly that, even if we should fail, after all, to understand it, at least we cannot misunderstand it. He is never vague, never "atmospheric", always decided, solid, definite...
>
> ...[He] is very emotional, but, not being sentimental, he does not substitute emotion for understanding like so many many famous [artists], but keeps it subordinate. He knows that the audience can be trusted to supply the emotion, [but he does not let that] limit him to the cast-iron, inhuman detachment that might endear him to our contemporary prigs. He does not affect impersonality.[9]

As apt as this description is, it does not touch the heart of his accomplishment, Basil Bunting's ability to 'dignify and perpetuate our common life'[10] with its varied experiences by elevating them to poetry as near as possible to the condition of music.

Notes

Abbreviations used in text and notes:

D	*Descant on Rawthey's Madrigal: Conversations with Basil Bunting*, edited by Jonathan Williams (Lexington, KY: Gnomon Press, 1968).
LZ	Letters to Louis Zukofsky, 1930-1964. Harry Ransom Humanities Research Center, University of Texas at Austin. All letters from Bunting to Zukofsky are from this collection, cited in text as LZ with date.
AG 16	*Agenda*, 16 no. 1 (Spring 1978): Basil Bunting special issue.
PI 19	*Poetry Information*, 19 (Autumn 1978): Basil Bunting special issue.
Clucas	Garth Clucas, 'Basil Bunting: A Chronology', PI 19.
83 Answers	'83 Answers...and Some Questions'. With Basil Bunting and Jonathan Williams, introduced by Eric Robson, BBC North East, 17 August 1984 and 19 April 1985.
Guedalla	Roger Guedalla, 'Basil Bunting: A Bibliography of Major Works and Criticism', PI 19.
Hall	Anthea Hall, 'Basil Bunting Explains How a Poet Works', *The Journal* (Newcastle), 17 July 1965, p.7.
Lesch	Barbara E. Lesch, 'Basil Bunting: A Major British Modernist', dissertation, University of Wisconsin (1979). This includes comments by Bunting not published elsewhere.
Measure	'Measure of Words'. With Basil Bunting, Tony Bilbow; introduced by Eric Mottram; director, James Whiteley; producer, Heather Ging; research, Derek Smith: *Come In*, Tyne Tees Television, 21 July 1983 and 21 April 1985.
Mottram	Eric Mottram, 'Conversations with Basil Bunting on the Occasion of His 75th Birthday', PI 19.
A Note	*A Note on Briggflatts* (Durham: Basil Bunting Poetry Archive, Durham University Library, 1989).
Read	'Basil Bunting: Music or Meaning?', *Agenda*, 4 (Autumn 1966).
Quartermain	'Basil Bunting Talks About *Briggflatts*', AG 16; interview first published, in slightly different form, in *Writing* (*Georgia Straight, Writing Supplement*), no. 6 (18-25 November 1970), Vancouver, B.C.
Statement	Basil Bunting, 'The Poet's Point of View', *Arts Diary*, Northern Arts (April/Summer, 1966); reprinted in full in D (see above), and in part on the sleeve of the LP record *Basil Bunting reads 'Briggflatts'* (Bloodaxe Books, 1980).

COLLECTED POEMS:

Basil Bunting's *Collected Poems* was first published by Fulcrum Press (London) in 1968. The second edition published by Oxford University Press in 1978 incorporates some corrections by Bunting and includes four additional poems: 'All the cants they peddle', 'Stones trip coquet burn' and '*At Briggflatts meetinghouse*, (*Odes* II-9, 10, 11) and 'You can't grip years, Postume' (*Overdrafts*). The first American edition published by Moyer Bell (Mt Kisco, NY) in 1985 includes one additional poem, '*Perche no spero*', first published in an earlier version dated 1977 in *Agenda*, 16 no. 1 (Spring 1978).

Introduction (pp.11-13)

1   Mottram, 6.
2   Hall.
3   See [D] above. References to this book (which has no pagination) will be indicated in the text.

Chapter 1: **Basil Bunting: A Life** (pp.15-69)

1   See [D] above. References to this book (which has no pagination) will hereafter be indicated in the text only.
2   Brian Swann, 'Basil Bunting of Northumberland', *St Andrew's Review* (Spring-Summer 1977), 40.
3   Mottram, 6. See Guedalla, 88, for mention of Bunting's first poem, 'Keep Troth', *The Leightonian* (December 1916), 87-88, and prizes for poem and essay published in a Leeds evening paper (1916-17).
4   Noel Stock, *The Life of Ezra Pound* (New York, 1970), 283.
5   83 Answers.
6   Lesch, 36.
7   Measure.
8   Clucas, 70.
9   Basil Bunting to Leippert, 30 October 1932. Ronald Lane Latimer Papers, University of Chicago Library.
10 1 December 1923. *Letters of Ford Madox Ford*, edited by Richard Ludwig (Princeton, 1965), 160.
11 (Cambridge, MA: Pym Randall Press, 1971, ix-x.
12 Bunting to Leippert, 30 October 1932.
13 Bunting to Sisley Huddleston, 14 October 1926. Carlton Lake Collection, Humanities Research Library, University of Texas at Austin.
14 83 Answers.
15 Bunting to Leippert, 30 October 1932.
16 Charles Norman, *Ezra Pound*, revised edition (New York, 1979), 300.
17 Conversations with Bourtai (Bunting), 1986-7.
18 83 Answers.
19 Norman, 316-17.
20 Conversations with Roudaba (Bunting), 1986-7.
21 Guedalla, 79.
22 Jenny Penberthy, 'Brief Words Are Hard to Find: Basil Bunting and Lorine Niedecker', *Conjunctions*, 8 (1985), 160.
23 *The Autobiography of William Carlos Williams* (New York, 1951), 264.
24 Bunting to Louis Zukofsky, 7 September 1932. See LZ above.

J

25 Reprinted in PI 19.
26 iii-iv.
27 Guedalla, 74.
28 Clucas, 71.
29 83 Answers.
30 83 Answers.
31 83 Answers.
32 Measure.
33 Tom Pickard, 'Serving My Time to a Trade', *Paideuma* 9 no. 1 (Spring 1980), 155.
34 'Letters of Lorine Niedecker to Cid Corman 1961-1970', edited by Lisa Pater Faranda, *Conjunctions*, 5 (1983), 156.

Chapter 2: Poetics (pp.70-77)

POETICS AND LITERARY CRITICISM
1 Mottram, 8.
2 Bunting's 'Statement' was first published under the title 'A Poet's Point of View' in *Arts Diary*, Northern Arts (April/Summer, 1966). It is reprinted in full in D, and in part on the sleeve of the LP record *Basil Bunting reads 'Briggflatts'* (Bloodaxe Books, 1980).
3 Michael Hamburger, *The Truth of Poetry: Tensions in Modern Poetry from Baudelaire to the 1960s* (New York: Harcourt Brace Jovanich, 1969), 273.
4 'Criticism and Music', *Outlook*, 61 (28 April 1928), 526-27.
5 ['Rapallo Jan 28th, anno XII'], 'Date Line', *Make It New* (London, 1934), 7.
6 Pound, 'Date Line', 3-4.
7 Both Bunting [28 February 1972] and Louis Zukofsky [27 June 1972] wrote to me that they were not aware that the essay was ever published.
8 Pound, 'Date Line', 5.
9 'Brancusi', *Literary Essays of Ezra Pound*, edited by T. S. Eliot, 2nd edition (London, 1960), 441.

FORM AND MUSIC IN POETRY
10 Quartermain interview.
11 'How to Read', *Literary Essays of Ezra Pound*, 25.
12 See Read, 4-10, who enlists Longinus, Stravinsky and Zuckerkandl in Bunting's defence.
13 Eldon, 'Next in Line as the Grand Old Man of Poetry?', *Evening Chronicle* (Newcastle), 9 June 1965, 6.
14 See Susan Sontag, 'Against Interpretation' and 'On Style', *Against Interpretation* (New York, 1947), 3-36.
15 Read, 4-5.
16 Jonathan Williams & Tom Meyer, 'A Conversation with Basil Bunting', PI 19, 39.
17 Mottram, 5.
18 'An Arlespenny: Some Notes on the Poetry of Basil Bunting', *King Ida's Watch Chain* (Newcastle, 1964), no pagination.

Chapter 3: Major Contemporary Influences (pp.78-82)

1 'The Music of Poetry', *On Poetry and Poets* (New York, 1961), 26, 30, 32.
2 'T. S. Eliot', *The Literary Essays of Ezra Pound*, 421.
3 Hamburger, 122.
4 Lesch, 26.
5 Hamburger, 122.
6 'How to Read', *The Literary Essays of Ezra Pound*, 25-26.
7 *The Literary Essays of Ezra Pound*, 437.
8 *ABC of Reading* (New York, 1934), 61.
9 *Autobiography* (New York, 1970); Louis and Celia Zukofsky, *Bottom on Shakespeare*, 2 vols (Austin, TX, 1963).
10 *Prepositions: The Collected Critical Essays* (New York, 1967), 17.
11 *Prepositions*, 27, 28.
12 *Prepositions*, 30-31.

Chapter 4: Odes (pp.83-108)

1 Conversations with Jaafar Moghadam and Khosrow Moshtarikhah, Iranian midshipmen, University of Notre Dame students, 1971-72.
2 Warren D. Anderson, *Ethos and Education in Greek Music: The Evidence of Poetry and Philosophy* (Cambridge, MA, 1966), 2.
3 'Ode', *Encyclopedia of Poetry and Poetics*, edited by Alex Preminger (Princeton, 1965), 585; 'Ode', *Dictionary of World Literature*, 2nd edition (Totowa, NJ, 1966), 289.
4 Renée Winegarten, *French Lyric Poetry in the Age of Malherbe* (Manchester, 1954), 4.
5 Willi Apel, *Harvard Dictionary of Music* (Cambridge, MA, 1947), 503.
6 Lesch, 36.
7 J. B. Leishman, *Translating Horace* (Oxford: Bruno Cassirer, 1956), 38.
8 Measure.
9 Lesch, 302.
10 Lesch, 303.
11 Ezra Pound and Marcella Spann (New York, 1958), p. 315-6.
12 'D. H. Lawrence', *The Literary Essays of Ezra Pound*, 387.
13 Kenneth Cox, 'The Aesthetic of Basil Bunting', *Agenda*, 4 (Autumn 1966), 22.
14 Cox, 22.
15 As a twenty-seven year old journalist in London, he wrote 'Squares and Gardens', *Outlook*, 59 (7 May 1927), 542, in which he vigorously defended their inestimable value.
16 Bunting wrote to Harriet Monroe, 1 May 1931, *Poetry Magazine* Papers, University of Chicago Library, about a 'repulsive' letter published in *Poetry*: 'Will people never learn that the business of poetry is poetry, and not social reform nor setting up the damaged selfesteem of diffident nations?' Forty years later he refused to contribute to a Special Issue of *Poetry*, 120 (September 1972), 'Against War': 'Poetry does not seem to me to have any business with politics....We are experts on nothing but arrangements and patterns of vowels and consonants...' (362).

17 'Let Them Remember Samangan' with 'Mesh Cast for Mackerel' are recorded by Bunting on *The Poet Speaks*, Argo Record PLP 1087.
18 *The Collected Poems of W.B. Yeats*, 2nd edition (London, 1950), 392.
19 Bunting to John Matthias, 23 March 1970.
20 Lesch, 129.
21 *Poetry*, 37 (February 1931), 260-61.
22 'Correspondence', *Poetry*, 28 (April 1931), 56.
23 Thomas Cole, 'Bunting: Formal Aspect', *Poetry*, 78 (September 1951), 368.
24 Cole, 366.
25 Cole, 366.
26 Bunting wrote to Zukofsky: 'I've been thinking...about how and where I got whatever I know and feel about poetry, and the more I think the bigger Malherbe's part in it seems...Malherbe produced all I afterwards found in Ezra's writing except what I'd already got from Horace' (6 August 1953).
27 Winegarten, 4.
28 E. Bretschneider, *Medieval Researches from Eastern Asiatic Sources* (London, 1887), 1, 9-24, 35-108.
29 Bretschneider, 10-12.
30 Bretschneider, 36-7.
31 See three strong statements in letters to Zukofsky, 5 March 1949, 1 December 1950, 10 May 1953.
32 Lesch, 40.
33 Leishman, 31.
34 Leishman, 149.
35 AG 16, 6.
36 Hall.
37 'The Northerners', *The Listener*, 84 (8 October 1970), 484.
38 Hall.

Chapter 5: **Translations and Adaptations** (pp.109-146)

1 'A Retrospect', *Literary Essays of Ezra Pound*, 7, 10.
2 'A Retrospect' 11.
3 Pound to W. H. D. Rouse, Rapallo, 23 March 1935. *The Letters of Ezra Pound: 1907-1941*, edited by D. D. Paige (New York, 1950), 274.
4 Pound to T. S. Eliot, Rapallo, 28 March 1935, *Letters*, 272.
5 Pound to Rouse, Rapallo, April 1935, *Letters*, 273.
6 15 (July 1936), 715-16.

LATIN TRANSLATIONS
7 *De Rerum Natura: Libri Sex*, edited by Wm. E. Leonard and Stanley Barney Smith. T. Lucreti Cari (Madison, WI, 1942), 199.
8 *Lucretius: On the Nature of Things: A Metrical Translation*, translated by Wm. E. Leonard (London, 1921), x, xi, 3.
9 *Lucretius*, translated by R. C. Trevelyan (Cambridge, 1937), 116.
10 Leonard, 3.
11 *Horace and His Lyric Poetry* (Cambridge, 1951), 116.

12 Robinson Ellis, *A Commentary on Catullus* (Oxford, 1976), 227.
13 Pound to Eliot, Rapallo, 28 March 1935, *Letters*, 272.
14 (Melbourne, 1959), 57.
15 *Horace: Odes and Epodes*, edited by Paul Shorey and Gordon Laing, 2nd edition (Chicago, 1919), 361.
16 Wilkinson, 152.
17 Joseph P. Clancy, *The Odes and Epodes of Horace: A Modern Verse Translation* (Chicago, 1960), 41.
18 Wilkinson, 133-34.
19 Shorey and Laing, xxvii.

ITALIAN ADAPTATION
20 (London, 1933), 73.
21 *Machiavelli: The Chief Works and Others*, translated by Allan Gilbert, 3 vols. (Durham, NC, 1965), I, x.
22 K. L. Goodwin, *The Influence of Ezra Pound* (London, 1966), 218-19.
23 Gilbert, 166-7.
24 Gilbert, ix.
25 Bunting to John Matthias, 23 March 1970.

PERSIAN TRANSLATIONS
26 This is a copy of a letter Bunting was sending in order to find a job during a time when his family was in severely straitened circumstances. William Carlos Williams was in possession of this letter also to try to locate a position for him.
27 Background information about Persian literature compiled from Reuben Levy, *An Introduction to Persian Literature* (New York and London, 1969); Jan Rypka, *A History of Iranian Literature* (Dordrecht, 1968); Omar Pound, *Arabic and Persian Poems* (New York, 1970); *Anthology of Islamic Literature from the Rise of Islam to Modern Times*, edited by James Kritzeck, (New York, 1964); A. J. Arberry, *Classical Persian Literature* (New York, 1958); E. G. Browne, *A Literary History of Persia*, 4 vols. (Cambridge, 1928-1930); E. Denison Ross, *A Persian Anthology*, translated by Edw. Granville-Browne (London, 1927); Najib Ullah, *Islamic Literature: An Introductory History with Selections* (New York, 1963).
28 Also in *Nine*, 4 (April 1956), 10, with this introductory stanza:

> The thundercloud fills the meadow with heavenly beauty,
> gardens with plants embroiders plants with petals,
> distils from its own white pearls brilliant dyes,
> makes a Tibet of hills where its shadow falls,
> San'a of our fields when it passes on to the desert.
> Wail of the morning nightingale, scent of the breeze,
> frenzy a man's bewildered, drunken heart.
> Now is the season lovers shall pant awhile,
> now is the day sets hermits athirst for wine.

This seems a wise omission from the *Collected Poems*.
29 Rypka, 102. See also his description of a Persian verse as 'a completely worked out and independent miniature', 101.
30 Arthur Upham Pope, *An Introduction to Persian Art since the Seventh Century A.D.*, (London, 1930).
31 'Modern Translation', *Criterion*, 15 (July 1936), 714.

32 Titled only in *Nine*, 2 (August 1950), 219.
33 Rypka, 101.
34 *Nine*, 4 (April 1956), 9; *Nine*, 2 (August 1950), 218-19.
35 A sample of this phonetic writing:

     Agar an turk i shirazi ba dast arad dil i ma-ra
     ba khal i hinduvush baksham Samarkand u Bukhara-ra.

     With these phonetic transcriptions, Bunting sent notes about pronuncia-
     tion and allusions.
36 Jaafar Moghadam and Khosrow Moshtarikhah, Iranian midshipmen
     studying at the University of Notre Dame, spent many hours with me
     sharing their knowledge of Persian literature, 1971-2. Khosrow located
     both poems which Bunting spelled out phonetically in Persian books of
     literature: 'Agar an turk' etc. in *The Inspired Tongue* (Khajehe Sham-
     saddin Mohammed Hafez Shirazi) edited by Pezhman Bakhtiari, 5th ed.
     (Teheran, 1345 [1966]), 4; and 'Gufta: Birun shdi ba tamashay i mah i
     no' in *The Complete Works of Hafez*, edited by Housian Bakhtiari,
     (Teheran, 1318 [1945]), 189. These served as a double check on
     Bunting's translations.
37 9 January 1938. *The Letters of Ezra Pound*, 305.
38 26 February 1951. Carlton Lake Collection, Humanities Research
     Library, University of Texas at Austin.
39 Foreword to Omar Pound, *Arabic and Persian Poems* (New York, 1970),
     11.
40 Foreword, *Arabic and Persian Poems*, 76.

JAPANESE ADAPTATION
41 Bunting to Leippert, 26 September 1932. Ronald Latimer Papers,
     University of Chicago Library.
42 Roger Bersihand, *Japanese Literature*, translated by Unity Evans (New
     York, 1965), 25.
43 *Anthology of Japanese Literature from the Earliest Era to the Mid-Nineteenth
     Century*, edited by Donald Keene, UNESCO Collection of Representa-
     tive Works: Japanese Series (New York, 1955), 197.
44 'Appreciating Present Conditions', *Conjunctions*, 8 (1985), 208.
45 *Introduction to Classic Japanese Literature*, edited by the Kokusai Bunka
     Shinkokai (Tokyo, 1948), 129.
46 Bunting to Morton Dauwen Zabel, 4 January 1933. Morton Dauwen
     Zabel Papers, University of Chicago Library.
47 *Poetry*, 43 (November 1933), 108.
48 Bunting to Zabel, 24 March 1933. Zabel Papers.
49 *Poetry* 42 (August 1933), 357.
50 Kokusai Bunka Shinkokai, 132.
51 Bunting to Zabel, 4 January 1933. Zabel Papers.
52 *Poetry*, 42 (August 1933), 357.
53 Keene, 93.
54 *Poetry*, 42 (August 1933), 356-57.
55 Robert H. Brower and Earl Miner, *Japanese Court Poetry* (Stanford,
     1961), 268, 269.
56 *Poetry*, 42 (August 1933), 356-57.
57 Bunting to John Matthias, 23 March 1970.

58 Keene, 197-98.
59 Hugh Kenner, 'A Resurrected Poet', *Poetry*, 78 (September 1951), 363.
60 *Poetry*, 42 (August 1933), 357.
61 20 November 1932. *Poetry Magazine* Papers.
62 "Bunting: Formal Aspects," *Poetry*, (September 1951), 367.
63 Anthony Suter, 'Time and the Literary Past in the Poetry of Basil Bunting', *Contemporary Literature*, 12 (Autumn 1971), 522.
64 Suter, 522.
65 Goodwin, 201.
66 20 November 1933. Besides Pound, Eliot and Yeats, Zukofsky and William Carlos Williams were early critics of the poem. See also Bunting to Leippert, 30 October 1932.
67 Pound to Zabel, 21 February 1933. Morton Dauwen Zabel Papers.

Chapter 6: **Early Sonatas** (pp.147-176)

1   *Poetry*, 39 (February 1932), 101, 110-11.
2   Quartermain interview.
3   Kenneth Cox, 'A Commentary on Basil Bunting's *Villon*', *Stony Brook*, 3-4 (1969), 59.
4   Lesch, 151.
5   See Cox ('A Commentary') for a different interpretation. Bunting wrote to me that he accepts 'no responsibility for Kenneth Cox's ideas, or for anybody's of what I am up to. I don't think in that sort of way. But he does perceive surprising things, and has a notion of what dictates structure. If he is often wrong in detail, at least he knows what *kind* of formal relations I've tried to put together.' [29 July 1972]
6   Anthony Suter, 'Time and the Literary Past in the Poetry of Basil Bunting', *Contemporary Literature*, 12 (Autumn 1971), 513-14.
7   Hamburger, 272.
8   *Poetry Magazine* Papers, University of Chicago Library (30 November 1930).
9   ' "London or Troy?" "Adest" ', *Poetry* 38 (June 1931), 161.
10 Cox ('A Commentary'), 68.
11 *Poetry Magazine* Papers, University of Chicago Library (13 July 1931).
12 'LXIII', *Catullus*, translated by Celia and Louis Zukofsky (New York, 1969), [no pagination].
13 Suter, 514.
14 *The Poems of Catullus*, translated by Peter Whigham (Baltimore, 1966), 139. Whigham retains Catullus' Cybebe form of Cybele, while Bunting regularises both to Cybele.
15 Ellis (Oxford, 1876), 209.
16 *Catullus* (Whigham), 26-27.
17 Dante Gabriel Rossetti, *The Collected Works of Dante Gabriel Rossetti*, edited by William M. Rossetti (London, 1888), II, 19.
18 *Catullus* (Whigham), 138.
19 *The Oxford Universal Dictionary on Historical Principles*, 3rd edition (1964), 'Ithyphallic', p. 1053.
20 Hamburger, 273.

21 Bunting to Harriet Monroe, 13 July 1931. *Poetry Magazine* Papers,
    University of Chicago Library.
22 Bunting's translation. See *Collected Poems*, 'Darling of Gods and
    Men, beneath the gliding stars'; see also, Bunting to Zukofsky, 28
    October 1935: ' *"Aequora pontis"*, Lucretius, *tibi rident aequora pontis*,
    i.e., for Venus'.
23 Geoffrey Hill, 'The Conscious Mind's Intelligible Structure: A Debate',
    Agenda, 9 (Autumn-Winter 1971-72), 14-23; Simone Weil, *The Need for
    Roots: Prelude to a Declaration of Duties Toward Mankind* (Boston), 216.

Chapter 7: The Spoils (pp.177-206)

1 The title on all the early drafts of *The Spoils*, Louis Zukofsky Collection,
   Humanities Research Library, University of Texas at Austin. All
   references to the early drafts are to this collection.
2 'I take it you have perceived that there are two separate moments in the
   breaking-camp sequence? Dawn, the camel wakes and lifts up his neck
   which has been stretched along the ground. There's no dung yet for the
   scarabs. That comes as the men saunter off after breakfast for a crap,
   pursued by scarabs, who cut the dung almost as it falls and shape it into
   balls with incredible speed and then roll it away, often before the man has
   finished. It is while this is at its height that the camels, now loaded, get up.
   I thought the soldier's satisfaction after breakfast worth noting.' [LZ, 3
   March 1951]
3 Suter, 522.
4 Ernest J. Grube, *The World of Islam* (New York, 1966), 172. See also
   Bunting's Foreword to Omar Pound, *Arabic and Persian Poems in English*
   (New York, 1970), 11.
5 Vincent Monteil, *Iran*, translated by Alisa Jaffa (London, 1965), 89;
   Grube, 70; Wilfred Blunt, *Isfahan: Pearl of Persia* (New York, 1966), 30;
   David Talbot Rice, *Islamic Art* (New York, 1965), 59.
6 Blunt, 30.
7 Blunt, 33.
8 Rice, 59.
9 E. G. Browne, *A Literary History of Persia*, 4 vols (Cambridge, 1928-30),
   II, 254-55.
10 Monteil speaks of 'Tughril Be, the "Sparrow-Hawk Prince" ' (*Iran*, p.
   114).
11 See Canto LIII: *The Cantos*, revised Collected edition (London: Faber &
   Faber, 1975), 265.
12 'Tradition and the Individual Talent', *Selected Essays*, 3rd enlarged edition
   (London: Faber & Faber, 1951), 13-22.
13 Quartermain interview; Hall; Bunting to Zukofsky, 'June the New
   Moonth'.
14 T. S. Eliot quoted by Bunting to Zukofsky, 22 June 1951.

Chapter 8: **Briggflatts** (pp.207-247)

1 Read, 7.
2 Bunting expresses his distaste for sentimentality in many statements; for example, see 'Recent Pianists', *Outlook*, 61 (11 February 1928), 177.
3 Read, 9.
4 Quartermain interview.
5 *A Note.*
6 Hamburger, 59.
7 Quartermain interview; Hall.
8 Quartermain interview.
9 *A Note.*
10 Charles Tomlinson, 'Experience into Music: the Poetry of Basil Bunting', *Agenda*, 4 (Autumn 1966), 15.
11 The Bloodaxe reading was recorded on 15 April 1977, with Scarlatti's B minor fugato sonata (L.33) mixed in with Bunting's reading to his instructions. The record, released to mark his 80th birthday in 1980, includes his statements on poetry, sound and meaning, in the sleeve-notes.
12 Tape recording of Bunting's reading of *Briggflatts*, University of British Columbia, 20 November 1970.
13 Hamburger, 273.
14 Read, 7.
15 11 July 1965. Edward Lucie-Smith Collection, Humanities Research Library, University of Texas at Austin. Bunting also mentions her in letters to his daughter Roudaba.
16 *Libro de Alexandre* quoted in Federico Carlos Sainz de Robles, *Historia y Antología de la Poesía Española (en Lengua Castellana) del Siglo XII al XX*, second edition (Madrid, 1950), 289.
17 Jose Manuel Blecua, *Historia y Textos de la Literatura Española* (Zaragoza, 1960), 42-43.
18 Fernando Valenti, record sleeve of *Sonatas for Harpsichord*, I (Westminster), XWN 18328.
19 Ralph Kirkpatrick, *Domenico Scarlatti* (Princeton, 1953), 210.
20 Quartermain interview. Hugh Kenner declares that 'Brag, sweet tenor bull' is 'the strongest opening in English since 'And then went down to the ship': *The Sinking Island: Modern English Writers* (New York: Knopf, 1988), 259.
21 Kenneth Cox, 'The Aesthetic of Basil Bunting', *Agenda*, 4 (Autumn 1966), 24.
22 Kirkpatrick, 259.
23 Kirkpatrick, 298.
24 Kirkpatrick, 287.
25 Read, 9.
26 'Out of Northumbria', *Sunday Times* (London), 12 February 1967.
27 Kirkpatrick, 161, 270.
28 William E. Brandt, *The Way of Music*, 2nd edition (Boston, 1968), 125.
29 Quartermain interview.
30 Kirkpatrick, 277.
31 Tape recording of Bunting's reading of *Briggflatts*, University of British

Columbia, 20 November 1970.
32 Quartermain interview.
33 Introduction to Bunting's reading of *Briggflatts* by Peter Quartermain, University of British Columbia.
34 Tomlinson, 16.
35 Tomlinson, 15-16.
36 Quartermain interview.
37 Tomlinson, 16.
38 J. B. Leishman, *Translating Horace* (Oxford, 1956), 42-48. In this section, 'Differences between Latin and English Prosody', the author studies in detail the slight possibilities of quantitative verse in English. However slight they may be, they help explain the "measure" of some of Bunting's poetry.
39 Kirkpatrick, 161.
40 *Sunday Times* (London), 3 December 1967. Connolly had reviewed *Briggflatts* previously in 'Out of Northumbria', *Sunday Times*, 12 February 1967.
41 'Private correspondence with the publisher', according to a letter from Deirdre Montgomery, Fulcrum Press, 1 July 1971. The quotation in which MacDiarmid praises Bunting's work appears on the jacket of Bunting's *Collected Poems*.
42 Robert Creeley, 'A Note on Basil Bunting', *Agenda*, 4 no.3 (Autumn 1966), 18-19. See also Robert Creeley, *A Quick Graph*, edited by Donald Allen (San Francisco, 1970), 143-48. Creeley travelled with Robert Duncan from San Francisco to Vancouver to hear Bunting's public reading of *Briggflatts* on 20 November 1970.
43 'Privately Published', *New Statesman*, 72 (4 November 1966), 672.
44 Kenneth Cox, 'The Aesthetic of Basil Bunting', *Agenda*, 4 no.3 (Autumn 1966), 27-28.
45 *A Note.*
46 H. A. Guerber, *Myths of Northern Land* (New York, 1895), 167-68.
47 Measure.

Chapter 9: **Conclusion** (pp.248-253)

1 'A Letter', *Agenda*, 10 (Autumn-Winter 1971-72), 12-13.
2 Measure.
3 *Letters of Ezra Pound: 1904-1914*, edited by D. D. Paige (New York, 1950), 277.
4 Measure.
5 Lesch, 148.
6 Lesch, 148.
7 Private correspondence with Deirdre Montgomery, Fulcrum Press, 1 July 1971.
8 (New York: Knopf, 1988), 258.
9 'Recent Pianists', *Outlook*, 61 (11 February 1928), 177.
10 Kenneth Cox, 'The Aesthetic of Basil Bunting', *Agenda*, 4 (Autumn 1966), 28.

Bibliography

Percy G. Adams: 'The Historical Importance of Assonance to Poets', *Publications of the Modern Language Association*, 88 (January 1973), 8-18.

Conrad Aiken: 'Review: *Active Anthology*', *Poetry*, 44 (August 1934), 276-79.

Michael Alexander (ed.): *The Earliest English Poems* (Baltimore: Penguin Books, 1966).

Keith Alldritt: *Modernism in the Second World War* (New York: Peter Lang, 1989).

Wilhelm Ambros: *The Boundaries of Music and Poetry* (New York: G. Schirmer, 1893).

Warren D. Anderson: *Ethos and Education in Greek Music: The Evidence of Poetry and Philosophy* (Cambridge, MA: Harvard University Press, 1966).

'Announcement of Awards', *Poetry*, 39 (November 1931), 96-111.

Willi Apel: *Harvard Dictionary of Music* (Cambridge, MA: Harvard University Press, 1947).

A.J. Arberry: *Classical Persian Literature* (New York: Macmillan, 1958).

—— (ed.) *Persian Poems: An Anthology of Verse Translations* (London: Dent, 1954).

Clive Bell: *Art*, Capricorn Books (New York: G.P. Putman's, 1958).

Robert M. Bender (ed.): *Five Courier Poets of the English Renaissance* (New York: Washington Square Press, 1969).

Thomas G. Bergin: *Dante* (New York: Orion Press, 1965).

Roger Bersihand: *Japanese Literature*, translated by Unity Evans (New York: Walker, 1965).

Jose Manuel Blecua: *Historia y Textos de la Literatura Española* (Zaragoza: Libreria General, Aula, 1960).

Harold Bloom: *The Visionary Company: A Reading of English Romantic Poetry*, 1st edition revised (Ithaca, NY: Cornell University Press, 1971).

William E. Brandt: *The Way of Music*, 2nd edition (Boston: Allyn & Bacon, 1968).

Geoffrey Brereton: *An Introduction to the French Poets: Villon to the Present Day*, University Paperbacks (New York: Barnes & Noble, 1956).

E. Bretschneider: *Medieval Researches from Eastern Asiatic Sources*, 2 vols (London: Kegan Paul, Trench, Trubner & Co., 1887), I.

Robert Brower and Earl Miner: *Japanese Court Poetry* (Stanford, CA: Stanford University Press, 1961).

Calvin S. Brown (ed.): *Music and Literature: A Comparison of the Arts* (Athens, GA: University of Georgia Press, 1948).

—— *The Reader's Companion to World Literature*, Mentor Book (New York: Dryden Press, 1956).

Edward G. Browne: *Literary History of Persia*, 4 vols (Cambridge University Press, 1928-30).

Basil Bunting: *Briggflatts* (London: Fulcrum Press, 1966).

—— *Briggflatts*, published in *Poetry*, 107 (January 1966), 213-37.

—— *Briggflatts*, LP record (Stream Records P1205, 1968).

—— *Briggflatts*, tape recording with Scarlatti sonatas, University of British Columbia, 20 November 1970.

—— *Briggflatts*, LP record with Scarlatti sonata in B minor, L.33, recording made 15 April 1977 (Newcastle upon Tyne: Bloodaxe Books YRIC 0001, 1980).

—— *A Note on Briggflatts* (Durham: Basil Bunting Poetry Archive, Durham University Library, 1989).

—— '*Chinese Lyrics* and *Some Greek Poems of Love and Beauty*', *Criterion*, 17 (April 1938), 557-59.

—— *Chomei at Toyama*, I-VII, *Poetry*, 42 (September 1933), 301-07.

—— *Collected Poems* (London: Fulcrum Press, 1968).

—— *Collected Poems*, second edition (London: Fulcrum Press, 1970).

—— *Collected Poems*, second edition, corrected, with four additional poems (Oxford University Press, 1978).

—— *Collected Poems*, first American edition, with one additional poem (Mt Kisco, NY: Moyer Bell, 1985).

—— 'Correspondence', *Hound and Horn*, 6 (January – March 1933), 322-23.

—— 'Correspondence', *Poetry*, 120 (September 1972), 362.

—— 'Directory of Current English Authors', *Front* (April 1931), 217-24.

—— '*Eheu Fugaces, Postume, Postume*', *Agenda*, 8 (Autumn – Winter 1970), 61.

—— 'English Poetry Today', *Poetry*, 39 (February 1932), 264-71.

—— 'Ezra Pound', *New English Weekly*, 1 (20 May 1932), 137-38.

—— 'Fearful Symmetry', *Poetry*, 39 (February 1932), 251.

—— 'Fishermen', *Poetry*, 45 (October 1934), 13.

—— 'Hugh MacDiarmid Lost', *Agenda*, 16 no.3 (Autumn–Winter 1978-79), 81-82.

—— (ed.) Joseph Skipsey: *Selected Poems* (Sunderland: Ceolfrith Press, 1976).

—— 'A Letter', *Agenda*, 10 (Autumn–Winter 1972-73), 12-13.

—— Letters to Bourtai Bunting. Personal collection.

—— Letters to Roudaba Bunting. Personal collection.

—— Letters to Edward Dahlberg; 11 May 1951; 30 June 1951. Edward Dahlberg Papers, Harry Ransom Humanities Research Center, University of Texas at Austin.

—— Letter to T.S. Eliot; 2 May 1951. Louis Zukofsky Collection, Harry Ransom Humanities Research Center, University of Texas at Austin.

—— Letters to S. Victoria M. Forde; 6 June 1971–19 March 1985; and conversations January–April 1982.

—— Letter to Sisley Huddleston; 14 October 1926. Edward Dahlberg Papers, Harry Ransom Humanities Research Center, University of Texas at Austin.

—— Letters to [James G.] Leippert; 26 September 1932; 30 October 1932. Ronald Lane Latimer Papers, University of Chicago Library.

—— Letters to Edward Lucie-Smith; 21 June 1965; 11 July 1965; 9 January 1969. Edward Lucie-Smith Papers, Harry Ransom Humanities Research Center, University of Texas at Austin.

—— Letter to John Matthias; 23 March 1970.

—— Letters to Harriet Monroe; 1931-33. *Poetry Magazine* Papers, University of Chicago Library.

—— Letter to Ezra Pound; 26 February 1951. Ezra Pound Collection,

Harry Ransom Humanities Research Center, University of Texas at Austin.
——— Letters to Morton Dauwen Zabel; 4 January 1933; 24 March 1933.
Morton Dauwen Zabel Papers, University of Chicago Library.
——— Letters to Louis Zukofsky; 1930-64. Harry Ransom Humanities
Research Center, University of Texas at Austin.
——— *Loquitur* (London: Fulcrum Press, 1965).
——— '*Modern Translation* by E. Stuart Bates', *Criterion*, 15 (July 1936),
715-16.
——— 'Mr T.S. Eliot', *New English Weekly*, 1 (8 September 1932), 499-500.
——— *Outlook*, weekly articles, 59 (19 February 1927)–61 (19 May 1928).
——— (trs.) *The Pious Cat* by Obaid-e Zakani (London: Bertram Rota, 1986).
——— *Poems: 1950* (Galveston, Texas: The Cleaner's Press, 1950).
——— Poems and notes, *ca.* 1930-64. Louis Zukofsky Collection, Harry
Ransom Humanities Research Center, University of Texas at Austin.
——— *The Poet Speaks*, LP record (Argo Records PLP 1087, 1967).
——— 'The Poet's Point of View', *Arts Diary*, Northern Arts (April/Summer,
1966); reprinted in full in D, and in part on the sleeve of the LP record *Basil
Bunting reads 'Briggflatts'*.
——— *Redimiculum Matellarum* (Milan, 1930).
——— '*The Rover* by Joseph Conrad', *Transatlantic Review*, 2 (August 1924),
132-34.
——— (ed.) Ford Madox Ford: *Selected Poems* (Cambridge, MA: Pym-Randall
Press, 1971).
——— *The Spoils* (Newcastle upon Tyne: Morden Tower Book Room, 1965).
——— *The Spoils*, in *Poetry*, 79 (November 1951), 84-97.
——— 'Thanks to the Guinea Worm', *Agenda*, 8 (Autumn–Winter 1970),
117-21.
——— 'Three Poems from the Persian', *Nine*, 2 (August 1950), 217-19.
——— 'Three Poems from the Persian', *Nine*, 4 (April 1956), 9-10.
——— 'To Violet', *Poetry*, 58 (September 1941), 304.
——— 'Two New Odes', *Agenda*, 4 no.3 (Autumn 1966), 3.
——— 'Valentine and Orson', *Poetry*, 40 (August 1932), 293-95.
——— *Villon*, in *Poetry*, 37 (October 1930), 27-30.
——— 'What about Herbert Read?', *Agenda*, 7 (Spring 1969), 41-45.
——— 'The Word', *Poetry*, 37 (February 1931), 260-61.
Basil Bunting Issue: *Agenda*, 16 no.1 (Spring 1978).
Basil Bunting Issue: *Bête Noire*, 2/3 (Spring 1987).
Basil Bunting Issue: *Georgia Straight Writing Supplement*, 6 (18-24 November
1970).
Basil Bunting Issue: *King Ida's Watch Chain: A Moving Anthology: Link One*
(Newcastle upon Tyne: Morden Tower Book Room, 1964).
Basil Bunting Issue: *Paideuma*, 9 (Spring 1980).
Basil Bunting Issue: *Poetry Information*, 19 (Autumn 1978).
Basil Bunting Issue: *Scripsi*, 1 nos. 3/4 (April 1982).
'Basil Bunting: Poet of Unique Strengths', *The Times* (19 April 1985), 14.
Sigurd Burckhardt: 'The Poet as Fool and Priest', *Journal of English Literary
History*, 25 (December 1956), 279-98.
Gaius Valerius Catullus: *The Complete Poems for American Readers*, translated by
Reney Myers and Robert Ormsby (New York: E.P. Dutton, 1970).

———— *The Complete Poetry*, translated by Frank O. Copley (Ann Arbor: University of Michigan Press, 1957).

———— *The Complete Poetry of Catullus*, translated by Roy Arthur Swanson (New York: Liberal Arts Press, 1967).

———— *The Poems of Catullus*, translated by Peter Whigham (Baltimore: Penguin Books, 1966).

———— *The Poetry of Catullus*, translated by C.H. Sisson (New York: Orion Press, 1967).

P.A. Chapman *et al* (eds.): *An Anthology of Seventeenth Century French Literature* (Princeton NJ,: Princeton University Press, 1928).

'Cino da Postoia', *The Collected Works of Dante Gabriel Rossetti*, with a preface and notes by William Rossetti, 2 vols (London: Ellis and Elvey, 1888), II, 163-77.

Joseph P. Clancy: *The Odes and Epodes of Horace*, Phoenix Books (Chicago: University of Chicago Press, 1960).

Thomas Clark: 'New Lines', *Poetry*, 109 (November 1966), 110-12.

Alasdair Clayre: 'Recent Verse', *Encounter*, 29 (November 1967), 74-76.

Thomas Cole: 'Bunting: Formal Aspects', *Poetry*, 128 (September 1951), 366-69.

Cyril Connolly: 'Critic's Choice of the Year', *Sunday Times* (3 December 1967).

———— 'Out of Northumbria', *Sunday Times* (12 February 1967).

Aaron Copland: *Music and Imagination* (Cambridge, MA: Harvard University Press, 1952).

Kenneth Cox: 'The Aesthetic of Basil Bunting', *Agenda*, 4 no.3 (Autumn 1966), 20-28.

———— 'Basil Bunting', *Scripsi*, 3 nos. 2 & 3 (August 1985), 1-5.

———— 'A Commentary on Basil Bunting's *Villon*', *Agenda*, 16 no.1 (Spring 1978), 20-36; *Stony Brook*, nos.3-4 (1969), 59-69.

Robert Creeley: 'A Note on Basil Bunting', *Agenda*, 4 no.3 (Autumn 1966), 18-19.

———— *A Quick Graph: Collected Notes and Essays*, edited by Donald Allen (San Francisco: Four Seasons Foundation, 1970).

John Cunliffe and Ashley H. Thorndike (eds.): *The World's Best Literature*, University edition, 30 vols (New York: Warner Library Co., 1917), XXV.

Donald Davie: *Ezra Pound: Poet as Sculptor* (New York: Oxford University Press, 1964).

———— 'Privately Published', *New Statesman*, 72 (4 November 1966), 672.

———— *Under Briggflatts: A History of Poetry in Great Britain 1960-1988* (Manchester: Carcanet Press, 1989).

Martin S. Day: *History of English Literature: 1660-1837* (Garden City, NY: Doubleday. 1963).

L.S. Dembo: 'Louis Zukofsky: Objectivist Politics and the Quest for Form', *American Literature*, 44 (March 1972), 74-96.

Babette Deutsch: *Poetry in Our Time* (New York: Columbia University Press, 1956).

Mora Dickson: *Baghdad and Beyond* (Chicago: Rand McNally & Co., 1961).

Martin Dodsworth (ed.): *The Survival of Poetry: A Contemporary Survey* (London: Faber, 1970).

'Eighty-three Answers...and Some Questions', *Coast to Coast*: with Basil

Bunting and Jonathan Williams, BBC Television, 17 August 1984 and 19 April 1985.

Eldon: 'Next in Line as the Grand Old Man of Poetry?', *Evening Chronicle* (Newcastle), 9 June 1965.

T.S. Eliot: *On Poetry and Poets*, Noonday Paperbound edition (New York: Farrar, Straus & Cudahy, 1961).

———— *The Sacred Wood: Essays on Poetry and Criticism*, University Paperbacks (London: Methuen, 1950).

Robinson Ellis: *A Commentary on Catullus* (Oxford: Clarendon Press, 1876).

'Exotic Northumbria', *Times Literary Supplement*, 16 February 1967.

Lisa Pater Faranda (ed.): 'Selected Letters of Lorine Niedecker to Cid Corman', *Conjunctions*, 5 (1985), 137-72.

Ferdowsi: *The Epic of Kings*, translated by Reuben Levy, Persian Heritage Series (Chicago: University of Chicago Press, 1967).

Sean Figgis & Andrew McAllister: 'Basil Bunting: The Last Interview', *Bête Noire*, 2/3 (Spring 1987), 22-51.

Firdausi: *The Shah Nameh of the Persian Poet*, translated by James Atkinson (London: George Routledge, 1892).

Agnes Kate Foxwell (ed.): *The Poems of Sir Thomas Wyatt* (New York: Russell & Russell, 1964).

Edward Gibbon: *The Decline and Fall of the Roman Empire*, 2 vols, Modern Library Series (New York: Modern Library, 1932), I.

Allan Gilbert (trs.): *Machiavelli: The Chief Works and Others*, 3 vols (Durham, NC: Duke University Press, 1965), I.

Allen Ginsberg: *Planet News* (San Francisco: City Lights, 1968).

K. L. Goodwin: *The Influence of Ezra Pound* (Oxford University Press, 1966).

David Gordon: 'A Northumbrian Sabine', *Paideuma*, 9 (Spring 1980), 77-87.

'Grand Old Man of British Poetry is Still Writing', *Seattle Times*, 10 July 1978, A10.

Theodore M. Greene: *The Arts and the Art of Criticism* (Princeton: Princeton University Press, 1940).

Harvey Gross: *Sound and Form in Modern Poetry: A Study of Prosody from Thomas Hardy to Robert Lowell* (Ann Arbor: University of Michigan Press, 1968).

Grove's Dictionary of Music and Musicians, 5th edition, edited by Eric Bloom, 10 vols (London: Methuen, 1954), I and VII.

Ernest J. Grube: *The World of Islam* (New York: McGraw-Hill, 1966).

Helene A. Guerber: *Myths of the Northern Lands* (New York: American Book Co., 1895).

Hafez: *The Complete Works of Hafez*, edited by Housian Bakhtiari (Teheran, 1945 [1318]). [Persian.]

———— *The Inspired Tongue*, 5th edition, edited by Pezhman Bakhtiari (Teheran, 1966 [1345]). [Persian.]

Nakamura Hajime: *A History of the Development of Japanese Thought: AD 592-1868*, 2 vols (San Francisco: Japanese Publications, 1970).

Anthea Hall: 'Basil Bunting Explains How a Poet Works', *The Journal* (Newcastle), 17 July 1965, 7.

Michael Hamburger: *The Truth of Poetry: Tensions in Modern Poetry from Baudelaire to the 1960s* (New York: Harcourt Brace Jovanovich, 1969).

Sam Hamill: 'Appreciating Present Conditions', *Conjunctions*, 8 (1985), 207-09.

Edith Hamilton: *Mythology*, Mentor Book (New York: New English Library, 1942).

Eduard Hanslick: *On the Beautiful in Music* (Bobbs, NY: Liberal Arts Press, 1957).

Michael Heyward: 'Aspects of *Briggflatts*', *Scripsi*, 1 nos. 3/4 (April 1982), 32-45.

Michael Heyward & Peter Craven: 'An Interview with Basil Bunting', *Scripsi*, 1 nos. 3/4 (April 1982), 27-31.

William W. Hoffa: 'Ezra Pound and George Antheil: Vorticist Music and the *Cantos*', *American Literature*, 44 (March 1972), 52-73.

Andrés Holguín (ed.): *La Poesía de François Villon* (Bogota: Ediciones Universidad de Los Andes, 1968).

John Hollander (ed.): *Modern Poetry: Essays in Criticism* (Oxford University Press, 1968).

Homer: *The Odyssey*, translated by Francis Caulfield (London: G. Bell & Sons Ltd, 1923).

E.A. Honigmann (ed.): *Milton's Sonnets* (London: Macmillan, 1966).

Francis Hope: 'The Authentic', *New Statesman*, 70 (17 December 1965), 976.

Richard Howard: 'British Chronicle', *Poetry*, 110 (June 1967), 195-98.

Glenn Hughes: *Imagism and the Imagists: A Study in Modern Poetry* (Stanford, CA: Stanford University Press, 1931).

C.C. Humiston: *A Comparative Study of the Metrical Technique of Ronsard and Malherbe* (Berkeley: University of California Press, 1941).

Iran Almanac and Book of Facts: 1971, 10th edition (Teheran: The Echo of Iran, 1971).

Iran-American Review: 1971-1972 (Scarsdale, NY: Iran-American Chamber of Commerce, 1972).

J. Isaacs: *The Background of Modern Poetry* (New York: E.P. Dutton, 1952).

A.V. Williams Jackson: *Early Persian Poetry from the Beginnings Down to the Time of Firdausi* (New York: Macmillan, 1920).

P. Mansell Jones (ed.): *The Oxford Book of French Verse*, 2nd edition (Oxford University Press, 1957).

Donald Keene (ed.): *Anthology of Japanese Literature from the Earliest Era to the Mid-Nineteenth Century* (New York: UNESCO, 1955).

Hugh Kenner: 'Never a Boast or a See-Here', *National Review*, 19 (31 October 1967), 1217-18.

—— *The Poetry of Ezra Pound* (London: Faber, 1951).

—— *The Pound Era* (Berkeley: University of California Press, 1971).

—— 'A Resurrected Poet', *Poetry*, 78 (September 1951), 361-65.

—— *The Sinking Island: Modern English Writers* (New York: Knopf, 1988).

Ralph Kirkpatrick: *Domenico Scarlatti* (Princeton, NJ: Princeton University Press, 1953).

—— (ed.) *Domenico Scarlatti: Sixty Sonatas in Two Volumes* (New York: G. Schirmer, 1953).

August Kleinzahler: 'Remembering Bunting', *Scripsi*, 3 nos. 2/3 (August 1985).

The Kokusai Bunka Shinkokai (ed.): *Introduction to Classical Japanese Literature* (Tokyo: The Kokusai Bunka Shinkokai, 1948).

Jaroslav Kosciuszko: 'Four Bottles of Glenfiddich and a Curry', *Bête Noire*, 2/3 (Spring 1987), 51-55.

A.L. Korn: 'Puttenham and the Oriental Pattern-Poem', *Comparative Literature*, 6 (Fall 1954), 289-303.

James Kritzeck (ed.): *Anthology of Islamic Literature from the Rise of Islam to Modern Times* (New York: Holt Rinehart and Winston, 1964).

Ernest Kühnel: *Islamic Art and Architecture*, translated by Katherine Watson (Ithaca, NY: Cornell University Press, 1966).

Susanne K. Langer: *Philosophy in a New Key: A Study in the Symbolism of Reason, Rite and Art*, Mentor Book (New York: New American Library, 1951).

J.B. Leishman: *Translating Horace* (Oxford: Bruno Cassirer, 1956).

John H. Lepper (trs.): *The Testaments of François Villon* (New York: Boni & Liveright, 1926).

'Leptis', *Encyclopaedia Britannica* (1971), XIII, 982.

Barbara E. Lesch: 'Basil Bunting: A Major British Modernist', dissertation, University of Wisconsin-Madison (1979).

Reuben Levy: *An Introduction to Persian Literature* (New York: Columbia University Press, 1969).

────── *Persian Poetry: An Introduction* (Oxford University Press, 1923).

D.B. Wyndham Lewis: *François Villon: A Documentary Survey* (Garden City, NY: Garden City Publishing Co., 1928).

Norman Lloyd: *The Golden Encyclopedia of Music* (New York: Golden Press, 1968).

Stephen H. Longrigg: *The Middle East: A Social Geography* (Chicago: Aldine Publishing Co., 1963).

Longus: *Daphnis and Chloe*, translated by J.M. Edmonds (Cambridge, MA: Harvard University Press, 1916).

Lucretius: *De Rerum Natura*, edited by William E. Leonard and Stanley B. Smith (Madison, WI: University of Wisconsin Press, 1942).

────── *The Nature of the Universe*, translated by R.E. Latham (Baltimore: Penguin Books, 1951).

────── *Of the Nature of Things*, metrical translation by W.E. Leonard (London: J.M. Dent, 1921).

Richard M. Ludwig (ed.): *Letters of Ford Madox Ford* (Princeton, NJ: Princeton University Press, 1965).

Andrew McAllister: 'Today's Posts . . .', *Bete Nôire*, nos. 2/3 (Spring 1987), 56-76.

George MacBeth: Letter to S.V.M. Forde, 4 June 1971.

Peter Makin: '*Briggflatts* & *Beowulf*', *Scripsi*, 4 no.3 (April 1987), 225-41.

W.H. Mallock: *Lucretius on Life and Death in the Metre of Omar Khayyam* (London: Adam and Charles Black, 1900).

John Matthias (ed.): *Twenty-Three Modern British Poets* (Chicago: Swallow Press, 1971).

'Measure of Words': with Basil Bunting, Tony Bilbow; introduced by Eric Mottram; director, James Whiteley; producer, Heather Ging; research, Derek Smith: *Come In*, Tyne Tees Television, 21 July 1983 and 21 April 1985.

Harriet Monroe: 'The French Influence', *Poetry*, 27 (October 1930), 44-49.

Vincent Monteil: *Iran*, translated by Alisa Jaffa (London: Studio Vista, 1965).

Eric Mottram: 'Conversations with Basil Bunting on the Occasion of His 75th Birthday', *Poetry Information*, 19 (Autumn 1978), 3-10.

Kenneth Muir (ed.): *Collected Poems of Sir Thomas Wyatt* (Cambridge, MA: Harvard University Press, 1949).

Edith Nesbit [Bland]: *The Story of the Amulet* (New York: Coward-McCann, Inc., no date).

William S. Newman: *The Sonata in the Baroque Era* (Chapel Hill, NC: University of North Carolina Press, 1959).

Maxim Newmark: *Dictionary of Spanish Literature* (New York: Philosophy Library, 1956).

Lorine Niedecker: 'The Ballad of Basil', *Stony Brook*, nos 3-4 (1969), 31.

Charles Norman (ed.): *Poets On Poetry* (New York: The Free Press, 1962).

Sydney Northcote: *Byrd to Britten: A Survey of English Song* (London: John Baker Publishers, 1966).

'The Northerners', *The Listener*, 84 (8 October 1970), 484.

'Ode', *Dictionary of World Literature*, edited by Joseph T. Shipley. Revised edition (Totowa, NJ: Littlefield, Adams & Co, 1966).

'Ode', *Encyclopaedia of Poetry and Poetics*, edited by Alex Preminger (Princeton, NJ: Princeton University Press, 1965).

John Osborne & Bruce Woodcock: 'Bunting, Olson and Modernism', *Bête Noire* 5 (Spring 1988) 116-34.

D.D. Paige (ed.): *Letters of Ezra Pound: 1907-41* (New York: Harcourt Brace & Co., 1950).

Walter Pater: *The Renaissance: Studies in Art and Poetry*, Mentor Book (New York: New American Library, 1959).

Reinhard G. Pauly: *Music in the Classic Period* (Englewood Cliffs, NJ: Prentice-Hall, 1965).

Tom Pickard: *High on the Walls*. Preface by Basil Bunting (London: Fulcrum Press, 1967).

'Poetry', *Library Journal*, 93 (August 1968), 2880.

Arthur Upham Pope: *An Introduction to Persian Art Since the Seventh Century A.D.* (London: Peter Davies, 1930).

Ezra Pound: *ABC of Reading*, New Directions Paperback (New York: New Directions, 1960).

———— *Active Anthology* (London: Faber & Faber, 1933).

———— 'A Few Don'ts by an Imagiste', *Poetry*, 1 (March 1913), 200-06.

———— *Guide To Kulchur*. Dedicated to Louis Zukofsky and Basil Bunting (Norfolk, CT: New Directions, 1938).

———— *Imaginary Letters* (Paris: Black Sun Press, 1930).

———— Letter to Basil Bunting, no date. Ezra Pound Papers, Harry Ransom Humanities Research Center, University of Texas at Austin.

———— Letters to Morton Dauwen Zabel, 1932-34. Morton Dauwen Zabel Papers, University of Chicago Library. [Letter to Harriet Monroe, 'St Patrick's Day', enclosed.]

———— *Literary Essays of Ezra Pound*, edited by T.S. Eliot (London: Faber & Faber, 1934).

———— *Make It New: Essays by Ezra Pound* (London: Faber & Faber, 1934).

———— *Quia Pauper Amavi* (London: The Egoist Ltd, 1919).

———— *Selected Poems* (New York: New Directions, 1957).

———— 'T.S. Eliot', *Poetry*, 10 (August 1917), 264-71.

Ezra Pound & Marcella Spann (eds.): *From Confucius to Cummings: An Anthology of Poetry* (New York: New Directions, 1958).

Omar Pound: *Arabic and Persian Poems in English*. Foreword by Basil Bunting. (New York: New Directions, 1970).

Kenneth Quinn: *The Catullan Revolution* (Melbourne: Melbourne University Press, 1959).

George L. Raymond: *Rhythm and Harmony in Poetry and Music*, 2nd edition, (New York: G.P. Putman's Sons, 1909).

Herbert Read: 'Basil Bunting: Music or Meaning?', *Agenda*, 4 no.3 (Autumn 1966), 4-10.

Kenneth Rexroth (ed.): *D.H. Lawrence: Selected Poems*, Viking Compass Book (New York: Viking Press Inc., 1959).

David Talbot Rice: *Islamic Art* (New York: Frederick Praeger, 1965).

Luigi Ronga: *The Meeting of Poetry and Music*, translated by Elio Gianturco and Cara Rosanti (New York: Merlin Press, no date).

E. Denison Ross (ed.): *A Persian Anthology*, translated by Edward Granville-Browne (London: Methuen, 1927).

Jan Rypka: *History of Iranian Literature* (Dordrecht, Holland: D. Reidel Publishing Company, 1968).

Federico Carlos Sainz de Robles: *Historia y Antología de la Poesía Española del Siglo XII al XX*, 2nd edition (Madrid: Aguilar, 1950).

Domenico Scarlatti: *Opere Complete per Clavicembalo*, Rivedute da Alessandro Longo, 10 vols (Milan: G. Ricordi, 1937), I,II,V,VI and Indice Tematico.

—— *Sonatas for Harpsichord played by Fernando Valenti*, 3 vols (Westminster Recordings, XWN 18328-18330).

—— *Sonaten für Cembalo*, Ralph Kirkpatrick (Archiv Produktion, 2533 072).

James Scully (ed.): *Modern Poetics* (New York: McGraw-Hill, 1965).

Roger Sessions: *The Musical Experience of Composer, Performer, Listener* (New York: Atheneum, 1966).

Charlie Sheard: 'Basil Bunting and Music', *The Present Tense*, 3 (Autumn 1982), 27-31.

Paul Shorey and Gordon J. Laing (eds.): *Horace: Odes and Epodes* (Chicago: Benjamin H. Sanborn, 1919).

Susan Sontag: *Against Interpretation and Other Essays*, Delta Book (New York: Dell Publishing Co, 1966).

Guiseppe Sormani (ed.): *The Illustrated Library of the World and its People: Middle East*, 2 vols (New York: Greystone Press, 1970).

Noel Stock: *The Life of Ezra Pound* (New York: Pantheon Books, 1970).

—— *Reading the Cantos: A Study of Meaning in Ezra Pound* (London: Routledge and Kegan Paul, 1967).

Igor Stravinsky: *Poetics of Music in the Form of Six Lessons*, translated by Arthur Knodel and Darius Milhaud (New York: Vintage Books, 1956).

Anthony Suter: 'Time and the Literary Past in the Poetry of Basil Bunting', *Contemporary Literature*, 12 (Autumn, 1971) 510-26.

Brian Swann: 'Basil Bunting of Northumberland', *St Andrew's Review*, 4 (Spring/Summer 1977), 33-41.

René Taupin: *4 Essais Indifférents pour Une Esthetique de l'Inspiration* (Paris: Les Presses Universitaires de France, 1932).

Carroll F. Terrell (ed.): *Basil Bunting: Man & Poet* (Orono, ME: National Poetry Foundation, 1980).

D.M. Thomas: Letter to S. Victoria M. Forde, 3 November 1971.

——— 'Three Poets', *London Magazine*, 7 (May 1967), 70-72.

Charles Tomlinson: 'Experience into Music: The Poetry of Basil Bunting', *Agenda*, 4 no.3 (Autumn 1966), 11-17.

Donald F. Tovey: *The Forms of Music* (New York: Meridian Books, 1957).

R.C. Trevelyan: *Lucretius* (Cambridge University Press, 1937).

Gael Turnbull: 'An Arlespenny: Some Notes on the Poetry of Basil Bunting', *King Ida's Watch Chain: A Moving Anthology: Link One* (Newcastle upon Tyne: Morden Tower Book Room, 1964).

——— 'Then is Now: Meeting Basil Bunting', *Scripsi*, 3 nos. 2/3 (August 1985).

Najib Ullah: *Islamic Literature: An Introductory History with Selections* (New York: Washington Square Press, 1963).

'Unfortified', *Times Literary Supplement*, 17 February 1966.

William W. Vernon: *Readings on the Inferno of Dante*, 2 vols, 2nd edition (London: Methuen, 1906), I.

François Villon: *The Poems of François Villon*, translated by H. de Vere Stacpoole (London: Hutchinson, 1913).

——— *The Poems of François Villon*, translated by Lewis Wharton (London: J.M. Dent & Sons, 1935).

John O. Ward (ed.): *The Oxford Companion to Music*, 10th edition (Oxford University Press, 1970).

Daniel Webb: *Observations on the Correspondence between Poetry and Music* (London: J. Dodsley, 1769).

Peter Whigham: 'Herbert Read: *Collected Poems*', *Agenda*, 4 no.3 (Autumn 1966), 77-78.

Donald N. Wilbur: *Contemporary Iran* (New York: Frederick Praeger, 1963).

L.P. Wilkinson: *Golden Latin Artistry* (Cambridge University Press, 1963).

——— *Horace and His Lyric Poetry* (Cambridge University Press, 1951).

Jonathan Williams (ed.): *Descant on Rawthey's Madrigal: Conversations with Basil Bunting* (Lexington, KY: Gnomon Press, 1968).

——— *An Ear in Bartram's Tree: Selected Poems 1957-67* (Chapel Hill, NC: University of North Carolina Press, 1969).

——— (ed.) *Madeira and Toasts for Basil Bunting's 75th Birthday* (Highlands, NC: Jargon Society, 1977).

——— (ed.) 'A Tribute to Basil Bunting', *Conjunctions*, 8 (1985), 148-223.

Jonathan Williams and Tom Meyer: 'A Conversation with Basil Bunting', *Poetry Information*, 19 (Autumn 1978), 37-47.

William Carlos Williams: *The Autobiography of William Carlos Williams* (New York: Random House, 1951).

Renee Winegarten: *French Lyric Poetry in the Age of Malherbe* (Manchester University Press, 1954).

R.S. Woof: 'Basil Bunting's Poetry', *Stand*, 8 no.2 (1966), 28-34.

Andrew Wylie: 'Basil Bunting', *Agenda*, 7 (Spring, 1969), 46-48.

William B. Yeats: *Collected Poems*, 2nd edition (London: Macmillan, 1950).

——— (ed.) *Poems of Spenser* (Edinburgh: T.C. & E.C. Jack, 1906).

Victor Zuckerkandl: *Sound and Symbol: Music and the External World*, translated by Willard R. Trask, Bollingen Series, 44 (Princeton, NJ: Princeton University Press, 1956).

Celia Zukofsky: *A Bibliography of Louis Zukofsky* (Los Angeles: Black Sparrow Press, 1969).

Louis Zukofsky: *All: The Collected Shorter Poems 1923-56* (New York: W.W. Norton, 1965).

—————— *All: The Collected Shorter Poems 1956-64* (New York: W.W. Norton, 1966).

—————— *Autobiography* (New York: Grossman Publishers, 1970).

—————— *Bottom: On Shakespeare*, 2 vols. Music for Shakespeare's *Pericles* by Celia Zukofsky (Austin, TX: University of Texas Press, 1963).

—————— 'Correspondence', *Poetry*, 38 (April 1931), 55-57.

—————— Letter to S. Victoria M. Forde, 2 February, 1972.

—————— ' "London or Troy?" ' "Adest" ', *Poetry*, 38 (June 1931), 160-62.

—————— *An 'Objectivists' Anthology* (New York: To Publishers, 1932).

—————— (ed.) *Poetry*, 37 (February 1931).

—————— *Prepositions: The Collected Critical Essays of Louis Zukofsky* (New York: Horizon Press, 1968).

—————— 'Program: "Objectivists", 1931', *Poetry*, 37 (February 1931), 268-72.

—————— 'Sincerity and Objectification I-III', *Poetry*, 37 (February 1931), 272-84.

—————— *A Test of Poetry* (New York: Jargon/Corinth Books), 1964.

—————— *Zukofsky at the American Embassy, London, 21 May 1969* (Newcastle upon Tyne: Ultima Thule, 1969).

Zukofsky, Louis and Celia: *Catullus* (London: Cape Goliard, 1969).

Publisher's Note: This bibliography includes some recent publications which have appeared since Victoria Forde wrote this book.

AUTHORS PUBLISHED BY
BLOODAXE BOOKS

FLEUR ADCOCK
ANNA AKHMATOVA
SIMON ARMITAGE
NEIL ASTLEY
SHIRLEY BAKER
GEREMIE BARMÉ
MARTIN BELL
CONNIE BENSLEY
YVES BONNEFOY
GORDON BROWN
BASIL BUNTING
CIARAN CARSON
ANGELA CARTER
JOHN CASSIDY
JAROSLAV ČEJKA
MICHAL ČERNÍK
SID CHAPLIN
RENÉ CHAR
GEORGE CHARLTON
EILÉAN NÍ CHUILLEANÁIN
KILLARNEY CLARY
JACK CLEMO
JACK COMMON
STEWART CONN
NOEL CONNOR
DAVID CONSTANTINE
JENI COUZYN
HART CRANE
ADAM CZERNIAWSKI
PETER DIDSBURY
MAURA DOOLEY
JOHN DREW
IAN DUHIG
HELEN DUNMORE
DOUGLAS DUNN
STEPHEN DUNSTAN
G.F. DUTTON
LAURIS EDMOND
STEVE ELLIS
ODYSSEUS ELYTIS
CHARLOTTE EVEREST-PHILLIPS
RUTH FAINLIGHT
RICHARD FALKNER

EVA FIGES
SYLVA FISCHEROVÁ
TONY FLYNN
VICTORIA FORDE
TUA FORSSTRÖM
JIMMY FORSYTH
LINDA FRANCE
ELIZABETH GARRETT
ARTHUR GIBSON
PAMELA GILLILAN
ANDREW GREIG
JOHN GREENING
PHILIP GROSS
JOSEF HANZLÍK
TONY HARRISON
DOROTHY HEWETT
FRIEDRICH HÖLDERLIN
MIROSLAV HOLUB
FRANCES HOROVITZ
DOUGLAS HOUSTON
PAUL HYLAND
KATHLEEN JAMIE
VLADIMÍR JANOVIC
B.S. JOHNSON
JOOLZ
JENNY JOSEPH
SYLVIA KANTARIS
JACKIE KAY
BRENDAN KENNELLY
SIRKKA-LIISA KONTTINEN
JEAN HANFF KORELITZ
DENISE LEVERTOV
HERBERT LOMAS
MARION LOMAX
EDNA LONGLEY
FEDERICO GARCÍA LORCA
PETER McDONALD
DAVID McDUFF
OSIP MANDELSTAM
GERALD MANGAN
E.A. MARKHAM
JILL MAUGHAN
GLYN MAXWELL

HENRI MICHAUX
JOHN MINFORD
JOHN MONTAGUE
EUGENIO MONTALE
DAVID MORLEY
VINCENT MORRISON
RICHARD MURPHY
SEAN O'BRIEN
JULIE O'CALLAGHAN
JOHN OLDHAM
TOM PAULIN
GYÖRGY PETRI
TOM PICKARD
DEBORAH RANDALL
IRINA RATUSHINSKAYA
DIANE RAWSON
MARIA RAZUMOVSKY
JEREMY REED
CAROL RUMENS
EVA SALZMAN
WILLIAM SCAMMELL
DAVID SCOTT
JO SHAPCOTT
JAMES SIMMONS
MATT SIMPSON
DAVE SMITH
KEN SMITH
EDITH SÖDERGRAN
PIOTR SOMMER
MARIN SORESCU
LEOPOLD STAFF
PAULINE STAINER
MARTIN STOKES
KAREL SÝS
RABINDRANATH TAGORE
JEAN TARDIEU
R.S. THOMAS
TOMAS TRANSTRÖMER
MARINA TSVETAYEVA
ALAN WEARNE
NIGEL WELLS
C.K. WILLIAMS
JOHN HARTLEY WILLIAMS

For a complete list of poetry, fiction, drama and photography books
published by Bloodaxe, please write to:

Bloodaxe Books Ltd, P.O. Box 1SN,
Newcastle upon Tyne NE99 1SN.